D1556905

FAULKNER AND THE GREAT DEPRESSION

TED ATKINSON

Faulkner and the Great Depression

Aesthetics, Ideology, and Cultural Politics

The University of Georgia Press | Athens and London

© 2006 by The University of Georgia Press
Athens, Georgia 30602
All rights reserved
Designed by Mindy Basinger Hill
Set in Sabon by Bookcomp, Inc.
Printed and bound by Thomson-Shore
The paper in this book meets the guidelines for
permanence and durability of the Committee on
Production Guidelines for Book Longevity of the
Council on Library Resources.

Printed in the United States of America
09 08 07 06 05 C 5 4 3 2 1

Library of Congress Cataloging-in-Publication Data

Atkinson, Ted, 1967–
    Faulkner and the Great Depression : aesthetics,
ideology, and cultural politics / Ted Atkinson.
        p. cm.
    Includes bibliographical references and index.
    ISBN-13: 978-0-8203-2750-1 (alk. paper)
    ISBN-10: 0-8203-2750-6 (alk. paper)
    1. Faulkner, William, 1897–1962—Knowledge—
History. 2. Literature and history—United States—
History—20th century. 3. Faulkner, William,
1897–1962—Political and social views. 4. Literature
and society—United States—History—20th century.
5. Social problems in literature. 6. Depressions in
literature. 7. History in literature. I. Title.
PS3511.A86Z587 2005
813'.52—dc22   2005014070

British Library Cataloging-in-Publication Data available

Contents

Acknowledgments

As I have come to realize in my study of literature, the production of a book involves much more than the solitary experience of writing. A wide range of influences acts on an author before and during the writing process to make the work possible. Bearing that in mind, I want to acknowledge those who have helped in myriad ways to bring this book to light.

First of all, I owe a debt of gratitude to the dedicated teachers who fostered my love of language, literature, and history over the years. Betty Simmons, Joan King, Ted Ownby, and Jack Barbera immediately come to mind when I think of influential teachers. Doreen Fowler gave me my first tour of Yoknapatawpha while I was enrolled in her undergraduate course on Faulkner at Ole Miss. It was nothing short of an epiphany to discover Mississippi's eighty-third county. Jay Watson continued the tour, demonstrating an enthusiasm for Faulkner and for teaching that still serves as a model to me in my research and pedagogy.

I have benefited greatly from the advice of readers at various stages in the writing process. Without the initial guidance and the continued support of Panthea Reid, this book simply would not have been possible. I also wish to thank Richard C. Moreland and Patrick McGee for their careful reading and thoughtful responses in the early going. Susan Donaldson's insightful comments and suggestions helped me to define the scope of this project more clearly and thus to improve its consistency. I appreciate as well her collegiality and kind words of support during my search for stable ground in academia. I also wish to thank Philip Cohen for his careful reading and constructive criticism during the review and revision phase. His advice helped me to sharpen the interdisciplinary focus of this study. Hugh Ruppersburg stepped in as a reader late in the game, and I am grateful for his time and effort at a crucial stage. Jeanée Ledoux is an extraordinary copyeditor. Her attention to detail and diagnosis of my "not only . . . but also" disease enabled my manuscript to become more reader friendly.

The scholarly community in Faulkner studies has been a valuable resource. Along the way, Faulkner scholars have offered intellectual stimulation, inspiration, and encouragement—sometimes knowingly, sometimes not. I want to thank the *Faulkner Journal* for publishing an essay that I revised and incorporated into chapter 1. The William Faulkner Society and the Faulkner and Yoknapatawpha Conference gave me opportunities to present material associated with this project and to receive useful feedback from other Faulknerians. I am grateful to Anne Goodwyn Jones and Kevin Railey for their genuine expressions of interest and encouragement. The scholarly contributions of John Matthews, Eric Sundquist, and Richard Godden to the field of Faulkner studies have been so influential that I consider them ex officio advisers.

Working with the staff at the University of Georgia Press has been a delight. I appreciate Nancy Grayson's enthusiastic response to this project from the outset and her always prompt, thorough, and straightforward manner of keeping me posted and responding to questions. I also wish to thank Jon Davies, an exceptional project editor, Sandra Hudson, Patrick Allen, John McLeod, Andrew Berzanskis, and Jane Kobres for their courtesy, creativity, and professionalism in dealing with a first-timer.

Over the years I have been fortunate to work with many wonderful people. When I reflect on the process of writing this book, I realize just how instrumental they have been. The LSU crew—Andrea Adolph, Meg Watson Barrett, Anne-Marie Thomas, Christine Cleveland, and Judi Kemerait Livingston—has provided much support, first as graduate school cohorts and now as longtime friends. Lillie Johnson, chair of the Department of Languages, Literature, and Communications at Augusta State University, gave me a port in the storm so that I could finish this project. For that I am more grateful than words can express. Mary McCormack, Grace Heck, and Betty House are kind and wise mentors to the junior faculty, and I appreciate their always taking the time to ask, "How's the book coming?" Christina Heckman and Christie Launius are ideal colleagues and the best of friends.

I must acknowledge the support of family and my "family." My parents both work with numbers, and so I am all the more grateful to them for accepting my love of words and for not making too much of a fuss when I acted on it by shifting professional gears dramatically. Caroline Langston Jarboe has been a constant source of wisdom, grace, and humor in my life. She is, in the immortal words of E. B. White, that rarest of combinations: "a true friend and a good writer." To the "ka-tet" in Augusta and to Peter Conroy, thanks for asking about the book and then helping to take my mind off of it. I offer my heartfelt appreciation to Douglas Joubert for the many votes of confidence and recognitions of achievement during an uncertain but ultimately transformative journey. Finally, I am grateful to Grant Williams for helping me to reach the end of this book and to imagine a new beginning.

Abbreviations

AA	*Absalom, Absalom!*
AILD	*As I Lay Dying*
CS	*Collected Stories of William Faulkner*
FAB	*Faulkner: A Biography*
FABOV	*Faulkner: A Biography, One Volume Edition*
H	*The Hamlet*
LA	*Light in August*
M	*Mosquitoes*
S	*Sanctuary*
SO	*Sanctuary: The Original Text*
SF	*The Sound and the Fury*
U	*The Unvanquished*

FAULKNER AND THE GREAT DEPRESSION

Placement and Perspective

Faulkner and the Great Depression

WILLIAM FAULKNER'S MOST HERALDED fiction emerged from a phase of creative inspiration and artistic achievement that rivals any in literary history. Remarkably, during a period roughly corresponding to the Great Depression, Faulkner wrote the novels and stories most often read, taught, and examined by scholars. At a time when the American economy produced little, Faulkner produced much. Even though these two significant developments in American history and culture occurred simultaneously, there has been no extensive study of their relationship to each other—until now. In redressing this critical oversight, *Faulkner and the Great Depression* functions, in the words of Addie Bundren, as "a shape to fill a lack" (*AILD* 172), exploring in the process how Faulkner's writing in the historical and cultural context of the Great Depression contributed to some of the most profound and enduring works of American literature.

Admittedly, in arguing a constitutive relationship between Faulkner and the Depression era, this study forges something of a revisionist path against the grain of literary history. For the most part, Faulkner's place in 1930s culture has been defined in terms of alienation, from both contemporaneous and retrospective points of view. During the Depression, Faulkner's fiction appeared out of touch with what many influential denizens of the literary establishment, energized by leftist activism, considered relevant and worthwhile. Driven by the urgency of the times, these critics placed a premium on literature that directly addressed social and political issues of the day and derided the "bourgeois" literary tradition for clinging to the false notion of "art for art's sake." Joseph Freeman's introduction to the 1935 anthology *Proletarian Literature in the United States* exemplifies this approach as well as the polemical nature of literary debate. Freeman points to the newfound primacy of social and political themes in the literature of the early thirties, asserting that trying conditions had attracted greater sympathy for the plight of the working class and had inspired those so inclined to become "more interested in unemployment, strikes, the fight against war and fascism, revolution and counter-revolution than in nightingales, the stream of the middle-class unconscious, or love in Greenwich Village" (16). Bearing witness to what he identifies as an intellectual and artistic shift to the cause of the proletariat, Freeman declares that "we have here the beginnings of an American literature, one which will grow in insight and power with the growth of the American working class now beginning to tread its historic path toward the new world" (28).

Predictably, William Faulkner was not among the featured writers in Freeman's anthology. After all, Faulkner hardly seemed a fellow traveler down the "historic path" Freeman envisions in his introductory remarks. For some critics on the left, elements of Faulkner's style associated with modernism marked him as irrelevant, a throwback to the "decadent" literary sensibilities of the twenties. For others, Faulkner tempted readers with a twisted form of escape from social reality, providing them with macabre and violent subject matter while demonstrating a chronic indifference to the evils of poverty and racism plaguing his native South. In a telling critical assessment, Alan R. Thompson issues what had become a standard line by the mid-1930s, acknowledging Faulkner's literary skill yet mourning his misguided direction in spearheading "the cult of cruelty" (477–87).

Emerging from the thirties with his books mostly out of print and his prospects for leaving a lasting impression on American letters appearing slim at best, Faulkner experienced a rapid rise in literary reputation. As it happened, many of the arguments that had been made to bury Faulkner in the thirties were made to praise him in the forties and fifties. Malcolm Cowley, who had aligned himself with both the "lost generation" of the twenties and the leftist cultural insurgents of the thirties, changed shades again to adapt to the conditions of postwar culture. Overseeing the publication of *The Portable Faulkner* in 1946, Cowley staged a resurrection of sorts, paving the way for the New Critics to champion Faulkner as the embodiment of consummate artistic genius and a skilled craftsman of the "well wrought urn." Once detriments, Faulkner's modernist style and his apparent indifference to current events were now his finest attributes, traits that distinguished him from what the New Critics deemed the politically motivated, and thus aesthetically compromised, literature of the thirties. As Lawrence H. Schwartz observes, Faulkner's fiction was "perfectly suited to the prevailing formalist aesthetics of the post-war era which claimed, in part, that literature in its fully realized form was universal and apolitical" (203). This formalism was in itself a reaction to the prevailing leftist aesthetic of the thirties, which aimed for integration of art and radical leftist politics in the form of a revamped and revitalized realism known by various names: "social realism," "socialist realism," and "proletarian literature," among others. Interpretations of Faulkner from both social realist and New Critical perspectives, then, reached the same conclusion: Faulkner's fiction was disengaged from the issues and concerns of the politically inflected literature prominent in the thirties.

Over time the notion of the apolitical Faulkner derived staying power not only from the politics of literary criticism but also from a persistent tendency to define his work in strictly regional terms. With *The Portable Faulkner*, Cowley set the stage, casting Faulkner as supreme chronicler of the southern saga. Likely fearing the designation too limiting, Faulkner described the influence of his native region as incidental rather than determining. In a letter to Cowley, Faulkner explained, "I'm inclined to think that my material, the South, is not very important to me. I just happen to know it, and don't have time in one life to learn another and write at the same time" (Blotner, *Selected Letters* 14–15). Despite such assertions, the southern label remained firmly affixed to Faulkner. *The American Writer and the Great Depression*, one of the earliest efforts to sift through the literature of the 1930s in the interest of canon formation, demonstrates how the regional fixation, particularly in assessments of Faulkner in the Depression, laid the foundation for the apolitical designation. In the introduction to this anthology, Harvey Swados looks back on the Depression and concludes that "America was a unified land, that its problems were national problems, that its misery was national, that solutions and resolutions would have to be national" (xvi). Significantly, Swados adds that "the writers, *with rare exceptions like William Faulkner* or Richard Wright (whose insistent focusing upon regional or racial drama was rarely recognized as containing elements of universality), addressed themselves to the national scene and presumed—for the first time—to speak *of* the nation at large and *to* the nation at large" (xvi; emphasis added). For Swados, the regionally challenged Faulkner is unwilling or unable to address matters of national consequence and so can be omitted from the anthology because his "works do not deal with the depression as such" (xxxiv).

Of course, the importance of place in Faulkner is apparent even from a cursory reading. After all, it was a change in setting that engendered the seismic shift in Faulkner's literary production when he moved from writing in the derivative vein of *Soldier's Pay* (1926) and *Mosquitoes* (1927) to *Sartoris* (1929), in which he founds Yoknapatawpha County. Faulkner's

Yoknapatawpha is much like Joyce's Dublin: the fictional place, analogous to an actual one, takes shape from a dialectical process that involves both productive inspiration and tormenting sorrow. In Joyce's Dublin, it is easy to become engrossed in vivid detail as we wander the streets and make our way into pubs, houses, and meeting rooms, all the while encountering the many colorful characters that the author brings to life. And so it goes in Faulkner's Yoknapatawpha as we cautiously travel the country roads of Beat Four, cruise the town square in Jefferson, and become acquainted with the various Compsons, Snopeses, Sartorises, McCaslins, Beauchamps, Sutpens, and others who return in story after story, novel after novel. While enriching Faulkner's fictional world, this vivid sense of place has contributed to a critical provincialism that imposes de facto limitations not only on Faulkner's scope but on the critic's as well. Significantly, this tendency runs the gamut of Faulkner scholarship—from the New Critics' praise of Faulkner for transporting the South to the universal and mythical realm of humanistic values to contemporary scholars' claims of Faulkner's subversion and/or support of southern patriarchal ideologies of race, class, and gender. However, what can be lost in the process is a more comprehensive understanding of how Faulkner's fiction weaves into the fabric of American history and culture. Recovering this loss requires a more expansive frame of reference based on the understanding that Faulkner's scope is, in the words of David Minter, "broad in its allusions, analogues, and reach. It brings the culture, society, and political economy of one imaginary North Mississippi county into the broad sweep of U.S. history" (217).

To move beyond the boundaries of critical provincialism, *Faulkner and the Great Depression* defines a frame encompassing the regional and the national to reveal that Faulkner's fiction during this period is, with all its southern inflections, very much attuned to the American experience. To aid this critical endeavor, part of the work here involves reconstituting key conditions of historical and cultural context that bring into relief relevant features of Faulkner's texts. In this regard, *Faulkner and the Great Depression* takes part in the ongoing reassessment of Depression cultural history that has been under way in earnest since the mid-1970s. Much of this work has served the mission of recovery, in the sense of attempting to rescue accounts of the period from a Cold War cultural politics that tended to downplay, or in many cases demonize, the influence of the Left. Accordingly, cultural critics and historians have tried through painstaking detail to reconstruct the thirties as a means of demonstrating how a leftist agenda shaped the broad spectrum of social thought and public policy.[1] Focused on literary debates in the context of Depression culture war, works such as James Murphy's *The Proletarian Moment*, James Bloom's *Left Letters*, and Barbara Foley's *Radical Representations* have challenged contemporaneous and received notions of intractable opposition between right and left, between formalism and social realism, to offer instead an integrated paradigm based on a field of interplay shadowing ideological, polemical, and often divisive exchanges between prominent writers and critics. Cultural criticism and literary analysis in this arena have been refined even further, setting sights on specific authors and genres.[2] This critical endeavor has taken some unexpected and ultimately beneficial turns. In *Modernism from Right to Left*, for example, Alan Filreis lends his hand to recovery with the unorthodox move of highlighting the influence of the Left by examining its impact on Wallace Stevens, a poet held up by critics in the thirties and beyond as an exemplar of high modernism. Eschewing the project of New Left recovery, however, Sean McCann's *Gumshoe America* and Michael Szalay's *New Deal Modernism* focus on genre to reveal how literature and related forms of cultural expression influenced and were influenced by the social, political, and economic endeavors of the New Deal. Both works admirably resist reductive historicism to offer instead innovative and complex models of how literature and politics interact. Accordingly, McCann offers this claim as the foundation of his study: "A pop genre, a cultural complaint, and a political myth, hard-boiled crime fiction thus became a symbolic theater where the dilemmas of New Deal liberalism could be staged" (5). Similarly relating literature and politics, Szalay surveys the broad political spectrum to argue that "an ideologically diverse group of writers from the left as well as the right were active participants in the reinvention of modern governance" (3).

In many respects, *Faulkner and the Great Depression* takes cues from and attempts to make worthwhile contributions to this productive body of scholarship. Consequently, it works to "fill a lack" not only in Faulkner studies but also in a revisionist project that has devoted little, if any, attention to Faulkner in trying to gain a fuller understanding of Depression cultural history and politics. To be clear, my primary objective is not recovery for the purpose of revaluing the worth of the radical Left by demonstrating its impact on a reputed lion of modernism. Such an approach is fraught with unintended consequences, not the least of which is accidentally perpetuating the false sense of binary opposition professed, but rarely practiced, in the literary climate of the thirties. Szalay astutely notes this unfortunate outcome in Alan Filreis's otherwise compelling treatment of Wallace Stevens, pointing out that it "does as much to reify the coherence and autonomy of modernism as the culturally conservative writing of the New Critics and the New York Intellectuals ever did" (7). Bearing that in mind, I mount a different kind of recovery project, designed to salvage to the extent possible the incoherence and upheaval that were Depression facts of life. Conjuring the multiplicity of voices and influences active at the time makes it possible to set aside the deceptively clear lens of reductive historiography and to fashion instead something of a kaleidoscope simulating the American cultural landscape confronting Faulkner and his audience at historical ground zero. This move affords a view of Faulkner as ideologically responsive to cultural politics rather than far removed by the conditions of modernist solipsism or regional isolation.

It is important to note as well that I am not trying to reconstruct William Faulkner as, of all things, an unwitting or unacknowledged proletarian writer. In a climate of professed opposition—left versus right, proletariat versus bourgeois, social realism versus formalism—Faulkner's complex works defied the sort of facile categorization promoted on the left and the right, even as they fell prey to its penchant for simplistic labeling. Though responsive to key social and political concerns, Faulkner's fiction lacked the element of topicality so much in demand in the Depression. After all, readers of Faulkner's novels and stories could find virtually no explicit references to matters deemed essential to enlightened social consciousness. In *Sanctuary*, Horace Benbow does not invoke the memory of Sacco and Vanzetti to make his case for the wrongfully accused Goodwin. Quentin Compson does not literally offer the saga of Thomas Sutpen in *Absalom, Absalom!* as a cautionary tale about the potential rise of fascism in America. Nor does Joe Christmas cite the Scottsboro trial in *Light in August* to highlight racial injustice. Talk on the front porch of Will Varner's general store in *The Hamlet* does not conspicuously turn to the plight of small farmers under the yoke of sharecropping. All of this is to say that Faulkner was indeed too much the artist to run the risk of his fiction reading as propaganda. However, a dearth of explicit references does not mean that Faulkner was tone deaf to the tenor of the times or preoccupied with formal experimentation to the point of obliviousness. On the contrary, Faulkner offers us remarkable insight into Depression history and culture on the basis of his expansive social vision as well as his forays into both "highbrow" literary style and the popular culture industry. During this time Faulkner maintained a far-reaching network of experiences and associations, encompassing the hills of north Mississippi, the studio front offices and back lots of Hollywood, and the inner circles of New York's literati.

Granting this access, Faulkner's fiction offers keen insight into the urgent imperative to bring order to the upheaval of Depression America. Of paramount concern in American society, this effort manifested most visibly in the flurry of initiatives that coalesced around Franklin Delano Roosevelt's New Deal. While this vast and unwieldy enterprise was determined less by action than reaction, as we shall see, FDR sought to give it meaning through the fundamental goal of realizing, as he declared in his Second Inaugural Address, a "new order of things" (par. 10). In a common rhetorical move, the president followed this statement with an appeal to common purpose, signified by his repeated use of the royal "we" in establishing point of view: "Our pledge was not merely to do a patchwork job with second-hand materials. By using the new materials of social justice we have undertaken to erect on the old foundations a more enduring structure for the better use of future generations" (par. 10). In my view, FDR's emphasis on shaping social material into coherent form is especially relevant, provoking intriguing connections between literature and politics—especially in the case of Faulkner. FDR's remarks in this instance and others betrayed a reliance on planned society that Faulkner came to view with increasing consternation as the Depression wore on into the mid-1930s. Apparent in aspects of his life and work, Faulkner's aversion to the emerging federal welfare state calls for examination not as an end in itself but rather as a means of understanding better how historical and cultural conditions provided him with impetus as well as material for the production of his own planned society in the pages of his novels and stories. This ambitious and vast project developed, with notable exceptions, in the realm of Yoknapatawpha, gaining staggering momentum as the Great Depression approached and unfolded.

To highlight this dimension of Faulkner's fiction, *Faulkner and the Great Depression* focuses on key issues shaping the cultural politics of the era: the "literary class war," a Depression cultural development stemming from turn-of-the-century roots; the discourse around fascism informed by public desire for strong leadership; invocations of agrarianism on both the left and the right, respectively promoting communal identity and re-asserting the value of rugged individualism; and representations of the Civil War as sites for addressing Depression concerns and for negotiating the terms of a reconstructed, post-Depression America. Under these banners, the application of dialectical themes exposes in selected novels and stories published between 1927 and 1941 intricate negotiations between aesthetics and ideology that offer enhanced perspectives on Faulkner's fiction and thus yield the opportunity to reconsider his place in 1930s culture.[3]

It is important to note as well that the thematic approach undertaken here is productive but by no means all encompassing. As with any study, but especially one uniting two such vast topics as Faulkner and the Great Depression, defining a manageable approach is necessary. Admittedly, noticeable absences occur in this study—novels such as *If I Forget Thee, Jerusalem*, *Pylon*, and *Go Down, Moses*, as well as several short stories— that could have figured prominently but, in the final analysis, do not. This outcome is not a sin of omission, I submit, but a product of the tough choices one inevitably faces during the process of design and execution. The overarching mission here is an interdisciplinary and thematic approach that fosters close reading of Faulkner's texts as works of art and as cultural artifacts. As a consequence of this methodology, some will likely view this study as complicit in an effort to dismantle the long-standing qualitative hierarchy of Faulkner's novels. As a preemptive response, I offer that my intention is not to argue that "bad" novels such as *Mosquitoes* and *The Unvanquished*, for example, can be redeemed as "good" based on traditional standards of literary merit and taste, but instead to apply altogether different standards. By emphasizing relevance to historical and cultural context and integrating aesthetic and ideological analysis, this study traces in Faulkner's literary production a consistent, though often inchoate, responsiveness to immediate developments in Depression society and culture. This aspect of Faulkner has been all too often ignored, resisted, or unsatisfactorily defined in a line of critical inquiry traversing the thirties, the reign of the New Criticism, the burgeoning of critical theory, and now postmodernism.

Along the way, Faulkner has been linked to diverse causes and movements such as modernism, southern exceptionalism, cultural conservatism, feminism, and perhaps most unexpectedly, political radicalism. These latter accounts tend to pose bold alternatives to traditional readings of Faulkner to adapt him to the politics of postmodern literary criticism. In *The Feminine and Faulkner*, for instance, Minrose Gwin defines Faulkner's vision as comprehensive, arguing that Rosa Coldfield's narrative in *Absalom, Absalom!* conveys "*both* woman's subversive power to speak the madness of patriarchal culture . . . and the *direst consequence* of female power and female desire: the annihilation of the female subject"

(65). On the strength of *Absalom*'s presentation of historiography as "a blatantly ideological art form," Joseph R. Urgo, in *Faulkner's Apocrypha*, claims that Faulkner is "probably among the most politically radical of all those whom America's literary establishment privileges as its major authors" (83). Likewise, in *Faulkner's Marginal Couple*, John Duvall charts queer territory on the outskirts of Faulknerian characterization. He asserts that in Faulkner's fiction, "We find not a world populated by she-women and he-men; rather, we discover curious traces of androgynous poses" (132). While such approaches are provocative and constructive, they do show signs of the struggle to rehabilitate Faulkner for the prevailing political climate of literary studies. In the throes of this effort, the desire to reconcile the irreconcilable can be considerable. This response is likely prompted by what Philip Cohen aptly describes as the "difficulty dealing with Faulkner's often simultaneous adherence and resistance to the repressive doctrines of his day, with the unceasing dialectic of progressive and conservative discourses of race, gender, and class that constitutes his work" (633). Wary of this challenge, I want to approach the political Faulkner by accepting, rather than trying to resolve, the dialectical forces of contradiction, thus reading his texts in context as sites of intense ideological negotiation and political struggle. Sylvia Jenkins Cook defines productive space for such an endeavor when she claims, on the one hand, that "in his treatment of poor whites and of southern society generally, Faulkner is as acutely class-conscious as any Marxist and as prone to patterns of economic sympathy and class allegiance" and, on the other hand, that Faulkner differs from his counterparts on the left in his refusal to blame class exploitation solely or fundamentally for the plight of the poor (39–40). Internally contentious, then, Faulkner's texts often defy the appearance of finished form, providing evidence of ideological interplay and political work in progress rather than stable or coherent positions. Understood in this way, Faulkner's literary production of the Depression enacts a process not unlike, but not simply reflective of, the monumental political effort to bring some semblance of order to a volatile mix of competing interests.

This analogy matters to *Faulkner and the Great Depression* because it opens a pathway to the time when Faulkner's political convictions were in development, existing in a malleable form that would take clearer shape in the public Faulkner of the postwar era. The myriad contradictions evident in this early phase are indicative of Faulkner's place in a dominant class inclined to sympathize with the plight of the poor but also fearful of joining their ranks. Experiencing high anxiety, the dominant class in the Depression longed for an overarching sense of stability and security and yet remained heavily invested in fundamental tenets of classical liberalism: self-reliance, state and local control, and private property rights. As this study reveals, the resulting crisis in this influential political philosophy registers with considerable force in Faulkner's literary production. Facing social and economic upheaval on a wide scale, Faulkner and a host of his peers turned urgently to the world of art, where the potential to affect lives in the course of overwhelming events, to achieve order out of apparent chaos, and to reassert the viability of self-reliance must have seemed far greater than in the upended realm of social reality. By its very nature, such a turn *away* is political—an attempt to achieve power and agency from the force of creative expression, regardless of the extent to which the writer believes art capable of transforming the material world. But, in dialectical form, it is also a move that is binding and thus inherently fraught with tension, insofar as it defines the "new order of things" in the text relative to forces active in its context. In the late twenties and early thirties, with society and culture in upheaval, the productive capability of this tension heightened considerably. Faulkner's literary production was a direct beneficiary, taking form to a significant degree as the author simultaneously thrived on ideological engagement and strived for aesthetic autonomy.

If literary production is, as this study assumes, informed by ideology and inherently social and political, then so is literary criticism. For a critic, the task of approaching the figure of William Faulkner is daunting enough, but add to that the elements of historical and cultural inquiry into the Depression and the practice of ideological analysis, and the prospect becomes even more so. Owing to the nature of the beast, setting out to perform ideological analysis as a way of understanding the political Faulkner compels the critic to gauge his or her own approach relative to the politics of literary criticism and to situate that approach accordingly. From the outset, ideologically concerned treatments of Faulkner have been defined largely in terms of opposition to longstanding interpretations considered thickly rooted in formalism or, more to the point, the New Criticism. Indicatively, Myra Jehlen's groundbreaking study *Class and Character in Faulkner's South*, the first sustained effort to bring ideological analysis to bear on Faulkner, takes dead aim at the scholarship of Cleanth Brooks. Where Brooks finds unity and order in Faulkner, Jehlen finds something different: "Faulkner's South is homogeneous only in the sense of adding up to a coherent community; but that community is itself deeply rent and its parts in constant play" (10). Producing this division, Jehlen argues, are "moral and ideological antagonisms rooted in a discordant class structure" (20). With this study, Jehlen forged a path for later scholars interested in exploring, either primarily or to some degree, the workings of ideology in Faulkner. This body of scholarship reflects a range of theoretical approaches and is responsible for many new and important insights into Faulkner's fiction.[4] Even so, the trend toward ideological analysis, occurring as it has in virtual lockstep with the development of literary theory and cultural studies, has led to some controversy in Faulkner studies.

When the Faulkner and Yoknapatawpha Conference, a useful barometer of trends in scholarship, convened to consider the theme of "Faulkner and Ideology," the give-and-take took center stage. The subsequent publication of the conference proceedings enacts in its textuality the politics of this debate, unfolding within the Faulknerian domain but also clearly influenced by broader issues and concerns in literary studies. From an editorial standpoint, the method of ideological inquiry is viewed with a skeptical eye. In the introduction, Donald M. Kartiganer calls into question the very critical practice employed by most of the featured scholars, basing his argument on Faulkner's self-professed lack of concern for contextual matters while engrossed in the writing process. Kartiganer thus declares, "If there is ideology in Faulkner's fiction, it is absent, as far as he is concerned, of much of the comprehensive and subtle force that Marx and more recent commentators have attributed to it" (ix). Kartiganer's critique sets the stage for a debate that takes its cues, in many respects, from the highly charged literary disputes of the 1930s that struggled, on the most basic level, to define the nature and purpose of literature relative to the material world. Making good on this implicit promise of recycled cultural conflict, the opening essay by André Bleikasten chastises the "new ideologues" in Faulkner studies for engendering a "relapse into the leftist pieties and platitudes of the 1930s" (4) and calls for a return to a more internalized approach to Faulkner based on the recognition that literature is about "the singular conditions and singular becomings of singular beings" (19).[5] In "William Faulkner: Why, the Very *Idea!*" a rhetorical bookend to what Kartiganer refers to as Bleikasten's "opening salvo against ideological analysis" (xxii), Louis Rubin Jr. urges scholars not only to acknowledge but also to embrace a form of academic elitism based on "an informed and cultivated taste in literature, which is the product of a college education and an acquaintance with a large body of literary work that most persons have never and will never read" (334). In a rhetorical manner worthy of 1930s polemics, Rubin lashes out at critics who "yearn for an ideological scheme, a theoretical absolute to anchor our all-too-diffuse traffic with literary imagination" and operate on the narrow-minded assumption that "whoever is not with us is *per se* against us" (337). With Kartiganer and Bleikasten leading off and Rubin batting cleanup, as it were, the form of the collection betrays what can best be called an organizational ideology, which guides the effort to discredit ideological analysis even as the text performs the presumably unintended task of confirming one of the method's basic claims: that ideology is instrumental in shaping form.

Binary opposition is rarely productive, or even sustainable, in literary criticism, despite professions to the contrary in the thirties or under the auspices of diagnosing the condition of Faulkner studies. In the case of *Faulkner and Ideology*, for example, Bleikasten's and Rubin's reluctance to concede any ground to ideological inquiry and to lodge charges against its practitioners at every turn is undermined by the reasonable conclusion that "these charges do not accurately characterize many of the other essays in this collection," as Cohen aptly notes (638). Indeed, the diversity and vitality of the featured essays signal the remarkable potential of ideological inquiry rather than confirm suspicions of its inherent danger as a reductive form of critical practice. To put it bluntly, the insistence on absolutes in the sound and fury over ideological analysis absolutely will not do. After all, if we look beneath the polemical surface, we find that both Bleikasten and Rubin do not dismiss ideological analysis entirely, but rather use strong rhetorical tactics in the interest of maintaining academic rigor. Furthering this cause, both scholars urge a responsible mode of ideological inquiry that retains still useful tools of the trade forged in the New Criticism. Moreover, they warn against the temptation of "forcing all of Faulkner's novels into their ideological straightjacket," as Bleikasten has it (14). Here we see the opportunity to move beyond the entrenchment that often attends theoretical and cultural disputes of this nature. This potential is the kind that Karl Zender aims to fulfill in *Faulkner and the Politics of Reading* as he sets out to "bring together the accepting and resisting halves of my response to the new methodologies" (xiv).

Faulkner and the Great Depression stems from a similar desire to bridge a gap, exploring how ideology informs literary production by giving aesthetics its due. Instead of viewing these concerns as independent, this study operates on the assumption that they are interdependent. The tendency toward segregation has been driven by the insistence that the "well wrought urn" brought down from its pedestal is sure to be damaged and, on the other end of the spectrum, that attention to form obscures understanding of art's social and political relevance. On the contrary, recognizing the inevitable negotiations between text and context, between aesthetics and ideology, between art and politics, can yield heightened appreciation of literary achievements. By applying this theory to Faulkner and exploring how his fiction engages a crucial historical and cultural moment, we stand to gain new insight into the ways that one of the most profound and complex American writers continues to engage us.

CHAPTER ONE

History and Culture
Faulkner in Political Context

WILLIAM FAULKNER ENDED the 1920s with the narrative frenzy of *The Sound and the Fury* and began the thirties, appropriately enough, with *As I Lay Dying*, the story of a harrowing journey toward an uncertain and ominous horizon. The titles alone suggest connections between these novels and the historical and cultural forces informing their production. On one level, it would seem, Faulkner sensed the last desperate gasp of one era as it succumbed to the reality of a lingering and painful demise. The young nation that had emerged from World War I to assume its role as world power and model of industrial capacity, enabled by the Icarus wings of speculation and conspicuous consumption, now found itself entering the 1930s in a chaotic downward spiral. The transition from the Roaring Twenties to the Great Depression was cruel and abrupt, bringing an end to the sort of recklessness that Jason Compson comments on as he otherwise ineffectually analyzes the stock market in the third section of *The Sound and the Fury*. Indeed, the crash proved devastating to the entire economy, as T. H. Watkins explains, because "the failure of the greatest speculative fever in American history profoundly weakened confidence in the basic soundness . . . of one of the nation's economic foundations" (75).

Economic indicators reflect the damage that extended to all sectors of the economy. From the high point of prosperity in 1929 to the low point of economic despair in 1933, GNP plummeted 29 percent, expenditures 18 percent, construction starts 78 percent, and investment 98 percent; unemployment rose from 3.2 percent to 24.9 percent (McElvaine 75). Once a well-oiled machine of production and consumption, the American economy had come to a screeching halt. Due to high tariffs and overproduction, warehouses were overstocked, farm markets were overwhelmed by the twin demons of high yields and low prices, and consumers were left with extremely diminished buying power. It would take an entire decade and another global war to bring about economic recovery. No other factor contributed more to shaping the historical and cultural context in which Faulkner produced his most celebrated fiction than this monumental crisis that ripped the fabric of American society and culture.

The term "depression" speaks well to the dimensions of this national catastrophe, for it can be measured in units both great and small. While the statistics tell much about the damage to the economy, they can do little to show the effects on those who lived through the experience. After all, it is one thing to take note of the substantial drop in consumption or the drastic rise in unemployment but quite another to be confronted with the wan look of despair on the human face of this disaster, as captured vividly by Dorthea Lange in her photograph *Migrant Mother*, perhaps the most recognizable image of Depression anxiety and suffering. Economic data lack the pathos evoked by Sherwood Anderson's account of "men who are heads of families creeping through the streets of American cities, eating from garbage cans; men turned out of houses and sleeping week after week on park benches, on the ground in parks, in the mud under bridges" (qtd. in Jellison 14). Such circumstances led to severe depression of the psychological kind in those most directly affected by the hard times. For the scores of Americans struggling to survive, there was the added burden of low self-worth exacting a huge psychological toll, as illustrated by this recollection from a Depression survivor: "Shame? . . . I would go stand on that relief line, I would look this way and that way and see if there's nobody around that knows me. I would bend my head low so nobody would recognize me. The only scar left on me is my pride, my pride" (Terkel 426). Measuring the Depression in terms of wounded dignity is a common refrain in accounts of the period, registering a depth of self-doubt extending from the individual to the national consciousness. Out of this hardship, there inevitably emerged in the early years of the Depression a growing sense of desperation and urgency in the land, leading many to ask the simple question from which social consciousness is born: What is to be done?

One answer to this question came in the form of reassessing core American values defining the relationship between the individual and society. This process exacerbated the identity crisis in American liberalism under way at least since the Progressive Era. In the nineteenth century classical liberalism, as it has been called by historians and political scientists, had reached the status of a dominant ideology in America on the strength of its fundamental principles of individual liberty, private property rights, local control, and laissez-faire economics. As Raymond Williams explains, a dominant ideology serves the interests of the dominant class, a cultural formation that has achieved a position of considerable power and influence by asserting through direct and indirect means that its values and practices are conditions of "natural" social order or reflections of "absolute truth" (121–27). As such, classical liberalism served as a powerful agent for democracy and, more to the point, capitalism; it promoted freedom from restrictive forces, a strong work ethic, and entrepreneurial ingenuity as virtually sacred American values, enabling those with access to productive capabilities to profit considerably. Emerson's championing of self-reliance, the expansive Whitmanesque poetic persona, and Thoreau's idealized visions of harmony between vocation and avocation stand as literary testaments to the century's faith in the seemingly unlimited potential of the individual.

With the machine of capitalist industrialism in overdrive in the mid- to late 1920s, classical liberalism appeared to have taken an ironic turn along the way. "Robber baron" industrialists seized on laissez-faire economic policies to exercise self-interest in ways that exposed the materialistic desires lurking beneath the surface of noble ideals. Despite efforts by magnates such as Andrew Carnegie to cultivate the philanthropic reputation, many Americans perceived an insatiable greed fed by unfettered individualism. With these men driving the engines of capitalism for unimaginable personal wealth, classical liberalism's professed open door seemed to be closed—except to those with enough capital to gain entry. This climate was conducive to proposals for social and economic reform that built upon those introduced by Theodore Roosevelt and the Progressives and extended during Woodrow Wilson's time at the helm of the vast military-industrial complex formed to mobilize America for World War I. Accordingly, social theorists such as John Dewey, Walter Lippman, Thorstein Veblen, and Charles A. Beard spoke out against unrestrained liberalism and laissez-faire economics, laying the groundwork for a reformed or progressive form of liberalism emphasizing communal values and centralization as antidotes to the social ills they viewed as inherent in capitalist society.

Once the crash of 1929 ushered in the Depression, opportunities to put these theories into practice seemed abundant, and classical liberalism was poised for a thorough overhaul. As Watkins points out, Americans were still clinging to this dominant ideology at the onset of the Depression: "Self-reliance, rugged individualism, and the primacy of local rule were articles of faith rarely questioned by most middle- and upper-class Americans at the beginning of the 1930s" (73). Nevertheless, as Patricia Sullivan explains, for this set of Americans, "individual self-reliance, a cultural bedrock, proved to be completely ineffectual in countering personal misfortune" as conditions grew worse (22). From their position of hegemony, supported by assured social status and relative economic security of the twenties, those in the dominant class had found it much easier to extol individualism as an essential American value. Conveniently, they could ignore the support from government—for example, federal land grants for farms and mining operations and tax incentives for industry—and choose instead to believe that success had come solely by virtue of hard work and individual initiative. However, with the Depression extending economic hardship far into the ranks of the middle class, self-reliance seemed less an agent of liberation and personal wish fulfillment than a cruel condition of social Darwinism, a naturalistic system in which only the fittest could survive. For many in the dominant class, then, faith in the individual to go it alone was becoming incompatible with the harsh realities of Depression life, a development leading to considerable anxiety, fear, and doubt.

This outcome compelled many middle-class Americans to have greater sympathy for those below them on the socioeconomic ladder, even as they remained wary of being counted among them in short order, and left them more open to viable alternatives rooted in cooperation and collectivism.[1] As a result, classical liberalism was in the process of what Leonard Williams calls "ideological change." Explaining this concept, Williams points to the critical habit of describing ideologies as static forces and dominant ideologies as monolithic ones. Instead, Williams argues, we should begin with the assumption that "ideological change is simply a fact of social and political life" (4). Thus a dominant ideology does not speak with one voice but opens up contested space in which many voices seek hegemony. Under these circumstances, Williams adds, "Ideological traditions similarly face demands both to accommodate novelty and to maintain their identity and thus are simultaneously pluri- and monovocal" (14). For Williams, then, the focus should not only be on how to subvert or gain freedom from a dominant ideology but also on "how a public philosophy can be transformed" (39).

An effective means of tracing this transformation in American liberalism as a way to comprehend Faulkner's responsiveness can be found in the field of rhetorical historiography. Emerging in the late sixties on the strength of Kenneth Burke's scholarship, this critical approach seeks to bring the past to life, to some degree, by studying the spoken and written words of political leaders. Applying this methodology to the first four years of the Depression, Davis W. Houck examines speeches and public remarks by Herbert Hoover and Franklin Delano Roosevelt to define "rhetoric as palpable currency" that can be analyzed to reveal how "thoughts, beliefs, and emotions constitute and create our economic realities" and how "markets are propped up on the edifice of discourse" (4). For the politician, especially in times of crisis, the value of this currency is measurable in narrative terms. If employed skillfully, political rhetoric can function as an ordering device, with leaders interpreting the past, trying to make sense of the present, and projecting images of the future as a means of bringing them about actually. An analogy can be made to the creative process that produces fiction: like the writer, the politician tries to conjure a world through the power of language, employing imagery, symbolism, and a range of rhetorical devices. As a result of this practice, citizens can turn to political rhetoric for relatively ordered narratives of what has happened, what is happening, and what could happen. What Faulkner and other Americans confronted in the rhetorical tactics of Herbert Hoover and Franklin D. Roosevelt in the early phase of the Depression was, in effect, a staging of the ideological change under way in American liberalism. While Hoover proposed staying the course of classical liberalism as an antidote to social and economic strife, FDR envisioned a reformed liberalism more attuned to communal and cooperative values.

For many years the reputation of Herbert Hoover was staked on the consensus that he responded ineffectually to the Depression, with historians describing that response on a range from timidity to pampered indifference. Subsequent historiography has featured revisionist efforts to redeem Hoover to varying degrees, arguing that he should be given more credit for his handling of the crisis and, even more ambitiously, that FDR merely picked up where Hoover left off and took the credit for recovery.[2] While Hoover's response to the Depression and his historical reputation are certainly debatable, his impassioned championing of classical liberal-

ism during the Depression is not, as even a cursory view of his speeches
and writing during the period confirms. In 1934, still stinging from a landslide defeat at the hands of FDR and trying to resurrect himself as a political figure, he published *The Challenge to Liberty*, a direct attack on the
programs and policies of the Roosevelt administration. The book enabled
Hoover to elaborate on ideas expressed in *American Individualism*, his
diminutive yet impassioned manifesto in favor of self-reliance published
in 1922. A major component of Hoover's mission, as he notes in the introduction, was to stop the "overthrow of Liberalism" by bureaucrats intent
on redefining its basic tenets and purposes (9). In a transparent rhetorical
move, Hoover identifies the "New Utopias" being advanced under fascism and Nazism on foreign soil, implicitly linking FDR to these projects
by veiled references to attacks on the judiciary and fearmongering that
enact "the harsh curbing of freedom" (16). Hoover warns repeatedly of
the threat to liberty posed by efforts to assert greater federal control and
bureaucracy over the lives of individuals under the auspices of national
emergency. Instead, Hoover presents a reaffirmation of the philosophy of
limited government, laissez-faire economics, and personal responsibility
that he promoted as president. Under this program, Hoover envisions a
society of "ordered Liberty," with government functioning as a system
of "traffic signals" through which "each citizen moves more swiftly to
his own individual purpose and attainment" (200). Hoover trumpeted
these ideas again in a major speech during the presidential campaign of
1936; however, his efforts were to no avail at a time when the maxim that
perception is reality rang especially true. Americans were resistant to the
message of basically unfettered individualism that the much-maligned ex-
president brought to the table, having decided to strike a New Deal with
Franklin Delano Roosevelt.

After FDR took office in January 1933, his administration feverishly
delivered policies and programs designed to alleviate the hardship at the
same time it struggled to convey the reassuring impression that the response was concerted, coherent, and consistent with fundamental American principles. Over the years historians have devoted a wealth of atten-

tion to the New Deal, seeking to understand its emergence and operation within the context of the Depression as well as its influence in the years that followed. Generally speaking, historical accounts have focused on determining the quality of FDR's leadership and thus his legacy, the extent of New Deal innovation and effectiveness as an instrument of economic recovery, and the New Deal's role in the formation of the modern welfare state. Like the New Deal itself, the body of scholarship on this monumental subject can be described as a panoply of alternatives. Over time the historiography has been informed as much by contemporaneous ideological and political concerns as by those active in the Depression. For this reason, FDR and the New Deal have often served as historical screens on which to project ideological responses in the service of current political agendas.[3] More useful are historical accounts that present the New Deal as something of a mixed bag, stressing FDR's leadership as pragmatic rather than visionary and the program's unfolding as an improvisational exercise. Typical of this moderate approach, David M. Kennedy divides the New Deal into halves, pre- and post-1935. The first hundred days of FDR's administration, Kennedy asserts, were a microcosm of the first half, with the New Deal's emergence as a series of "ramshackle, hastily assembled" measures (152–53). However, by 1935 the program evolved into something more manageable, to the point that it could deliver on its mission to bring a tangible sense of stability to many ordinary Americans (247). Alan Brinkley defines the New Deal's development as a process of evolution that involved "innumerable small adaptations that gradually but decisively accumulated." Brinkley adds that by the end of this process in the late 1930s, "it had become evident that the concrete achievements of the New Deal had ceased to bear any clear relation to the ideological rationales that had supported their creation" (*End* 3). For Daniel T. Rodgers, such inconsistency presents students of the New Deal with the vexing dilemma of "how to square its energy . . . with its monumental confusions." Rodgers elaborates: "Without intellectual and ideological passion, the New Deal is all but inexplicable, yet virtually every quest for the New Deal's logic seems only to unravel in contradictions. The riddle of the New Deal is how to understand the marriage of such striking success with such massive apparent incoherence" (412). Treatments that emphasize the chaos are informed significantly by serious doubts in postmodern historiography about the ability to define social and political formations in stable terms. Rather than obscuring our historical view, however, embracing the incoherence yields a constructive vantage point from which to survey the New Deal as it played out in full view of Faulkner and other Americans in its original historical context.

On the grounds of rhetorical precision rather than audience receptiveness, Houck gives Herbert Hoover higher marks than FDR, arguing that the latter struggled to shape his rhetoric in a fundamentally meaningful way. Houck's evaluation calls to mind one of the most common charges against rhetorical historiography: that its tendency to privilege word over deed creates an imbalance rendering the method insufficient for getting to the heart of material history. While this charge may hold true in some cases, it does not in the case of ideological analysis, which is compelled to view the word as equally important to the deed, if not more so. As rhetorical historiography instructs so well, though, if Americans were to make any sense of the New Deal, the most obvious place to start was with FDR, who became for countless citizens the focal point for the struggle to overcome the Depression and to move toward a future of renewed hope and possibility. In my view, what Houck identifies as inconsistencies and contradictions in FDR's rhetorical strategy are actually marks of an improvisational style that was ideologically responsive to numerous concerns: debates within the administration over social and economic policy and political strategy, points of criticism made from both the right and the left, and, most important, the fears and hopes of an American public suffering through hard times. This condition was apparent from the outset in the strained rhetorical attempt to redefine liberalism from a philosophy of self-reliance, local autonomy, and states' rights into one that would work ideologically to promote decisive and centralized action from the federal government.

FDR began this project before taking office for his first term, tap-

ping into the growing identification with the downtrodden and dispossessed now prevalent well into the ranks of the dominant class. In his
famous 1932 radio address, "The Forgotten Man," Roosevelt sounded
a populist theme, focusing not on a specific individual as his protagonist but rather on a Depression Everyman. With noticeable attention to
form, FDR promised measures that would rescue his neglected hero by
"build[ing] from the bottom up and not from the top down" to bene-
fit "the forgotten man at the bottom of the economic pyramid" (par. 5).
Later, in his first Nomination Address, Roosevelt returned his attention to
form by way of metaphor—albeit a mixed one. On behalf of the American
people, FDR asked why the Hoover administration had failed to realize
that all sectors of the pyramid, from top to bottom, were mutually dependent, each affecting "the whole financial fabric" (par. 25). With this
revised understanding of social structure, Roosevelt began the process of
advancing and naturalizing a significant change in social thought, declaring adamantly that "we are going to make the voters understand this year
that this Nation is not merely a Nation of independence, but it is, if we are
to survive, bound to be a Nation of interdependence" (par. 25). This declaration of interdependence, as it were, informed both the emerging New
Deal and its signature programs—from the National Recovery Agency
(NRA) to the Civilian Conservation Corps (CCC) to the Works Progress
Administration (WPA) to Social Security—that were designed to change
the relationships between the various sectors of the pyramid but not, it
would seem, to alter its form too dramatically.

While trumpeting the theme of interdependence, Roosevelt and the
crafters of the New Deal did not abandon self-reliance altogether, resulting in a noticeable amount of irony and paradox in the attending
rhetoric. This condition was evident in FDR's remarks on federal expansion, which were almost always delivered with a dose of individualistic
flair. This rhetorical strategy reflected the need to make an activist federal
government more palatable to the dominant class and to ease what Houck
calls FDR's "abiding fears of centralization" (106). In Roosevelt's view, it
was the responsibility of Washington to provide support out of a concern

for the greater good rather than to seize control of local authorities. So in his first Nomination Address, for example, Roosevelt made a renewed pledge to carry out Washington's natural function without a shift in the fundamental balance of powers: "I say that while the primary responsibility rests with localities now, as ever, yet the Federal Government has always had and still has a continuing responsibility for the broader public welfare. It will soon fulfill that responsibility" (par. 56). This paradoxical understanding was on full display in the "self-help cooperatives," a programmatic contradiction in terms administered by the WPA. The Roosevelt administration applied its own logic in trying to resolve the paradox, as evident in Eleanor Roosevelt's plea on behalf of the program. In "Helping Them to Help Themselves," she insisted that "everybody must do his own work," but always with the clear sense that "you cannot work for yourself alone" (par. 17). Individual profit, then, would not exist in isolation, but instead for a collective purpose. For as the First Lady added in aphoristic style, "The more you help others, the more you really gain yourself" (par. 17). In a statement with obvious ideological implications, she added that this was "good doctrine to inculcate in the citizens of a great democracy" (par. 17).

The success of the New Deal depended to a large degree on promoting a sense of order and stability by instilling in the nation's citizens—particularly those who comprised the dominant class—a belief that a commitment to the administration's policies and programs was the natural course of action for the unfolding plot. The preoccupation with imposing and maintaining order was reflected in agencies such as the NRA, which was initiated in the early years of the New Deal to regulate economic activity in support of what Brinkley calls an "associative ideal," or an effort to achieve "a stable concert of interests among the state, business, and labor" (*End* 32). This program, as well as others, reflected a rhetorical strategy to universalize the New Deal or, in Houck's words, to carry out an "organic plan" conceiving the nation as a whole unit (118). Accordingly, Roosevelt repeatedly insisted that times of national crisis required unified and decisive action unhindered by the sort of fractious debate that would threaten momentum. In stating his philosophy of recovery, Roosevelt declared, "This is no time to cavil or to question the standard set by this universal agreement" ("Purpose" par. 30). Order and stability would proceed from a "great common effort" to shape the many voices into one that would speak to the challenging task at hand. Americans could support the New Deal, Roosevelt assured, because it was "in complete accord with the underlying principles of orderly popular government which Americans have demanded since the white man first came to these shores. We count, in the future as in the past, on the driving power of individual initiative and the incentive of fair private profit, strengthened with the acceptance of those obligations to the public interest which rest upon us all. We have the right to expect that this driving power will be given patriotically and wholeheartedly to our nation" ("Greater" par. 10). By this reasoning, the New Deal was an extension of Manifest Destiny—or in narrative terms, an installment marked by tragedy, but only part of the broader American epic guided as ever by the triumphant conclusion that was assuredly this nation's due. Of course, this was the story written by and for a dominant class that saw its position threatened. It is no wonder, then, that Roosevelt's promises of immediate relief in the service of preserving established order came mostly as reassurances that the pyramid would remain intact. For this reason, alterations in social and political form were not radical revisions but instruments of reproducing the means of production for a dominant class interested in maintaining its prerogative.

While accomplishing this feat required both ideological and material endeavors, it also demanded, as we have seen, nearly impossible feats of political rhetoric. Roosevelt's speeches during the Depression constantly addressed issues of political, social, and economic reform, in keeping with the sense of desperation and urgency that gripped the nation. Rather than advocating revolutionary change, however, FDR appropriated revolutionary rhetoric for the cause of the New Deal. Accordingly, moments of firebrand oratory were tempered by statements of caution and reserve. This rhetorical strategy was exhibited in Roosevelt's first Inaugural

Address, as early on he sounded the notes of class conflict characteristic of socialism: "The money changers have fled from their high seats in the temple of our civilization. We may now restore that temple to the ancient truths. The measure of the restoration lies in the extent to which we apply social values more noble than mere monetary profit" (par. 4). Invoking memories of the Great War, Roosevelt cautioned against uprising, advising instead that "we must move as a trained and loyal army willing to sacrifice for the good of a common discipline" and stand "willing to submit our lives and property to such discipline, because it makes possible a leadership which aims at a larger good" (par. 17). Such rhetorical maneuvering was influenced in no uncertain terms by FDR's previously expressed concern that the misguided response of the Hoover administration to the Depression "may degenerate into unreasoning radicalism," which was exhibited in the growing chorus of social protest resounding in the country ("Nomination" par. 8).

The early years of the Depression were marked by a radical spirit that grew out of economic catastrophe and widespread social unrest—evident from rural areas of the country such as Faulkner's Mississippi, where Depression-like conditions had existed before the thirties, to urban centers where organized bands of unemployed citizens looted stores. This social unrest came to a head in the summer of 1932 when auto workers rioted in Dearborn, Michigan, and disaffected veterans of World War I gathered in Washington for the Bonus March, camping out in tents and demanding that the federal government make good on promised benefits. Roosevelt took the Oath of Office for his first term with talk of revolution in the air; after a reprieve during the first year of his initial term, this social unrest resurfaced. By 1934 forces were stirring in opposition to Roosevelt's New Deal. From the right, critics accused FDR of threatening traditional American values; from the left came disaffected charges that he had not acted decisively enough to provide relief and institute lasting social and economic reform. As Raymond Williams observes, though, any successful hegemonic endeavor remains ever wary of movements on the fringes that threaten its dominance and thus moves to appropriate or stifle the forces of opposition (113). Along these lines, FDR's rhetoric took on a sense of great urgency bred of political necessity as he sought to propel the New Deal forward in his first term. Speaking in favor of his work relief program, Roosevelt implored, "This is a great national crusade to destroy enforced idleness which is an enemy of the human spirit generated by this depression. Our attack upon these enemies must be without stint and without discrimination" ("Works" par. 23). The analogy between the economic recovery effort and wartime mobilization had its advantages, not the least of which was rallying the citizen-troops to the cause of the New Deal by casting it as a necessary response to a national crisis. In this time of emergency, Roosevelt argued, citizens must accept the fact that "a rounded leadership by the Federal Government had become a necessity of both theory and fact." He also employed aesthetic means to further the crusade, urging citizens to become "soldiers [who] wear a bright badge on their shoulders to be sure that comrades do not fire on comrades"; the badge was emblazoned with the declaration, "We do our part" ("Purpose" par. 25).

For obvious historical reasons, this martial rhetoric coming from the federal level resonated with unique implications in Faulkner's native South, the region of the country with arguably the most ideologically conflicted response to the New Deal. Since the founding of the country, the effort to maintain a proper balance between the power of the federal government and the authority of state governments and localities had shaped not only classical liberalism but also the political identity of the South, contributing primarily to its troubled relations with Washington. In the Great Depression, the tendency of southerners in the dominant class to point an accusing finger at FDR with one hand while holding out the other for federal money was vividly on display, if rarely acknowledged. Informed by a southern-inflected version of self-reliance, this contradictory practice influenced and was influenced by degenerating relations between the president and southern Democrats. As Kari Frederickson explains in *The Dixiecrat Revolt and the End of the Solid South*, the New Deal exacerbated tensions between the material and the ideological, pitting need for relief against an ever-increasing fear that the "New Deal and the accompanying growth of federal power in the 1930s and 1940s threatened the South's ideal of states' rights and limited federal government" (12). Frederickson adds that at the same time prominent southerners were able to reap significant profits from agricultural subsidy programs administered at the local level, they "viewed warily the potential of New Deal programs to threaten the region's economic dependence on cheap labor while stirring the democratic ambitions of the disenfranchised and undermining white supremacy" (12). In FDR's first term, this concern was muted, with the need for immediate relief outweighing the ideological imperatives. Consequently, FDR was able to maintain a high level of popularity in the South and thus to count on the loyalty of southern Democrats when it came to key votes in Congress. By the mid-1930s, however, fault lines began to emerge, serving as faint harbingers, we now know, that the Democratic "solid South" would crumble in the decades to come.

For many white southerners, initial concerns about the direction and implications of the New Deal grew more acute in the mid- to late thirties, taking on the form of worst fears realized. For one, the scores of new voters attracted to the Democratic Party by the popularity of FDR and the New Deal led southern Democrats to question by the election of 1936 whether they would be able to wield the same amount of influence. The abolishment of the two-thirds rule in the presidential nomination process at the convention that year answered the question definitively. In the South, blacks and working-class whites were emboldened by the hard times and by the rhetoric of class conflict to mount greater resistance to the status quo, resulting in heightened activity in the arenas of civil rights and labor union formation (Biles 45–50; Frederickson 13). While the level of activity was by no means comparable to other regions of the country, it did fuel anxiety in the dominant class over a potential redistribution of power under the driving force of the New Deal. Two further developments in FDR's second term exacerbated tensions with conservative southern Democrats. An increasing readiness on the part of these law-

makers to oppose New Deal programs, particularly those deemed a threat
to white supremacy, prompted FDR's infamous and ultimately failed attempt to "purge" the party as a means of bolstering what he viewed as
a liberal southern voting bloc in Congress (Frederickson 25). Moreover,
in 1938, the Roosevelt administration released the *Report on Economic
Conditions of the South*, citing the region as the nation's foremost economic problem. While many southern lawmakers were in support of key
recommendations in the report, they and many of their influential con-
stituents objected to what they perceived as a condescending tone harking
back to the era of Reconstruction.[4] While the degenerating relationship
between FDR and conservative southern Democrats was significant for
laying the groundwork for the eventual rise of the Republican Party in the
South, it was in the Depression era a case of ideological tension that could
be overlooked in the service of political pragmatism. Insofar as New Deal
measures were crafted by the Roosevelt administration and perceived by
southerners as agents of relief and progress, they could attract support
in the South. If, however, the specter of a federal social agenda emerged,
particularly in terms of upsetting the racial hierarchy, whites in power
became resistant and reactionary—a response that registers in Faulkner's
fiction.

Despite the appearance of these tensions, they were not strong enough
in the thirties to provoke southerners to jump the Democratic ship and
climb aboard the Republican one, loaded as it was with considerable historical baggage—of the carpet variety, naturally. Even if southern Democrats had wanted to switch party affiliation, they would have found
themselves in a party marked by retreat and disarray. The Republicans
spent the first years after FDR's landslide victory reeling from defeat and
suffering under the cloud cast over the party during Hoover's final years
in office. With Republicans marginalized in government and public discourse, the party's attempts to challenge FDR came as temporal instances
of coalition building with dissenting Democrats. In 1934, for example,
the American Liberty League formed as a bipartisan effort to propose an
alternative to the New Deal; it was conceived by and targeted mainly for

those not feeling the blows of the Depression. This organization emerged from a series of letters between the former Democratic National Committee chairman John Raskob and R. R. M. Carpenter, vice president of the Du Pont Corporation. Motivated by the loss of "good help" to agencies such as the CCC, Carpenter enlisted Raskob in the effort to prevent Roosevelt from leading the country toward irreversible social and economic reform. The former New York City mayor and presidential candidate Al Smith, who by this time had drifted from his working-class roots to cast his lot with corporate executives, served in the initial group of directors of the Liberty League.

As the name of the organization suggests, the American Liberty League was steeped in the fundamentals of classical liberalism. The organization sounded themes consistent with the reservations expressed by Hoover, arguing that the New Deal was an attempt by the federal government to encroach on the sacred American virtues of individual liberty. Setting a tone that would characterize the 1936 presidential election, the league insisted that Roosevelt's policies would create a nation of dependents addicted to the dole rather than capable of self-sufficiency in the "traditional" American way. A headline in the *New York Times* on August 23, 1934, stated the league's twofold mission: "League is Formed to Scan New Deal, 'Protect' Rights." The ideological position of the league was made clear in the prepared statement delivered by Executive Chairman Jouett Shouse, who declared the organization's promise "to defend and uphold the Constitution of the United States . . . to teach the duty of government, to encourage and protect individual and group initiative and enterprise, to foster the right to work, earn, save and acquire property, and to preserve the ownership and lawful use of property when acquired" ("American" par. 3–5). Like FDR, Shouse emphasized form in his rhetorical strategy, as he sought to convey the league's social, political, and economic ideas. Instead of a pyramid, though, Shouse likened government to a tree—a solid trunk with individual branches extending in all directions. Although the league vehemently opposed the policies of the New Deal, it shared the same resistance to fundamental alteration of social structure.

Articulating a political aesthetic, Shouse explained, "We do not oppose change, but we would not sacrifice the form of government under which our country has grown strong and prosperous. There have been abuses. They must not be allowed to recur. There have been inequities. They must be righted. But the tree must not be destroyed merely because some branches need to be removed" ("American" par. 26). Faced with the nation's general move leftward in response to the crisis at hand, the Liberty League expressed an urgent need to cling to the individualistic values so popular in the dominant class during times of stability and prosperity. But, like Hoover, the league was clearly too out of step with the times to gain enough support for stemming the tide of FDR's New Deal. The values that the league wanted to preserve with a sort of fundamentalism were meeting the forces of ideological change.[5]

While the Great Depression pushed the Right to the margins of political discourse, the Left experienced a time of unprecedented vibrancy— socioeconomic conditions made its social policies and political concerns more relevant and appealing than at any other time in the nation's history. Marginalized during the bacchanalian reign of capitalism in the twenties, the Left viewed the despair of the thirties as an opportunity to advance an agenda of fundamental reform in American social, economic, and political life. The nature of this reform ranged from communist calls for a proletarian revolution to the proposals of socialists for redistribution of wealth and strict governmental control over the economy to the more moderate aims of a transforming liberalism to bring about greater social equality and economic justice. The Depression, in one sense, allowed the radical Left to say "We told you so" to a nation that had refused to heed warnings against unchecked capitalism as the Industrial Age unfolded. Though perhaps hard to imagine now, the prevailing cultural climate during the Depression was largely determined by the successful efforts of the Left to influence political debate and, in effect, to define social consciousness for an American public more attuned to these concerns by sheer force of experience. In many ways the Depression was the finest hour for radicals, who spoke passionately to an American public never more willing to listen, even if it was not ultimately prepared to vote for the sort of radical change that would fundamentally restructure American society along the lines of socialism. Consequently, Americans like Faulkner, who were not predisposed to the Left, had to contend with its revitalized political agenda made all the more relevant by the circumstances of the Depression.

Two years into FDR's first term, with the New Deal in its infancy, the federal government made visible efforts to provide relief and to restore confidence in the American economy. In spite of these efforts, however, those to the left of FDR politically were not satisfied that his measures would be sufficient to achieve lasting reform. For this reason, a rift emerged by the latter half of 1934, occurring essentially along the lines described by Robert Morse Lovett nearly a decade earlier. In "Liberalism and the Class War," Lovett defines a fundamental point of contention between radicals and liberals as a threat to progressivism. For Lovett, a radical would define society in terms of class conflict brought about by "the domination of an upper class, through control of religion, education, social recognition, ethical standards, literature, art, and government" (191). On the contrary, Lovett writes, a liberal "is by theory and tradition opposed to the Class War, as he is opposed to everything that intensifies the difference between the classes" (191). What Lovett explains here is essentially hegemony, with liberals exerting a sort of omnipresent control that prevents radicals from asserting a view of society centered on class conflict. Lovett's model can be applied as well to the political dynamics on the left during the implementation of the New Deal, as proponents tried to stem radical challenges intended to move the country ever closer to collectivism.

Class conflict was at the heart of significant movements exerting pressure on FDR to move further leftward. For one, the labor unions became more active, culminating in 1934 with widespread strikes, perhaps the most famous of which was staged by the longshoremen in San Francisco. Led by the charismatic Harry Bridges, chairman of the Joint Maritime Strike Committee, the strike garnered national attention and epitomized labor discontent across the nation. In Faulkner's South, the Southern Tenant Farmers' Union (STFU) formed in the small Arkansas Delta town of Tyronza, and the Share Cropper's Union (SCU) in rural Alabama, extending to the mid-1930s a pattern of labor unrest that had surfaced most visibly with the 1929 Gastonia riots in North Carolina. Reinvigorated labor activism and protests resulted not only from the frustrations accompanying economic hardship but also from a new attitude in the working class. After FDR took the reins of power from Hoover, the blend of rhetoric stressing the "forgotten man" and policy measures providing relief heartened a labor movement that saw the initial years of FDR's first term as a time for decisive action to bring about a lasting shift in the balance of power between labor and management. Labor urged Roosevelt left and closer to the collectivism he had been approaching moderately. When it became clear that FDR was willing to go only so far, social unrest intensified.

Also fanning the flames was an insurgent populism that swept the land, as demonstrated by high-profile movements seeking to translate social unrest into political action. Two movements in particular demonstrate the widespread appeal of populism in Depression politics and culture. In Detroit, Father Charles Coughlin, a Catholic priest and radio personality, launched a populist movement that gained national prominence. Next door to Faulkner's Mississippi, Huey Long, the Louisiana governor–turned–U.S. Senator, mounted a grassroots campaign that enabled him eventually to pose a serious threat to FDR's reelection campaign in 1936. Coughlin and Long drew support by using the rhetoric of class warfare. Each in his own way repeatedly called for programs that would redistribute the wealth and thus move America closer to collectivism than FDR's New Deal envisioned. Americans responded to both men in large numbers. At the height of his popularity, the "Radio Priest," as Coughlin was widely known, reached an estimated audience of thirty to forty million and received an average of eighty thousand letters per week (McElvaine 238). Likewise, Long's Share Our Wealth (SOW) program generated an average of sixty thousand letters per week to his Senate office; in 1935, a year after the founding of SOW, officials claimed there were twenty-seven thousand clubs in existence (246). Early on Coughlin stressed social justice, vilifying the "robber barons" who placed individual wealth above concern for the collective good. In order to set the country on the right track, Coughlin argued, the exploited working class would need to share more in the fruits of its labor. While not calling for an end to private property, Coughlin argued that social justice and responsibility should take precedence over the profit motive. Every bit the personality that Coughlin was, and more, Long stressed specifics: his SOW program, in the true spirit of Robin Hood, called for literally taking from the rich (those with fortunes over one million dollars) and giving to the poor. Extending the tradition of rural populism that had heavily influenced him, Long berated the guilty profiteers and promised to return what had been plundered from the working class. In this time of severe crisis, the message was welcome; as a result, these messengers acquired substantial amounts of political influence and cultural capital.

While the rise of these very public figures speaks volumes about restlessness in the mid-1930s, they are no less compelling for what they reveal about the imperiled condition of self-reliance as an ideological concept. Despite agendas based ideologically in collectivism, perceptions of Coughlin's and Long's movements became less about the policies they proposed than about them as enigmatic and controversial figures. This focus led increasingly toward an inconsistency typical of movements defined more by the ego of the leader than the ideological base.[6] But it is important to remember that, at the height of their popularity, it was the emphasis on the values of cooperation, social justice, and economic redistribution that caught the attention of Americans who saw in their radicalism a fervor that was missing in FDR's New Deal, rooted as it was in the context of an emerging progressive liberalism.

In more urgent terms, Coughlin and Long appealed not only to the working class but also to those in the middle class for whom sharing the wealth seemed preferable to having no wealth at all. For these Americans, preserving the form of the pyramid did not seem as essential as improving social and economic conditions in quick measure. An essential difference between the New Deal and radical opposition movements such as those staged by Coughlin and Long was apparent in the fundamental bases of support they tried to attract. As we have seen, the New Deal defined a broader scope of appeal, ranging from the class of the "forgotten man" to the upper- and middle-class alliance that had emerged from the 1920s as dominant. However, Coughlin and Long encouraged a greater affinity between the lower middle class and the working class, based on shared hardship and a commitment to fundamental changes in American society inspired by collectivism. This alliance is what Marx, in *The Eighteenth Brumaire of Louis Bonaparte*, calls a transition class—that is, a union forged in immediate response to external conditions, professing to transcend class antagonisms but really suspending them out of expediency (47). In these times of despair, Coughlin and Long injected a radical fervor into political discourse, coaxing the middle class toward a potentially new hegemonic position in union with a long-exploited working class. The individualism that tempted them ever closer to demagoguery as they promoted this alliance should not obscure the collectivism that contributed in the main to their mass appeal. The popularity of such programs exposed and exacerbated dominant-class anxieties that, in turn, informed the transformation of classical liberalism and affected the course of the New Deal.

While these enigmatic figures loudly trumpeted the potential for a new and powerful alliance, the most expressive visions of this transition class came from the broad social and cultural formation known as the Popular Front. For the most part, radical political beliefs were channeled by the mid-1930s into this de facto alliance of intellectuals, artists, politicians, and social activists. Faulkner witnessed this movement firsthand during stints in Hollywood and visits to New York—hotbeds of Popular Front activity, as exiled intellectuals streamed in from Europe in advance of and during Hitler's conquests. In *The Cultural Front: The Laboring of American Society in the Twentieth Century*, Michael Denning defines a force as notable for its eclecticism as for its activism:

> The Popular Front was the insurgent social movement forged from the labor
> militancy of the fledgling CIO, the anti-fascist solidarity with Spain, Ethiopia,
> and China, and the refugees from Hitler, and the political struggles on the left
> wing of the New Deal. Born out of the social upheavals of 1934 and coinciding
> with the Communist Party's period of greatest influence in US society, the Pop-
> ular Front became a radical historical bloc uniting industrial unionists, Com-
> munists, independent socialists, community activists, and émigré anti-fascists
> around laborist social democracy, anti-fascism, and anti-lynching. (4)

Although it may have been born in 1934, the conception of the Popular
Front came much earlier. Its roots can be traced back at least as far as the
anticapitalist social activism practiced by the International Workers of
the World (IWW), or Wobblies, and the anti-institutional tactics of avant-
garde artists. Although the Popular Front advanced a socialist agenda, its
very nature as a self-professed radical movement demanded a collective
identity outside and against the status quo.

For the Popular Front, the preferred course of action was to center
on high-profile issues and incidents that could demonstrate the chronic
injustice of American society and, in turn, promote an alternative vision
of social justice. Thus the plight of dispossessed migrant farmers exposed
the systemic injustice of free-market capitalism wreaking havoc on agrarian communities; the brutal suppression of striking dock workers in San
Francisco or mill workers in Gastonia effectively spoke to the exploitation of the working class by management; the trial of Sacco and Vanzetti
suggested a darker interpretation of the founding principle that "justice is
blind"; and the case of the "Scottsboro Nine" or the disturbingly common
practice of lynching demonstrated brutal racism in America. Whereas
Coughlin, Long, and other charismatic figures relied heavily on personality to advance their visions, often resulting in egocentric movements, the
Popular Front cut a broader swath in its march toward radical reform
in America. In the spirit of the collectivism it espoused, the many parts
working for the whole characterized the social and political form of the
Popular Front.

Of course, cultural historians have varying opinions about the nature of the Popular Front and the extent of its influence.[7] But it is safe to say that its impact on FDR's New Deal, and thus on American society and culture, was substantial. Faced on his left flank with this formidable social movement and the vocal populist challenges from opponents like Coughlin and Long, FDR had no choice but to accommodate what McElvaine aptly calls the "thunder on the left" (224). And he did so in launching what has come to be known as the Second New Deal.[8] Initially hopeful that an expanded role for the federal government would bring an immediate recovery and thus make the expansion temporary, Roosevelt saw that, if he was to be reelected in 1936, he would have to toss the proverbial bone to those on his left. This tactic allowed FDR to temper resistance and thus to consolidate support for the New Deal. The fiery spirit of radicalism, as Richard Pells observes, was channeled into the Fireside Chats, which emanated warmth and stability and signaled to the dominant class that established order would prevail, despite a much-expanded role for the federal government in American life (86). By the end of the 1930s, radical activism would fade, the idealism and activism of the early years no match for the sobering defeat in the Spanish Civil War and the inevitable cynicism after the signing of the Nazi-Soviet Non-Aggression Pact. The Popular Front steadily charted its course of cultural politics into the larger progressive tide that was the New Deal, forming a pragmatic alliance that enabled it to take advantage of the ideological crisis directing social thought away from unqualified assertions of self-reliance and thus to shape public discourse in ways that heightened social consciousness.

The social formation of the Popular Front illustrates the high level of integration between political discourse and forms of cultural expression prevalent at the time. For radical artists and intellectuals committed to challenging the status quo based in capitalism, the Depression provided an unprecedented opportunity, ironically, to use capitalist modes of cultural production to stage a persuasive cultural politics for an audience generally more receptive to themes of social, economic, and political justice. These creative activists mounted an inspired effort to highlight issues and causes they deemed relevant. In this endeavor, leftists employed the various media prevalent at the time—namely literature, painting, theater, periodicals, photography, radio, and film. They took advantage of both "high" culture and a burgeoning popular culture industry in advancing this fusion of art and politics. Margaret Bourke-White's resonant photographs documenting the plight of the dispossessed; Clifford Odets's agitprop drama with its scathing portrayals of capitalist "robber barons" and calls for solidarity with the working class; King Vidor's testament to cooperative farming as a response to a harsh capitalist marketplace in his idealistic film *Our Daily Bread*; Mary Heaton Vorse's vivid accounts of the strikes in Gastonia; Richard Wright's stories full of visceral descriptions of urban squalor, rural violence, and systematic racism—these cultural products and others like them together wove a tapestry depicting America as a land of inherent injustice rather than unlimited opportunity. And they set standards for the times against which Faulkner and other emerging writers were measured.

The heightened emphasis on social consciousness fueled debates in the literary establishment over the purpose and function of art, one of the most prominent being the "literary class war" that brought formalism and social realism to blows in a cultural conflict that had been shaping up since the early twenties. This aesthetic and ideological dispute will be the subject of more comprehensive analysis in chapter 2. For now it suffices to say that by the time Michael Gold followed up several years of polemical criticism by staging this war's equivalent of Fort Sumter in the pages of the *New Republic* in 1930, the climate of American letters had already become politically charged and polarized. Gold's attack on Thornton Wilder effectively drew the battle lines between a host of leftists—young, socially conscious writers, some of them from the working class, and radical moderns still tapped into the avant-garde, expatriates from the twenties whose energy for social experimentation was now redirected toward political radicalism—and their formalist counterparts on the right, who held to traditional conceptions of art as removed from immediate concerns. For leftist writers, advocating the mission of the John

Reed Clubs to wed poetics and politics, boundaries between art and activism needed to be removed. Creating art was not to be the isolated act of creative genius confined to the bourgeoisie but a form of social praxis aiding in the cause of the proletariat. In the tradition of Communist Party writers in the Soviet Union, many American writers adopted social realism as the prescribed literary device for aiding in societal transformation. It was time, as the clarion call sounded, for writers to take up the cause of the working class in an effort to transform America based on communal values and social responsibility. This awakening of social conscience resulted in a flurry of activity in the literary establishment, including the birth of periodicals such as the *Partisan Review* and the *New Masses*, which provided a forum for radical politics and, in part, prompted liberal publications such as the *New Republic* to revise their editorial positions leftward.[9] Also, the publication, in 1935, of the anthology *Proletarian Literature in the United States* announced the arrival of a vibrant literary movement thriving on the radical spirit of social and political reform and urging influential critics to demand the same from writers of the period— a factor that had direct bearing on critical reception of Faulkner in the thirties.

Wary of such an overt mixture of art and politics, intellectuals on the right reasserted literary formalism as part of a larger formation of cultural conservatism. Taking their cues from T. S. Eliot, self-prescribed American "humanists" such as Irving Babbitt and Paul Elmer More urged the nation to respond to the hard times by turning inward for spiritual strength and resolve against the totalizing forces of science, industry, capitalism, socialism, and the developing New Deal welfare state. In many instances, intellectual conservatives fought fire with fire, attempting to claim the mantle of radicalism so popular in the thirties. When Seward Collins launched the *American Review*, for example, he proclaimed that the journal would be "providing a forum for the views of . . . 'Radicals of the Right' or 'Revolutionary Conservatives' " (126). The development of this journal demonstrated how the rhetoric of radicalism could easily lead to extremism, though. During the journal's six-year run, its editorial policy reflected a strict adherence to individualism, resulting in untenable political positions such as a call for monarchy and, finally, support for fascist regimes. Predictably, many of the *Review*'s contributors cut all ties to the journal, preferring instead to wage culture war in more moderate publications, such as those to which Faulkner contributed early in his career: the *Hound and Horn*, a popular forum for conservative dissent, and the *New Republic*, in which left could meet right at a noticeably left-of-center front. However, like the political conservatives mounting a challenge to the Left, intellectual conservatives in the thirties ultimately faced the harsh reality that their cultural project was no match for a severe socioeconomic crisis that was forcing Americans to the left.

Prolific with novels, stories, poems, plays, and articles, leftists tried to fashion aesthetic practices to meet the political demands of the time. Authors associated with high modernism and literary formalism were charged with emphasizing artistic self-reliance, berated as a relics of ego-centric bourgeois individualism, and deemed supportive of an oppressive capitalist system. For many leftists, works thought to be aligned with the bourgeois literary tradition appeared useless to the growing mass of the poor and downtrodden and to the cause of social and political re-form. Instead of striving for what Stephen Dedalus, in Joyce's *A Portrait of the Artist as a Young Man*, calls stasis—a suspended state of artis-tic appreciation—and replicating the solitary workings of interior (bour-geois) experience, advocates of social realism celebrated its lack of for-mal refinement and sophistication and looked urgently outward to the material world for inspiration. Rather than prompting the sort of active, yet totally aesthetic, response that Dedalus terms kinetic, this new litera-ture of the masses was meant to tout the collective struggle for social jus-tice fueled through political action. Writing in the *New Masses* in 1932, Philip Rahv described this proletarian catharsis as a new spirit "break-ing through the wall that separates literature from life" (281). Rahv gave voice to the central aesthetic concern of insurgent leftist writers coming into their own in the Depression and changing the literary establishment in the process: how to bridge the gap between art and social reality that had appeared to grow ever wider under the auspices of high modernism.

Each position staked out in this cultural debate was rooted in what Terry Eagleton has called the ideology of the aesthetic—a theoretical concept that accounts for the infusion of politics into debates over art. As a result of this condition, Eagleton explains, "The construction of the modern notion of the aesthetic artefact is thus inseparable from the construction of the dominant ideological forms of modern class-society, and indeed from a whole new form of human subjectivity appropriate to that social order" (*Aesthetic* 3). In this light, formalism can be connected with classical liberalism. The aesthetic concept of the autonomous text, for example, is implicated in the ideology that validates the system of private property, and the discourse surrounding creative genius bears striking resemblance to professions of individual liberty and enterprise. Likewise, the aesthetic of social realism can be aligned with progressive liberalism as well as more radical political conceptions, sharing an emphasis on communal values and collective representations of human identity and experience. In the thirties, then, aesthetics was returning to its pre-Enlightenment roots, brought from a Kantian realm of abstraction closer to material experience by a brand of cultural politics insisting that art develop social awareness in keeping with the times in order to be relevant.

Despite the prescriptive nature of social realism and the polarized climate of literary debate, however, it was not unusual to find authors with proletarian sympathies employing some of the same formal practices as writers considered irredeemably "bourgeois." Writers such as John Dos Passos, Tillie (Lerner) Olsen, Richard Wright, and Muriel Rukeyser, all of whom were praised in the pages of the radical and liberal journals of the thirties, used many of the same modernist techniques as those vilified as formalists—Eliot, Wilder, Hemingway, and Faulkner, to name a few. Simply put, both advocates of social realism and formalists who championed art for art's sake in the thirties and beyond insisted on a strict division in theory that simply did not hold up in practice.

Such artful negotiations produced fundamental questions that dominated cultural and literary debate in the 1930s: What is the relationship between forms of cultural expression and the social, historical, and political conditions surrounding them? Do aesthetic practices inevitably create a gap between art and social reality? If so, can that gap be closed with a revised aesthetic that takes into account the ideological and political dimensions of art? In the context of this revised aesthetic, what is the function of the "bourgeois" literary tradition? These questions not only served as fodder for left and right in the literary class war but also framed important developments in cultural theory on the left. On the whole, leftist writers and critics and the formalists who resisted the literature of social realism responded ideologically to cultural concerns and thus took part in the broader political struggle over whether or how to redefine American society during the Depression. Under these conditions, the ideological crisis facing the concept of self-reliance was translated into aesthetic terms. While formalists tended to hold firm to the rugged individualism of solitary creative genius and the autonomous text, leftists tended to promote a sort of aesthetic collectivism in trying to bring art closer to the experiences of the masses and thus to make it accessible and politically functional as an instrument of social transformation.

Faulkner's literary production bears the marks of its engagement with this dynamic cultural politics. Gauging the depth of impact calls for the kind of theoretical foundation enabled by Theodor Adorno in *Aesthetic Theory* as he articulates a revised method of immanent critique expanding the range of formal analysis to cover both text and context. With this critical approach, Adorno poses a challenge to reflection theory for the purpose of redeeming the social value of modern art from reductive attempts within Marxism to cast it aside in favor of a brand of realism purportedly able to reflect social reality for the purpose of critique and reform. Drawing on negative dialectics, Adorno envisions not reflective but rather intricately constitutive relations between art and social reality: "Art negates the categorical determinations stamped on the empirical world and yet harbors what is empirically existing in its own substance" (5). For Adorno, this is a material process in which art internalizes and reconfigures external influences to the point that we can define "aesthetic form as sedimented content" extracted from social reality (5). Having said that, Adorno cautions against the simplified view that "art's autonomous

realm has nothing in common with the external world other than borrowed elements that have entered into a fully changed context" (5). Instead, reinforcing the longstanding claim of Marxist cultural theory that
"the development of artistic processes, usually classed under the heading
of style, corresponds to social development," Adorno contends that art
remains perpetually responsive to the material world, ironically and di-
alectically by means of artistic autonomy (5). He further explains, "Even
the most sublime artwork takes up a determinate attitude to empirical
reality by stepping outside of the constraining spell it casts, not once and
for all, but rather ever and again, concretely, unconsciously polemical
toward this spell at each historical moment" (5). To grasp this perpetual
dynamic, Adorno argues, we must think of art as an inversely independent form and examine its properties accordingly: "That artworks as win-
dowless monads 'represent' what they themselves are not can scarcely be
understood except in their own dynamic, their immanent historicity as a
dialectic of nature and its domination, not only of the same essence as the
dialectic external to them but resembles it without imitating it" (5). Under
these conditions, the autonomous claim made in support of "art for art's
sake" is not grounds for dismissal of the "bourgeois" tradition but, on
the contrary, a way of exposing it as always already socially inscribed
and politically inflected, in spite of the most strident attempts by artists
or critics on the right or left to insist otherwise. For Adorno, as always,
the key to a productive aesthetic theory is forged from a dialectical mold:
"Art's double character as both autonomous and *fait social* is incessantly
reproduced at the level of its autonomy." Only through a practice of immanent critique that mediates textual form and content and social reality,
insists Adorno, can we realize that in works of art, "tension is binding in
relation to the tension external to them" (5).

Adorno's aesthetic theory shows the influence of debates in the 1930s
raging within Marxism and, by extension, in broader cultural forums over
the use value of the "bourgeois" literary tradition at a time of heightened social consciousness. Building on this tradition, Frederic Jameson
sets forth his definition of the "political unconscious" as a comprehensive

and fundamental human story, such as the struggle for freedom, fragmented by repressive forces at work as history is translated into narrative form. For the critic, then, the objective is to define relevant features, fill in gaps, and highlight contradictions in an effort to expose a surface of fuller meaning that extends from text to context. As Jameson argues, this critical practice involves defining "the multiple paths that lead to the unmasking of cultural artifacts as socially symbolic acts" (*Political Unconscious* 20). This analytical process traverses three concentric frames of reference: the contemporaneous historical context of the work, the social order as defined in terms of class relations, and the progression of human history as a whole. Toward this end, Jameson builds on Adorno's aesthetic theory, revising the practice of mediation traditionally used in Marxist cultural theory to integrate "formal analysis of the work of art and its social ground" as a means of exposing what he terms the "ideology of form" (39). This concept refers to an inherent state of contradiction arising from an artistic process in which literary texts respond to the contextual circumstances of their production. This blend of aesthetic and ideological inquiry applies readily to Faulkner's work leading up to and encompassing the Depression.

In performing ideological analysis, one of the most significant challenges is to negotiate the variations in meaning now attached to key concepts. The concept of "ideology" is a case in point. Initial use of the term, as in *The German Ideology* by Marx and Engels, refers to ideology as a "false consciousness" binding individuals to particular social formations and thus preventing them a comprehensive view of society from which to challenge received class structure. Elaboration of the concept in later Marxist theory, however, stresses ideology as a determinant of social relations rather than chiefly a cognitive function. In "Ideology and the Ideological State Apparatuses," Louis Althusser borrows from Lacanian psychoanalysis to define the systematic workings of ideology. Through State Apparatuses (government agencies, courts, military and police units) and Ideological State Apparatuses (churches, families, political parties, and forms of cultural expression, including art and popular media), ideology shapes or "interpellates" individuals, fashioning them as subjects willing to accept the conditions favorable to the dominant class. This approach exemplifies a common tendency in Marxist theory to view in ideology an inherent deceptiveness that serves the interests of a dominant class over an exploited working class.

However, as Eagleton and other contemporary theorists have cautioned, the insistence on false consciousness can lead to a reductive determinism hindering ideological inquiry. If, as Eagleton and others have asked, ideology is deceptive to the point of totality, how can one ever find a space outside ideology in order to interrogate it? Furthermore, must ideology be inherently false? These questions, among others, prompt Eagleton to offer a series of progressively refined definitions of ideology that retain much of what earlier Marxist theorists contribute to the discussion—Althusser's cogent discussion of the systematic workings of ideology, for instance—but also enable avoidance of determinism. Two of these definitions pertain to the understanding of ideology applied here to Faulkner's literary production. First, in *Ideology: An Introduction*, Eagleton explains that ideology is a system of ideas and beliefs, regardless of veracity, that "symbolize[s] the conditions and life-experiences of a specific, socially significant group or class" (29). Acknowledging the inevitability of inter- and intraclass conflict, Eagleton adds a qualification that such ideology "attends to the *promotion* and *legitimation* of the interests of such social groups in the face of opposing interests" (29). Thus ideology both reflects the beliefs and values of a given class and acts on behalf of that class as it enters into conflict with others in the realm of social relations.

These issues arising from the interplay of aesthetics and ideology not only affected Faulkner's literary production and critical reception as he emerged on the Depression cultural scene but also have remained pertinent to analysis of his work ever since. Of particular importance is the understanding of art as an autonomous form of expression, a view that Faulkner articulated in terms of his own creative process. As an addendum to *Absalom, Absalom!* he included a hand-sketched map of Yoknapatawpha County with an inscription reading, "William Faulkner, Sole Owner & Proprietor." This claim of ownership is one of the most widely quoted references Faulkner made to his fictional domain—second only, perhaps, to his later recollection of its genesis in an interview:

> Beginning with *Sartoris* I discovered that my own little postage stamp of native soil was worth writing about and that I would never live long enough to exhaust it, and by sublimating the actual into the apocryphal I would have complete liberty to use whatever talent I might have to its absolute top. It opened up a gold mine of other peoples, so I created a cosmos of my own. I can move these people around like God, not only in space but in time too. (Meriwether and Millgate 255)

Significantly, the process of sublimation that Faulkner describes shares in common with Adorno's aesthetic theory the notion that fiction takes its form from social relations and, despite the resulting condition of interdependence, is paradoxically able to declare independence. However, unlike Adorno, Faulkner places greater emphasis on the author than the text, equating individual liberty with the prerogative to wield absolute authority over the fictional realm. With this power, the author as Creator brings the fictional world into being. In Faulkner's view, however, this process of creation does not happen ex nihilo or in a vacuum, as Romantic and formalist fetishes of genius insist, for it bears repeating that he acknowledges the constitutive role that social reality plays. Engaged in social relations, the author collects material to translate, reshape, and fashion into literary form. By virtue of this process, Faulkner declares, the author emerges with an indisputable right to ownership. Faulkner's claim is significant for many reasons, not the least of which is the direct parallel it establishes between the aesthetic and the ideological by rendering art analogous to the concept of private property upheld as virtually sacrosanct in capitalist society.

While the primary concern of this study is with relations between the textual and contextual, rather than biographical factors, it is beneficial to understand Faulkner's social and political profile in the Depression. During this period Faulkner was aligned economically and, in many respects, ideologically with the dominant class. Compared to the casualties of the Depression, however, Faulkner seemed to be on a reverse trajectory, by outward appearances at least: he was all but broke in the twenties but was able to improve his financial standing just as the Depression took root. Money from his writing enabled Faulkner to become a property owner for the first time, a major personal and professional milestone for the man known by many in his hometown as "Count No Count." In April 1930, less than a year after the crash, Faulkner purchased an estate that he named Rowan Oak. Feelings of accomplishment and security that came with this purchase, however, were dampened by the serious financial difficulty that Faulkner experienced subsequently. In the years of the Depression, he teetered constantly on the brink of financial disaster due to faulty investment strategies, dual tax obligations in California and Mississippi, and a list of dependents.

Faulkner's correspondence throughout the Depression is peppered with urgent references to impending financial doom. In a 1940 letter to Robert Haas, his editor at Random House, Faulkner describes a correlation between diminishing creative and monetary resources, leading him to conclude that "maybe a man worrying about money cant write anything worth buying. . . . I'm a lug of the first water; what I should do (or any artist) is give all my income and property to the bloody govt. and go on WPA forever after" (Blotner, *Selected Letters* 120–21). In a subsequent letter to Haas, Faulkner pleads his case for a sizeable advance. Without the money, he warns, "I will have to liquidate myself, sell some of my property for what I can get for it, in order to preserve what I might. I wont hesitate to do this when I come to believe that I have no other course" (127). With the shaky confidence of a postcrash stock broker, Faulkner adds, "At present I still believe I have something to sell in place of it—namely, the gamble on my literary output for the said two years, provided these two years will be free of pressure" (127). After a detailed accounting of his debts in the form of a chart, Faulkner writes with a strange mix of self-deprecation and self-confidence, "Obviously, this is too high a rate of spending for my value as a writer, unless I hit moving pictures or write at least six commercial stories a year. I am still convinced that I can do it, despite the fact that I have not so far" (127). As the letter closes, Faulkner turns poignantly away from the material to express to Haas the symbolic value of the estate he wants so desperately to keep: "It's probably vanity as much as anything else which makes me want to hold onto it. I own a larger parcel of it than anybody else in town and nobody gave me any of it or loaned me a nickel to buy any of it with and all my relations and fellow townsmen, including the borrowers and frank sponges, all prophesied I'd never be more than a bum" (128–29). This urgent missive to Haas, like so many others Faulkner wrote, shares much in common with the scores of other pleas made during the hard times of the Depression, at once serving as a call for relief and invoking a history of self-reliance and the promise of hard work in the future. Not surprisingly, socioeconomic themes pervade Faulkner's fiction of the Depression. One of the most common is the inherent tension between independence and interdependence, suggesting connections not only to the experiences of his life but also to those of many Americans at the time, as well as to trends in contemporary social thought and politics.

Throughout the Depression, Faulkner found himself confronted with difficult ideological dilemmas posed by the crisis and by efforts to alleviate the suffering—notably, the ideas and policies converging in the New Deal. As this vast federal initiative channeled the forces of ideological change and modernization that had begun to alter the social and political landscape of America and of the South after World War I, it manifested in tangible ways for Faulkner and his circle of family and friends. In turn, it shaped Faulkner's political profile in the Depression significantly, with the effects lasting for the remainder of his life. By any measure, the New Deal was the largest expansion of the federal government in the history of the United States. In Faulkner's region of Mississippi, the development of the Tennessee Valley Authority (TVA) constituted a major federal incursion, the likes of which had not been seen since the one that came under much different circumstances during the Civil War and Reconstruction. Faulkner could bear witness to the work of the WPA as well—substantial improvements to the airport in Oxford, where Faulkner's love of flight took off, and his brother John's stint with a construction project, which provided both a much-needed job and material for his novel *Men Working*, were cases in point. That Faulkner chose not to acknowledge the tangible benefits afforded by the federal government can be viewed as a function of ideology. While responsible for untold improvements, especially in the lives of the rural poor, the TVA, the WPA, and other federal initiatives smacked of social engineering, an anathema to the sense of regional and individual self-reliance repeatedly exhibited in Faulkner's life, if not always so assuredly in his fiction.

Because he was intensely private and not yet the public figure he would become later in his career, Faulkner's anti–FDR/New Deal tendencies played out on the personal stage and thus come to us as anecdotal evidence. Along these lines, Joseph Blotner documents Faulkner's displeasure with having to obtain a Social Security number. "For a man who took a pessimistic view of programs such as the WPA and anything which tended to emphasize the group over the individual," writes Blotner, "it must have seemed some kind of ultimate affront" (*FAB* 2: 953). When the 1936 campaign rolled around, Faulkner marked the occasion by naming two of his mules after Eleanor Roosevelt and Jim Farley, FDR's campaign manager (Blotner, *FABOV* 412). In 1938 Faulkner responded angrily to FDR's decision to move the date of Thanksgiving Day, based on a request by the National Retail Dry Goods Association. Faulkner's wife, Estelle, recalled his saying later, "I never did care much for Thanksgiving after Mr. Roosevelt got through messing around with it" (Blotner, *FAB* 2: 1030). Sounding a more conciliatory note that same year, Faulkner asked Robert Haas to convey his appreciation to Bennett Cerf at Random House for sending the full five-volume set of *The Public Papers and Addresses of Franklin Delano Roosevelt* and later requested another set for his longtime friend Phil Stone, a well-connected Democrat and great admirer of FDR (Blotner, *Selected Letters* 106; *FAB* 2: 1003).

As this evidence suggests, when it came to taking political stands in the thirties, Faulkner was cut from a different mold than, say, his regional counterparts who dubbed themselves the "Southern Agrarians."

Sharing some of the same concerns as Faulkner, they mobilized publicly under one banner to publish *I'll Take My Stand* in 1930 as a manifesto against what they perceived as northeastern hegemony, destructive industrialization and modernization, and dehumanizing scientific theories of sociology and economics. On these grounds, the Southern Agrarians continued throughout the Depression era to oppose on both cultural and political fronts the New Deal as well as efforts from the far left to achieve socialism. Emily S. Bingham and Thomas A. Underwood do well to describe this coterie of writers and thinkers as "generals preparing for a battle" and as men who "orchestrated a series of political and intellectual skirmishes" in seeking to execute that plan (4). While not apolitical, Faulkner viewed such skirmishes from the sidelines, thus rendering his fiction the best place to pursue the political Faulkner of the Depression. Nevertheless, in terms of party affiliation, Joseph Blotner offers us the apt description of Faulkner as an "anti-radical Democrat," contrasting him with the writer and ardent Marxist Dashiell Hammett, with whom Faulkner developed a fast friendship on a jaunt to New York in 1931 (*FAB* 1: 740–43).

Despite a general reticence to speak out politically, Faulkner was capable of noticeable departures, as in a 1931 interview with the *New York Herald Tribune*. Provoked by what he later described as a climate of mutual dislike, Faulkner gave the reporter provocative answers, claiming that under slavery "Negroes would be better off because they would have someone to look after them"—a comment that drew controversy and prompted Faulkner to assert later that he had been misquoted (Meriwether and Millgate 19). The reporter described Faulkner as "interested in politics, but not national politics," noting that Faulkner was aware that the Democrats would likely take control of Congress but reacted to the prospect as if it were "the election of a very distant relative to office" (21). Playing up the angle of deficient political acumen, Faulkner declared, "I vote Democratic because I'm a property owner. Self-protection" (22). Performances such as this one early in Faulkner's career, driven by his intense desire to guard his privacy and likely by his aversion to interviews, lend an air of uncertainty to Faulkner's political views, making it all the more difficult to situate him comfortably in the context of the binary political opposition prevailing in the Depression. This project becomes even more challenging when we delve deeply into the fiction. We find, for example, that while Faulkner's own financial troubles and the sympathy for the poor and dispossessed often on display can be aligned with the burgeoning social consciousness inspired by hard times, his ideological investment in classical liberalism and his consequent wariness of collectivism can best be understood in the light of broader concerns expressed by the Right in the debate over the New Deal. Indeed, based on his New Deal skepticism, Faulkner shared much in common with the southern lawmakers FDR sought to purge. Like them, Faulkner was an increasingly dissatisfied Democrat who basically had nowhere else to go when faced with the immediate alternatives confronting him on the American political scene.

Times of such immense social and economic upheaval inevitably bring uncertainty and produce a climate of ever-shifting political allegiances. As we have seen, the desire for order and stability was imperative once the Depression threw the proverbial wrench into the American economic machine. Under these conditions, forces in political conflict tried to mobilize large numbers of Americans, attracting them to the fold with promises of relief and restored order in the present and greater security in the future. For the various social and political formations—from the New Deal to the American Liberty League to Southern Agrarianism to the Dixiecrat revolt to the Communist Party to the Popular Front—the fundamental challenge posed was quintessentially American: how to make the many voices speaking out in plurality function as a whole. In turning from the dynamics of this world to plan "a cosmos of my own," Faulkner represents this dilemma as a problem of form. Time and time again in this phase of his career, Faulkner attempts to bring multiple perspectives to order under the design of narrative unity. *The Sound and the Fury*, *As I Lay Dying*, and *Absalom, Absalom!* present an array of narrators with alternative accounts of the same events. Implicit in the form are the assertions that a collective purpose can be served and that a whole story can be told. *The Unvanquished* is composed of previously published material revised and collected under a singular textual banner, a show of unity consistently undermined by the tensions between and within the individual sections. *Light in August* features contrapuntal narratives that forge divergent paths in the context of one narrative terrain, often resulting in an unstable condition. Ideological tension and contradiction are inscribed even at the most basic level of form in Faulkner's texts, with bold assertions of autonomy from the author and his characters belied by a flow of clauses that engender perpetual deferment and yield layers of dependence. Moving along the spectrum of the form-content dialectic, we find that Faulkner's characters populate a fictional world in which family and community are gatherings of alienated individuals existing under nominal unity; in which cooperation happens fleetingly, when it happens at all, and gives way quite easily, with a few exceptions, to the pursuit of self-interest; in which characters reach out to one another but arrive frequently at intractable moments of difference, defined in terms of race, class, and gender.

When he cocked an ear toward American society and culture in the late twenties and thirties, Faulkner recorded a cacophony of voices singing different songs but moving toward the common refrain that greater cooperation and unity were essential for achieving a "new order of things." William Faulkner's "planned society" presented Depression readers with a more unstable, complex, and sobering alternative. Faulkner's fictional property stood in contrast to the society envisioned by the rhetoric of political idealism used to instill hope and confidence and to mobilize the American public. Faulkner gave to Depression readers an order of things in which totalizing conceptions of unity, organic wholeness, and harmony exist not as achievable ends but rather as tenuous constructs inherently vulnerable to the more "natural" human desire to pursue individual liberty—sometimes nobly, sometimes unscrupulously. This vision started to take form as Faulkner surveyed the national scene during the intensification of a major cultural conflict that would chart the course of literary debate for years to come.

CHAPTER TWO

Decadence and Dispossession
Faulkner and the "Literary Class War"

THE RISE IN social consciousness among artists and intellectuals in the 1930s began as a reaction to what had come to be viewed
as transgressions in the 1920s—namely the unchecked capitalism of the
"robber barons" and a frivolous bourgeoisie and the expatriate impulse
that had sent many Americans to the more enriching cultural climes of
Europe. With a sort of Lenten devotion, artists and intellectuals repented
of their past excesses, publicly renouncing past attitudes and practices
driven by bohemian and often hedonistic indulgences. Acknowledging
the decadence in life and art so pervasive in the twenties, many in the
"lost generation" welcomed the dose of reality prescribed by a new era of
hardship. Now these former "expats" would emerge from the insulation
of European cafés and the inner recesses of the creative mind to reinvent

themselves as social beings. This collective project of self-transformation inspired a new aesthetic ideology as well. If artists were to reestablish ties between the life of the mind and social reality, however, they would need an artistic form appropriate to the task. Determined to forge a bond between art and activism, those committed to a revitalized social realism essentially waged what Edmund Wilson aptly called the "literary class war"—a cultural conflict in formation since the aftermath of World War I brought rapid socioeconomic change to Europe and the United States ("Literary" 319).

For a young writer such as William Faulkner, who was struggling to make his mark in the late twenties and early thirties, getting caught in the politically charged crossfire was difficult to avoid. Certainly this sort of action was not what the young Faulkner craved when he enlisted in the Royal Air Force in Canada after deficiencies had prevented his joining the U.S. Air Force. Faulkner's service in World War I ended prematurely after a few weeks of training, yielding only a spiffy uniform and the affected limp that he cultivated upon returning home to Mississippi. Faulkner's experience with the forces converging in the literary class war, however, would prove much more productive.

Literary history has tended to define this encounter with laconic ease, relegating it to little more than a footnote in the story of Faulkner's development as a writer. Robert Penn Warren, for example, offers an explanation of why Faulkner was "not irrelevant, but inimical" to the Depression literary establishment (6). In Warren's view, Faulkner's fiction "clearly was not a literature in tune with the New Deal; the new post office art, the new social conscience, the new Moscow trials, or the new anything. It was, simply, new: that is, created. And in some circles, at all times, for a thing to be truly created, is to be outrageous" (7). A telling ideological assumption here is that the autonomy of Faulkner's fiction—that is, its distance from what Warren identifies as the "leftism" (6) of the thirties—stands as testimony to his integrity as an artist who needed only to persevere through a momentary lapse of reason in American literary history before his brilliance was rightfully acknowledged.

The gist of Warren's assessment long stood as a matter of record in Faulkner studies, gaining a sense of authority through the sheer power of repetition—one of the most effective devices in the politics of historiography. But it should be the task of the critic, if not to rewrite literary history, at least to revise it so as to question received assumptions that obscure more than they reveal. In my view, the problem with the traditional account of Faulkner's engagement with the cultural politics of the literary class war is that it denies the complexity of this relationship and especially its significant role in the production of Faulkner's early fiction. In order to achieve fuller understanding, this study challenges key false assumptions: (1) that the literary class war was rooted in binary opposition between formalism (or modernism) and social realism (or proletarian literature) and (2) that Faulkner remained distant from a cultural context increasingly focused on literature of heightened social conscience. Reconstituting the development of the literary class war so as to emphasize negotiations between formalism and social realism that occurred despite professions of absolute division exposes Faulkner's fiction not as disengaged from but rather highly active in this cultural formation.

On a basic level, the literary class war was an aesthetic and ideological dispute over the relationship between art and politics. In many respects, this debate mirrored the one surrounding classical liberalism, with the forces of ideological change producing competing visions of art and the creative process. With reinvigorated leftists continuing the call for art of political engagement focused on collective experience and social reform, many cultural conservatives reaffirmed principles of formalism that defined art as autonomous from social relations and as a privileged form of expression forged from the individual creative mind. These fundamentally different beliefs contributed to a sense of polarity, inspiring the rhetoric of entrenchment insistent on strict division along aesthetic and ideological lines. This intricate cultural politics centered not only on the literary giants of the time but also on emerging writers such as Faulkner.

Because Faulkner's early novels exhibited traits associated with modernism—specifically, formal experimentation, stream of consciousness passages, and deep psychological exploration—many advocates of social realism reacted with predictable consternation. These modernist qualities suggested to them that Faulkner had an affinity for the literary tradition of the twenties and that his opposition to the emergent aesthetic ideology of social realism could be assumed. After all, Faulkner's fiction seemed a far cry from the aesthetic vision fashioned by Michael Gold in his 1930 article "Proletarian Realism," a reaffirmation of the aesthetic and ideological vision he had been espousing for more than a decade. Predictably, the genre Gold describes in the article is essentially an antidote to the aesthetic practices of high modernism. True to Marxist theory, Gold posits culture as a reflection of class society and holds forth the dominant literary tradition of the twenties as evidence of a bourgeoisie in decline. For the mobilized proletariat intent on assuming power, Gold envisions a new literary form to reflect the revolutionary project at hand. Insisting that proletarian realism should resist prescriptive constraints, Gold nevertheless identifies various demonstrable aspects of this revolutionary form. Instead of focusing on "idle Bohemians" in the manner of Proust, the "master-masturbator of the bourgeois literature," Gold advises, proletarian realism should document the lives and work of the proletariat accurately ("Proletarian" 206). Aiming for a minimalist style, Gold adds, proletarian writers should strive for a brand of realism marked by "swift action, clear form, the direct line, cinema in words" (207). Fundamentally, depictions of social reality should be honest, focusing on the plight of the working class in order to awaken readers to the inherent injustices of capitalism and thus to inspire support for the revolutionary cause. In effect, Gold injects social realism with the more specific political agenda of proletarianism to arrive at an aesthetic ideology—that is to say, an artistic vision heavily influenced by the Marxist philosophy that Gold and a host of intellectuals had come to accept as essential to achieving greater social and economic justice in America. Gold was by no means alone in articulating such a vision: Granville Hicks, Philip Rahv, and Joseph Freeman, among others, also articulated ideas intended to bind art more tightly to social reality in general and a leftist political agenda in particular.

Hicks wrote one of the earliest critical studies of Faulkner's fiction outside the genre of the book review, and it now stands as an exemplary document of the initial response to Faulkner from the left. His treatment of Faulkner was plainly influenced by the emergent aesthetic ideology of social realism. In *The Great Tradition* (1933), Hicks takes Faulkner to task for not writing "simply and realistically about southern life" (266). In the eyes of Hicks and other advocates of social realism, Faulkner demonstrates a tendency to sensationalize the plight of the rural poor but no commitment to expose and indict the real social conditions responsible for that plight. Hicks contends that if Faulkner would aim for "a more representative description of life," he might be able to probe "the kind of crime that is committed every day, and the kind of corruption that gnaws at every human being in this rotten society" (266). Failing that, Hicks concludes, Faulkner is left "to pile violence upon violence in order to convey a mood that he will not or cannot analyze" (266).

In *Writers in Crisis* (1942), Maxwell Geismar devotes a chapter to Faulkner and follows Hicks's line of reasoning to its "logical" conclusion. Displaying the either/or reasoning common to the more polemical critics of the thirties, Geismar asserts that a writer unwilling to operate under the framework of social realism will wind up an advocate of fascism. Ironically, Faulkner could take heart in the fact that he had arrived in at least one respect: he had warranted the charge that leftist critics reserved only for writers whom they took seriously. Generally speaking, then, influential critics in the Depression, inspired by the aesthetic ideology of social realism, lodged two charges against Faulkner on a consistent basis. First, they criticized him for writing in a style derivative of high modernism, emphasizing formal experimentation and the "aristocratic obliviousness" of quasi aristocrats such as the Sartorises and the Compsons (Trilling 70). Second, critics cited Faulkner for injecting gratuitous violence into his novels and stories for apparent shock value.

These two primary criticisms implied the common charge of escapism—for radical critics, an aesthetic effect indicative of complicity in a fading bourgeois literary tradition. In "Wilder: Prophet of the Genteel

Christ," the article Wilson credits with intensifying the literary class war, Gold articulates this charge forcefully, taking Thornton Wilder to task for being "the poet of a small sophisticated class that has recently risen in America—our genteel bourgeoisie" (202). For Gold, Wilder is a servant of the dominant bourgeois class seeking to "forget its roots in American industrialism," because his fiction "disguises the barbaric sources of their income, the billions wrung from American and foreign peasants and coolies. It lets them feel spiritually worthy of that income" (202). For advocates of social realism, violent content functions in much the same way, offering an escape route to the bourgeois reader seeking freedom from social responsibility. Citing *Sanctuary* as an example, Hicks criticizes Faulkner for providing cheap thrills that obscure the unjust social conditions contributing to violence in the South. Instead of urging his readers to probe the roots of violence, Faulkner "helps them to forget, for a few hours, their petty cares" (Hicks 268). What Gold identifies in Wilder and Hicks in Faulkner is, in effect, an aesthetic ideology masking social reality for the dominant bourgeois class. Entranced in bourgeois decadence, the argument goes, the reader can deny material social conditions through a false consciousness induced by the aesthetic effects of the text.

Responsive to such attacks on established and emerging writers alike and wary of the overt mixture of art and politics promoted on the left, intellectuals on the right immediately reasserted an aesthetic ideology of formalism as part of a larger expression of cultural conservatism. In a series of articles written for the *New Republic*, the Southern Agrarian Allen Tate proved himself a worthy adversary to Gold. In "Poetry and Politics," one of the installments, Tate criticizes the effort to make art a political instrument, insisting that art and the artist are devalued and compromised in the process. Tate elaborates on this philosophical concern in aesthetic terms, identifying three motivations in contemporary writers: (1) the scientific spirit/practical will, (2) romantic irony, and (3) the creative spirit. In "Three Types of Poetry," the initial essay, Tate explains that the scientific spirit in art had yielded a "positive Platonism, or a naïve confidence in the limitless power of man to impose practical abstractions upon the world" (126). Inevitably frustrated by this attempt to replace the imagination with the practical will, Tate adds, the writer adopts romantic irony to express disillusionment. Instead, Tate encourages the artist to cultivate the individual creative spirit, which "occupies an aloof middle ground" between the practical will and romantic irony (126). Wary of a threat posed by what Tate perceives as disturbing literary trends, he points to an alarming "critical apparatus . . . known at present as the revolutionary or social point of view" (128). Finally, Tate articulates the aesthetic ideology of formalism, essentially reaffirming the notion of "art for art's sake." As Tate explains, poetry "has no useful relation to the ordinary forms of action" (read: to social reality or political causes); instead, "poetry finds its true usefulness in its perfect inutility, a focus of repose for the will-driven intellect that constantly shakes the equilibrium of persons and societies with its unrelieved imposition of partial formulas upon the world" (240).

While negative reception of Faulkner in the early days came largely from the left, appreciation of his work was informed by those steeped in the aesthetic ideology of formalism. The Fugitives, soon to be Southern Agrarians, were among the first to express admiration for Faulkner, casting his concern with form as an attribute rather than a detriment. Faulkner's first novel, *Soldier's Pay* (1926), caught the attention of Donald Davidson, whose assessment foreshadowed the coming divisions of the literary class war. In a review of the novel, Davidson hails Faulkner as "an artist in language, a sort of poet turned into prose; he does not write prose as Dreiser does, as if he were washing dishes; nor like Sinclair Lewis, who goes at words with a hammer and a saw" ("William Faulkner" 13). Instead, Davidson sees in Faulkner a devotion to the craft that makes him "distinctly a 'modern'" (13). A year later, in a review of *Mosquitoes*, Davidson picks up where he left off, praising Faulkner's "wonderful dexterity in the technical management of words" ("Grotesque" 20). The publication of *Sartoris* (1929) prompts Davidson to declare that "as a stylist and an acute observer of human behavior, I think that Mr. Faulkner is the equal of any except three or four American novelists who stand at the very top" ("Two Mississippi" 27). Davidson's treatment of Faulkner is indicative of the fervent commitment to aesthetic principles that would drive those on the right to fashion a "radicalism" of their own, once the literary class war erupted.

Conrad Aiken's spirited defense of Faulkner serves as an even more telling example of this aesthetic and ideological response at work. Determined to deflect the emphasis on depravity and violence in Faulkner's fiction, Aiken, in "William Faulkner: The Novel as Form," stresses its aesthetic merits. Unlike advocates of social realism, Aiken insists that "what sets [Faulkner] above—shall we say it firmly—all his American contemporaries, is his continuous preoccupation with the novel as *form*" (139). Owing to the density of Faulkner's writing—the complex narrative structures and the extended sentence patterns—Aiken contends that "the reader must therefore be steadily *drawn in*; he must be powerfully and unremittingly hypnotized" (138). Aiken's assessment could not be more firmly opposed to Gold's definition of the purpose and function of art. With his emphasis on form and the arresting effect of Faulkner's novels, Aiken essentially praises Faulkner for not applying the techniques of social realism and, in turn, for providing the reader with a means of escapist pleasure.

As traditional literary history would have it, then, Faulkner's initial critical reception was determined by the polarity that was taking hold of the literary establishment. Caught between two diametrically opposed aesthetic ideologies, Faulkner was fated to be condemned by one and praised by the other. The problem with this account, however, is that it fails to capture for the sake of posterity the complexities that make the literary class war every bit as hard to read as the literal kind. To say categorically that advocates of social realism dismissed Faulkner, while cultural conservatives recognized the value of his art, is to tell only part of the story. While this interpretation has served various purposes—foremost, perhaps, a political agenda active in the late forties and fifties and thus beyond the scope of concern here—accuracy is certainly not among them. In actuality, by the mid-1930s, recognition of Faulkner's worth as a writer was registered by some of the most unlikely people—outspoken advocates of proletarianism, for example—and in some of the most unlikely places—notably, the *New Masses*. This continually diminished and usually ignored component of Faulkner's critical reception in the thirties warrants serious consideration, not only for the added insight it lends to Faulkner's fiction in the historical and cultural context of the literary class war but also for the questions it raises about literary historiography.

Recognition of Faulkner's talent among advocates of proletarianism tended to come initially in the form of begrudging acknowledgment of his potential mixed with constructive criticism. While Faulkner's technical genius was obvious to many critics on the left, they predictably wanted him to expand a potentially keen social insight that they perceived as currently bound by an upper-class frame of reference. Such was the case with James T. Farrell, author of the *Studs Lonigan Trilogy*, as demonstrated by his review of *Light in August* for the *New Masses*. Farrell is especially impressed with the "powerful writing, particularly some of the passages that describe the life of Joe Christmas, a life heaped with injustice" (84). Predictably, Farrell mentions Faulkner's preoccupation with violence and mental disturbance; nevertheless, he remains confident that such concerns will wane in time. Implicitly recognizing Faulkner's talent for probing social reality, Farrell mourns the fact that for now "he is limiting himself" (84).

In a similar vein, Muriel Rukeyser's review of *Dr. Martino and Other Stories* for the *New Masses* is a blend of pointed criticism and recognition of vast promise. Rukeyser places Faulkner among "those writers of vignettes of the macabre who portray a civilization without explaining it" (115). Although she praises Faulkner for resisting didacticism, Rukeyser faults him for not clearly articulating one of the remaining alternatives: "to drive his characters implacably by outside forces, or to dignify them giving them enough consciousness to make meanings in their lives" (115). If Faulkner is "to assume the proportions his work still shadows," Rukeyser declares, he will have to develop the "emotional sophistication which he now lacks" (115). Achieving that, Rukeyser concludes, "his work will be what he is ambitious for it now to seem, having the living dimensions of the society he draws" (115).

By the time *The Hamlet* was published in 1940, it would seem that Faulkner had completed the task assigned by Rukeyser, at least for Edna Lou Walton in her review of the novel for the *New Masses*. Summarizing what leftists had cited repeatedly as Faulkner's main detriments— a derivative modernist style and an emphasis on violence and perversity—Walton proclaims Faulkner's redemption. Once misguided imitation, now Faulkner's "frequent use of stream of consciousness method . . . is admirably suited to his purpose of portraying almost completely inarticulate and shrewdly instinctive mentalities" (216). On the second count as well, Faulkner now demonstrates maturity because "his distortion can function when used to portray a distorted or disintegrating social scene" (216). Focused on the element of class conflict, Walton interprets Faulkner's novel as "a study of the methods (totally amoral and petty and vicious) by which the shrewder of the once tenant or small farmers of the hills turned the tables against the older traders" (216). Walton goes so far as to assign Faulkner a revolutionary vision, concluding that his treatment of the Snopeses demonstrates "that the small dog can eat the larger dog— if nothing, not even kinship (the greatest loyalty among landowners), is sacred" (216). All told, these reviews suggest that Faulkner's value as a writer was measured on the left in terms of his ability to move beyond perceived aesthetic and ideological limitations toward progressive social depictions.

Recognition of Faulkner along these lines was not an aberration but a by-product of evolution in the aesthetic ideology of social realism in the mid-1930s. By that point in the decade, controversy over "leftism" had surfaced in the radical journals committed in part to debates over aesthetics—most prominently the *New Masses*, the *Partisan Review*, and the *Daily Worker*. James F. Murphy explains that the term "leftism" had transformed into "an epithet characterizing certain attitudes and practices that were considered unacceptable" (1). Foremost among them were partisan attacks on writers considered deficient in social consciousness and the belief that writers committed to social realism and proletarianism stood to gain nothing from the bourgeois literary tradition. Moreover, "leftism" was associated with disregard for aesthetics and with the practice of a reductive brand of sociological literary criticism.

A major catalyst for this less strident aesthetic ideology was the publication of letters written by Marx and Engels on the relationship between art and the proletarian cause. Particularly influential was the publication of a letter by Engels to the British socialist writer Margaret Harkness, which appeared in English translation for the first time in *International Literature*, a respected journal among American radical writers and critics. In the letter, Engels stresses the contradictions in Balzac's work as evidence of his value to a writer intent on comprehending class conflict: "That Balzac was . . . compelled to go against his own class sympathies and political prejudices, that he saw the necessity of the downfall of his favorite nobles and described them as people deserving no better fate; that he saw the real of the future where, for the time being, they alone were to be found—that I consider one of the greatest triumphs of realism, and one of the greatest features in old Balzac" (114). While a writer such as Balzac was obviously more concerned with conflict between the upper class and a rising bourgeoisie, he nevertheless could prove worthy of emulation by proletarian writers as they set out to depict social relations in America in a more comprehensive way. The views of Marx and Engels on the uses of the bourgeois literary tradition inspired intellectuals on the left to revise the aesthetic ideology of social realism and to find new meaning and purpose in writers whom they had previously deemed irrelevant. American intellectuals were joining their European counterparts in reconsidering the bourgeois literary tradition for what it could teach writers committed to leftist causes. Of course, a writer's ability to anticipate and represent social dynamics, particularly class conflict, determined his or her value to a revised aesthetic ideology of social realism. For this reason, critics on the left could see the kind of potential in Faulkner that Engels saw fulfilled in Balzac: a writer at odds with his own class sympathies whose work was thus riddled with tension and contradiction and yet, for that very reason, a writer capable of yielding prophetic and comprehensive insight into social relations.

This kind of interpretation was in keeping with efforts to reevaluate modernism and to revise the definition of "realism" to claim more writers for the cause of radical reform. Involved in these undertakings were the Marxist theorists of the Frankfurt School—Adorno, Max Horkheimer, and Walter Benjamin—who challenged traditional Marxist conceptions of modernism as an antisocial form incapable of shedding productive light on class struggle. Georg Lukács was a key figure as well. Lukács set out to widen the conceptual net of socialist realism by defining the categories of "critical realism" and "bourgeois realism" to redeem the social value of previously dismissed or emerging authors and works not thought to toe the party line. For Lukács, one way for authors to achieve "great realism" is by demonstrating great foresight. In so doing, Lukács explains, these authors form

> the authentic ideological avant-garde since they depict the vital, but not im-
> mediately obvious forces at work in objective reality. They do so with such
> profundity and truth that the products of their imagination receive confirma-
> tion by subsequent events—not merely in the simple sense in which a successful
> photograph mirrors the original, but because they express the wealth and di-
> versity of reality, reflecting the forces as yet submerged beneath the surface,
> which only blossom forth visibly at a later stage. ("Realism" 47–48)

Despite aiming for a broadened scope, Lukács does not extend the critical bridge to writers perceived as hopelessly bound by high modernism—Joyce and Faulkner, for example. But this refusal does not preclude the possibility of extending the bridge in retrospect.

For this critical endeavor, Peter Bürger's *Theory of the Avant-Garde* is useful. In this landmark study, Bürger questions a longstanding tendency to fuse modernism and the avant-garde, suggesting instead the need to draw distinctions between the two movements. Under this revised understanding, modernism challenges the artistic status quo primarily in terms of style and form, while the avant-garde targets art as a social institution in need of "creative destruction" that can make way for reformation, to apply a Dadaist paradigm. For Bürger, the foundation of this avant-garde approach is derived from art's widely perceived autonomous status in bourgeois society: "its (relative) independence in the face of demands that it be socially useful" (24). Bürger elaborates on the consequences of this condition: "Art in bourgeois society lives off the tension between the institutional framework (releasing art from the demand that it fulfill a social function) and the possible political content . . . of individual works" (25). Under such conditions, the claim of autonomy means that "art necessarily becomes problematic for itself," which then "provokes the self-criticism of art" in relation to social context (27).

The mode of critique and resulting tensions described by Bürger were contributing factors in the literary class war, as formal and stylistic practices associated with modernism came under increasing scrutiny and the antiestablishment impulses of the avant-garde were channeled by radicals on the left to challenge bourgeois traditions and to promote cultural production as a form of social praxis. Focusing on the themes of decadence in *Mosquitoes* and dispossession in *The Sound and the Fury* offers constructive means of examining how Faulkner's fiction of the mid- to late twenties grapples with issues that would dominate literary debates in the thirties. By reading these texts in the light of this historical and cultural context, we stand to gain fuller understanding of the timely insight and sometimes remarkable prescience of Faulkner's fictional voice. Richard Gray offers an apt assessment of this capability when he observes that the "young Faulkner . . . was able to read the conflicts and tensions implicit in his society and to make a reasonably educated guess (based on knowledge of earlier and similar developments in other places) as to the social formations to which those conflicts would eventually lead, and the terms in which these tensions would (however temporarily) be resolved" (20). On these grounds, we can align Faulkner in key respects with the "authentic ideological avant-garde," as Lukács has it, viewing him not as a mere bystander to the literary class war but instead as a writer with his finger on the pulse of American cultural politics.

Many critics grant *Mosquitoes* the dubious distinction of being Faulkner's worst novel. Among the numerous flaws cited, the blatant posturing of this early work as a novel of ideas bears repeating. Typical of this genre, *Mosquitoes* contains repeated digressions serving no apparent purpose but to allow a budding novelist to express thoughts on various topics of interest, particularly the nature of art and the role of the artist in modern society. From this perspective, the characters in the novel function as thinly veiled mouthpieces and rhetorical devices through which Faulkner attempts to articulate a coherent aesthetic vision. But the novel also falls under the category of roman à clef, given that it emerged from Faulkner's stint in New Orleans in the mid-1920s. There Faulkner cultivated, but mostly observed, a bohemian and avant-garde lifestyle by sitting at the feet of Sherwood Anderson, who was, for a while, a mentor and advocate. On one level, *Mosquitoes* marks Faulkner's declaration of independence from this tutelage, expressed through the rather unflattering depiction of Dawson Fairchild, the Falstaffian novelist generally recognized as Anderson's analogue.

These two strains in the novel—the expression of ideas and the inclusion of autobiographical data (even a famous cameo appearance by Faulkner himself)—have led critics to conclude that *Mosquitoes* renders, in effect, a portrait of Faulkner the artist as a young man.[1] From this perspective, critics interested in ideas expressed in the novel have tended to focus on the most prominent themes as evidence of what preoccupied Faulkner at the time—specifically, the relationship between art and sex and problems of language and representation.[2] Treatment of these ideas is often accentuated by the connections between Faulkner's experiences in New Orleans and the events of the novel, which become allusive pieces of this roman à clef puzzle in need of assembling. While such critical practices have explained much about *Mosquitoes*, they ultimately contain the novel in a fixed set of references to Faulkner's ideas or to his biography. My objective is to broaden the scope by situating the novel in the larger cultural context of changing attitudes toward art and the role of the artist in the twenties that fueled the literary class war of the thirties. In fact, reading the novel as ideologically responsive to the theme of decadence so much in discussion in the late twenties reveals *Mosquitoes* as a text heavily influenced by competing aesthetic ideologies and thus highly active in the cultural politics of its time.

One of the most eloquent expressions of the changing convictions among artists and intellectuals in the late twenties and early thirties came from Faulkner's eventual champion Malcolm Cowley. Cowley's *Exile's Return* (1934) joined Edmund Wilson's *Axel's Castle* (1931) and a host of other articles and books in speaking for a "lost generation" committed to finding itself once more. Cowley's attack on the twenties was driven noticeably by the realization that the decadence in life and art that had come to define the decade was finally running its course. A chronicle of cultural transformation from one era to another, Cowley's book is useful for gauging the relevance of Faulkner's second novel to similar concerns. *Exile's Return* is a nostalgic autobiography documenting the experiences and sentiments of expatriates who fled America—some literally, some figuratively—believing that there was no clear role for the creative spirit in a post–World War I society that had grown increasingly materialistic. However, in keeping with the prevailing mood of the time, Cowley moves from the introspection of autobiography to comment incisively on the attitudes and behaviors of the expatriates and particularly the social implications of their self-imposed exile. For Cowley, writers in the twenties suffered from a chronic solipsism caused by a selfish desire to protect individuality as perhaps the most cherished possession. The consequences of this stance for the artist could be measured in the work of writers such as Eliot, Joyce, and Proust, all of whom Cowley takes to task for privileging solitary concerns to the detriment of social awareness and responsibility. Cowley thus offers his version of the mea culpa sounded by so many of his peers in reflecting on the twenties: "Once the artist had come to be regarded as a being set apart from the world of ordinary men, it followed that his aloofness would be increasingly emphasized. The world would more and more diminish in the eyes of the artist, and the artist would be self-magnified at the expense of the world. These tendencies, in turn, implied still others. Art would come to be treated as a self-sustaining entity, an essence neither produced by the world nor acting upon it: art would be *purposeless*" (143). Cowley's cultural critique is an indictment of the principle of "art for art's sake" as construed by the aesthetic ideology of formalism. In contrast to that view, Cowley insists that the relationship of the artist to society and culture, the essence of politics and political identity, is inextricably bound to and expressed by aesthetics.

Cowley defines the decadence of the twenties in terms of both the prevailing aesthetic ideology and the conflicted relationship between artists and capitalist society. Ironically, expatriates found themselves carrying out the unintended purpose of producing art as a commodity for the very bourgeois set from which they had tried to claim autonomy through dissident movements such as the avant-garde. In turn, they became too accustomed to the easy money that seemed everywhere in abundance in the twenties. Cowley mourns the loss of artistic integrity resulting from decadent complicity: "We became part of the system we were trying to evade, and it defeated us from within, not from without; our hearts beat to its tempo" (227). For art and artists to be redeemed, Cowley argues, the exiles must return from the bohemian cafés on the continent, tear themselves away from the narcissistic gaze, and strive to acknowledge the ties that bind them to a society riddled with social injustice and defined by class struggle. *Mosquitoes* stands as testament to the fact that the reevaluation of the artist's role in art as a social institution at the time of the novel's production was not lost on the young Faulkner, whose derivative second novel virtually forms in response to this cultural development. This mode of critique was engendered by the iconoclastic tactics of the avant-garde that were now being redirected toward the social consciousness and political activism that would dominate the Depression literary establishment.

One need look no further than the basic concept of the novel to discern connections to the evolving cultural politics thus far defined. *Mosquitoes* tells the story of a voyage on Lake Pontchartrain orchestrated by Mrs. Maurier, a dilettante New Orleans society matron who plans the cruise to be a sort of floating salon removed from the constraints of society. In a bit of social engineering, Mrs. Maurier carefully selects a group of artists for the cruise, believing they will hold erudite aesthetic discussions for her to consume with relish. Leaving virtually no genre without representation, she includes among her guests Dawson Fairchild, a raucous novelist; Gordon, a hypermasculine sculptor; Mark Frost, a brooding and unprolific poet; and Dorothy Jameson, a painter. For the artists, this arrangement is beneficial in the sense that Mrs. Maurier will take care of their material needs but potentially compromising in terms of undermining artistic integrity. By supplying Mrs. Maurier's demand, these artists become complicit in the sort of decadence that she represents and thus run the risk of turning themselves and their art into commodities. Not only that, but the artists must contend with the other guests, who embody various attitudes toward art: Ernest Talliaferro, an effete and foppish women's clothing salesman whose aesthetic "appreciation" is part of a carefully cultivated bohemian personality; Julius Kauffman, the "Semitic man" who dismisses art as a pale comparison to actual life experience; Patricia and Josh Robyn, Mrs. Maurier's niece and nephew, who further raise questions about the utilitarian value and commodification of art; and Pete and Jenny, the working-class characters, who virtually stumble aboard the yacht and proceed with a lack of pretentiousness that contrasts them with the other passengers. Aboard the aptly named *Nausikaa*, an allusion to Joyce's *Ulysses* that calls to mind despair and ennui, these characters enable Faulkner to explore, in the words of Frederick Karl, "how the artist may survive on a ship of fools" (4), which is in many ways a microcosm of the decadent society and culture prevailing in the late twenties.

Viewing the yacht in this representative light makes its journey all the more compelling. While the name of the ship calls to mind, in the words of Kierkegaard, "a sickness unto death," the lack of progress and motion points to the fact that the way of life contained on the *Nausikaa*—what Fairchild calls the "charming futility" (*M* 52) of the bohemian lifestyle—

has lost its vitality and momentum. Traditionally in American literature, taking to the water is associated with liberation and self-discovery, *Moby Dick* and *Huckleberry Finn* being perhaps the most obvious examples. On the water, freedom and movement—two American obsessions—provide means of transformation: the character who arrives at the docks is presumably a more rounded version of the one who set sail, having concluded the voyage and thus accomplished the inner progression the journey symbolizes. Steeped in this archetypal construct, the characters in *Mosquitoes* are initially hopeful that this outing on the yacht can provide them with a break from the constraints of society and ample opportunity for self-discovery. This hope for renewed growth is reinforced early on by the course of the *Nausikaa*, which moves "youthfully and gaily under a blue and drowsy day" (*M* 58). However, Faulkner almost immediately mounts a tide of resistance to the archetypal voyage, dating back at least as far as *The Odyssey*, by crafting (in every sense of the word) what Edwin T. Arnold rightly calls "a sterile, static world" in the novel (282). In this world, movement does not necessarily mean progress, a condition illustrated by the fact that the "*Nausikaa* forged onward without any sensation of motion" (*M* 83). Fairchild acknowledges the general lack of direction when he responds to a question about where the yacht is headed: " 'Why nowhere,' answered Fairchild with surprise. 'We just came from somewhere yesterday, didn't we?' " (85). What began as a yearning for freedom and movement has now become a tacit acceptance of confinement and stasis expressed in an explicit lack of purpose. Rather than serving as a means of liberation, as Eva Wiseman perceptively observes, "motion seems to have had a bad effect on the party" (110). Finally, the yacht ceases even its literal movement, running aground on a sandbar and resting "motionless, swaddled in mist like a fat jewel" (164). At this point, the novel explicitly contrasts the romanticism of the voyage with the reality of the antivoyage. As a result of this dilemma, discovery, progress, and motion enter into conflict with repetition, digression, and stagnation, thus creating an overarching formal tension between movement and stasis that frames the critique of decadence offered in *Mosquitoes*.

One way that the novel engages the theme of decadence is through its concern with issues of representation. A case in point is the repeated emphasis on the manipulation of language, particularly the discrepancy between word and deed. Here Faulkner translates a longstanding theme in literature—that language is a poor substitute for action—into contemporary terms. Fairchild initially introduces this theme in the context of gender relations, advising Talliaferro on the motivation of women: "They ain't interested in what you're going to say: they're interested in what you're going to do" (*M* 112). Ironically, Fairchild, whose craft is to employ language, expresses the recognition of its ultimate futility. When Fairchild derides Talliaferro's faith in language, Julius Kauffman, the skeptic when it comes to artistic appreciation, offers a spirited logocentric defense. Surprised that Fairchild, "a member of that species all of whose actions are controlled by words," should be diminishing the power of language, Kauffman defends its power: "It's the word that overturns thrones and political parties and instigates vice crusades, not things: the Thing is merely the symbol for the Word" (130). Interestingly enough, this vital defense of language is expressed in terms of its potential to bring about actual—in this case, political—transformation. In assigning literature a revolutionary function, Kauffman's understanding of language coincides with the aesthetic ideology of social realism.

Instead of subscribing to Kauffman's view, though, Fairchild holds firm to the concept of language as abstraction. And, on the *Nausikaa*, the abstract nature of language is taken to the extreme. In this rarefied and inert environment, in which there is apparently little tangible connection between word and deed, language is reduced to mere babble. "Talk, talk, talk: the utter and heartbreaking stupidity of words," bemoans the narrator after the yachting party holds a lengthy discussion about the inability of art to convey the unpredictable nature of reality. "It seemed endless, as though it might go on forever. Ideas, thoughts, became mere sounds to be bandied about until they were dead" (*M* 186). The arbitrary and impotent nature of words and ideas among this set is reinforced by the fact that Kauffman and Fairchild reverse positions once they have returned to land from the *Nausikaa*. Back in Gordon's studio, involved in a discussion of aesthetics, Fairchild testifies to the power of art to suspend time—a sentiment that Kauffman credits to Fairchild's "unshakable faith in words," adding that language has the same numbing effect as morphine (319). The discourse on language recurring in the novel is demonstrative of the superficiality that Faulkner assigns to Fairchild, whose faith in art apparently stems from sentimentality and a need to overcome the deficiencies of humble origins rather than genuine commitment. This criticism is in line with a major complaint that Cowley and others would lodge against the literature of the lost generation: that its decadence stands exposed in the excessive amount of idle chatter that separates word from deed and betrays a general lack of conviction among artists.

The theme of the limited capacity of language in *Mosquitoes* is augmented by Faulkner's treatment of visual representation. As with issues of language, aesthetic principles of form find initial expression in terms of gender. To apply a Lacanian paradigm, as the elusive object of desire, Woman symbolizes what is lacking and thus serves as the impetus for expression and articulation of ideas in the novel. (This component is, of course, even more pronounced in *The Sound and the Fury*, as feminist criticism of the novel has repeatedly shown.) Much is made in *Mosquitoes* of the female torso sculpted by Gordon. The epitome of idealized and arrested form, the sculpture is "the virginal breastless torso of a girl, headless, armless, legless, in marble temporarily caught and hushed yet passionate still for escape, passionate and simple and eternal in the equivocal derisive darkness of the world" (*M* 11). But the sculpture is also a rhetorical device that allows Faulkner to explore issues of perception, particularly the disparity between objectivity and subjectivity. When Patricia Robyn and Mrs. Maurier view the statue, they are compelled to discuss its meaning. While Mrs. Maurier defers to Gordon for an explanation of the torso's symbolic value, Patricia argues that the point is moot, given what she sees as the ultimately subjective and arbitrary nature of perception: "What do you want it to signify? Suppose it signified a—dog, or an ice cream soda, what difference would it make?" (26). Mr. Talliaferro presses the case even further, adding that the sculpture need not have "objective significance" but instead must exist as art for its own sake, as "pure form untrammeled by any relation to a familiar or utilitarian object" (26). However, as the artist, Gordon insists on having the ultimate authority, on being the sole proprietor of his creation. Asserting the "objective significance" of the sculpture, Gordon proclaims, "This is my feminine ideal: a virgin with no legs to leave me, no arms to hold me, no head to talk to me" (26). Gordon's ideal is ultimately an abstraction, though, a woman whose means of utility and agency have been dissembled. The "objective significance" here is determined in actuality by Gordon's (the artist's) supreme act of subjectivity, rendering the object of desire completely passive, woefully lacking, and thus dependent on the creator for completion and meaning.

Gordon plainly embodies the notion of the artist as solitary and supreme creator of "pure" art—a fundamental component of the aesthetic ideology of formalism that artists and intellectuals converted to social activism in the thirties would associate with the decadence of the twenties. If art exists for its own sake, the thinking goes, then it is the artist who endows art with this existence. Faulkner's novel exposes the basis of this aesthetic principle in terms of a gendered ideology that defines creativity as a masculine impulse. When Mrs. Maurier arrives at Gordon's studio early in the novel to view his sculpture, she pines, "Ah, to be a man, with no ties save those of the soul! To create, to create" (*M* 18). Later, in the epilogue, this masculine aesthetic principle is elaborated by Fairchild, who contrasts artistic creativity with human reproduction. Noting that biology determines man's deference to woman for most of the life-giving process, Fairchild contends that in art "a man can create without any assistance at all: what he does is his" (320). The element of ownership is a key component: for the individual artist, the work of art is a form of private property. Though Fairchild deems this arrangement a "perversion," he insists that "a perversion that builds Chartres and invents Lear is a pretty good thing" (320).

Like so many ideas in Faulkner's second novel, however, this aesthetic principle of the sole creator stands directly challenged. Patricia Robyn rather obviously is the living form meant to expose the inadequacy of the ideal one that Gordon supposedly creates ex nihilo and infuses with "objective significance." Her flat, boyish look calls to mind the androgyny of Lady Brett Ashley in Hemingway's *The Sun Also Rises*, which was published a year before *Mosquitoes*, and is a source of mystification and intrigue for Gordon. The sexual tension between Patricia and Gordon is apparent in one of their initial encounters aboard the *Nausikaa* when Gordon helps Patricia out of the lake after a swim. This tension is compounded by the fact that each tries to objectify the other through the power of perception. In Patricia's eyes, Gordon is the embodiment of his work—a living sculpture chiseled with a "high hard chest" (*M* 82). In turn, Gordon tries to control and then arrest Patricia's movement, just as he would one of his stone creations. Holding Patricia motionless above the deck, Gordon is struck by her "taut simple body, almost breastless and with the fleeting hips of a boy, . . . an ecstasy in golden marble" (82). A pattern is thus established in which Patricia is described in terms that evoke the image of the sculpture. However, unlike the torso that Gordon has captured in stone, Patricia is capable of leaving him. And so she does immediately after Gordon releases her from his grip: "Then she was gone, and Gordon stood looking at the wet and simple prints of her naked feet on the deck" (82).

Through his encounters with Patricia Robyn, his statue come to life, Gordon develops a less abstract aesthetic vision, eventually acknowledging constitutive ties between art and social relations. In effect, Gordon realizes the potential benefits of reconnecting to the world around him, rarefied though it may be aboard the *Nausikaa*. A telling encounter between Gordon and Mrs. Maurier and the sculpture that results from it illustrate Gordon's revised aesthetic. Mrs. Maurier envies Gordon for having a vocation that insulates him from the cruelty of the world: "To live within yourself, to be sufficient unto yourself. . . . To go through life, keeping yourself from becoming involved in it, to gather inspiration for your Work—ah, Mr. Gordon, how lucky you who create are" (*M* 153).

But Mrs. Maurier's praise has quite the opposite of its intended effect: instead of convincing Gordon of her enlightened understanding of art and the function of the artist, the remarks expose her desperate need for confirmation and prompt in Gordon a crucial revelation. Instead of believing that art emerges from the creative impulse of the solitary artist, he recognizes the role of social relations in artistic production. Fortified by this epiphany, Gordon sees Mrs. Maurier with a new intensity. Studying the contours of her face, "learning the bones of her forehead and eyesockets and nose through her flesh" (154), Gordon, in effect, chisels away the constructed facade that she presents to the external world. For Mrs. Maurier, the encounter proves devastating, shining the harsh light of reality into her refuge, the *Nausikaa*, "that island of security that was always waiting to transport her comfortably beyond the rumors of the world and its sorrows" (163). For Gordon, by contrast, the encounter enables him to produce a work approaching realism—the clay mask of Mrs. Maurier that greets the onlooker "with savage verisimilitude" (322) and captures the despair of her existence, which no one else has seen.

Faulkner highlights this transformation in Gordon by having the sculptor undergo what Julius Kauffman aptly deems a "resurrection" (*M* 267). Shortly after the aforementioned encounter with Mrs. Maurier on the *Nausikaa*, Gordon disappears and is presumed by the guests and crew to have drowned. However, he makes a sudden return, which fittingly coincides with the appearance of the tugboat sent to free the *Nausikaa* from its stagnant position on the sandbar. On one level, the tugboat rescue has symbolic value: rescued from "exile," the *Nausikaa* and the guests it contains must now return from a rarefied environment to social relations. For the "resurrected" Gordon, this transition occurs in terms of the relationship between life and art. After returning to the yacht, Gordon has another encounter with Patricia Robyn. In this scene, Faulkner intersperses the story of a king who leaves his marble court, breaking free from the *"dreaming lilac barriers of his world"* (269) to move among his subjects—an obvious analogue to Gordon's revised aesthetic. Gordon cites another story to Patricia of an author who "traps" his lover by writ-

ing about her in a book. Patricia immediately associates the story with
the sculpted torso, charging that Gordon's intention must have been the
same. Instead of the abstract woman represented in stone, Patricia inquires of Gordon, "Wouldn't you rather have a live one?" (270). This
query initiates negotiation between the two characters in a scene that
parodies exchange in various forms. For one, Patricia tries to purchase
Gordon's prized sculpture, effectually assigning it exchange value so as to
assume control over the object. While Gordon's power to confine objects
to abstraction is artistic, Patricia's is financial: she can impose her own
form of abstraction on the sculpture through the process of commodification. But Gordon predictably refuses the offer and tries to assert his own
form of control by perceiving Patricia once again as the living form of the
sculpture. Lifting Patricia and carrying her across the deck, he playfully
spanks ("sculpts") her in response to the challenge she has mounted. A
form of virtual sex, this exchange represents the consummation of the
artist's renewed attention to social relations and his awareness that life
and art must meet on material and physical terms rather than remaining
distanced by abstraction.

   A further challenge to the notion of the self-sustaining artist comes
in the form of Patricia's brother Josh, whose work exhibits an alternative aesthetic principle—the utilitarian conception of art. Fundamentally,
Josh is a counterpoint to Gordon in terms of the way he views his craft.
Rather than a maker of the "pure" form, the kind of artist that Gordon
initially tries to be and that Talliaferro repeatedly exalts, Josh is a living
example of what Gordon imagines in stream of consciousness as "the soul
horned by utility" (*M* 47). Josh is a sculptor of sorts, though his artistic
material is wood rather than clay. Unlike the torso, which exemplifies
Cowley's notion of "purposeless" art (*Exile's* 143), Josh's creation—a
cleaner-smoking pipe—is functional. Not only does Josh take pride in
the outcome, but he also feels a tangible connection to his work. Deriv-
ing satisfaction and a sense of fullness from his artistic labor, Josh does
not experience the kind of reified despair that Gordon suffers in relation
to the abstract torso. For Josh, the creative process yields simple pleasure.

Pressed by Major Ayers to explain the ulterior (i.e., profit) motive driving his work ethic, Josh cites mere pleasure as the source of his inspiration: "Say, I'm just making a pipe, I tell you. A pipe. Just to be making it. For fun" (*M* 173). Major Ayers, ever the venture capitalist, cannot comprehend this sentiment. For this reason, Josh faces much the same challenge from Major Ayers that Gordon faces from Patricia. Ready to abandon his plan for a surefire laxative to clear America's chronic constipation, a condition that in itself expresses incisive social commentary, the major tries to convince Josh to let him market the pipe. Like Patricia, Major Ayers attempts to assign an exchange value to the object, though his motivation is pure profit rather than obtaining the upper hand in a relationship. Still, for Josh the worth of the pipe is measured in terms of its use value and the sense of satisfaction that he derives from its production.

The depictions of Gordon and Josh as artisans, rendered from the perspectives of two seemingly opposed aesthetic ideologies, articulate essentially the same message: the purest art derives from the tangible connection between the creative process and the material world and maintains its integrity by resisting the bourgeois mentality that reduces art to the level of base commodity. The aesthetic principle that Faulkner imagines here suggests that he was testing ideas associated with the aesthetic ideology of social realism circulating in the cultural context of the novel. But to say that Faulkner embraces this aesthetic ideology would clearly overstate the point. Instead, *Mosquitoes* reveals the young Faulkner as responsive to cultural politics to the point that the critique of decadence in his second novel in many ways anticipates the intense conflict between alternative aesthetic ideologies that would mark the literary class war. In my view, Faulkner's response to this conflict goes a long way toward explaining the contradictions that riddle *Mosquitoes* and, in effect, serve as staging devices for the fiction to come.

One of the most visible contradictions in the novel is the way that it treats class relations. Obviously, the dominant perspective in this novel is upper class, whether focused from the standpoint of a character such as Mrs. Maurier, who holds a position in this class, or one such as Talliaferro, who is granted access to it because of his careful cultivation of acceptable social mores. While the *Nausikaa* represents an effort to gain freedom from the constraints of society, it also suggests the futility of this undertaking and the naturalization of social stratification, which ultimately renders the notion of classless society idealistic. Though the novel often expresses longing for encounters and spaces beyond class, it also exposes the rigidity of a social structure defined by class differences. This aspect of the novel is evident in the brief relationship that develops between Patricia Robyn and David West, the yacht's steward. In aesthetic terms, we might say that Patricia's attraction to David is initially a response to form. Patricia descends below the deck to the engine rooms, where she condescends to David's level, with the yacht in this instance representing socially stratified society. Patricia admits to David that she first noticed him when he jumped into the lake fully clothed to the aid of Major Ayers, who had flung himself overboard after losing a bridge hand. She further stresses his subservient role in the hierarchy of the yacht by repeatedly observing that he has to work long hours at the service of the guests, who are able to enjoy themselves at leisure. For Patricia, the interest in David stems from the same rebellious nature on display when she invites Pete and Jenny to join the cruise. After all, Patricia is motivated less by genuine regard for David or for Pete and Jenny than by a self-satisfying desire to disrupt the stratified form of the yacht and to spoil the intentionally sophisticated aura of the yachting party.

Through what can be termed formal experimentation, Patricia seeks to blur the lines of social division represented by the upper and lower decks of the *Nausikaa*. Because the relationship between Patricia and David is a vehicle for exploring the possibility of transcending class distinction, these characters are compelled to leave the yacht. Initially, Patricia suggests a rendezvous so that she and David might enjoy "swimming around in the moonlight" (*M* 135). When they do meet, David performs his assigned duty, rowing Patricia in one of the smaller boats for her midnight dip in the lake. Though Patricia urges David to join her for a swim, he is at first reluctant, preferring instead to remain as the faithful steward with oars in hand. But Patricia is insistent that David remove his uniform, an outward signifier of his social function, and enjoy the soothing water. In this fluid environment, a direct contrast to the rigidly stratified yacht, the separation between these two characters is at least aesthetically obscured, enabling them to interact more freely. Fortified by the prospect of greater equality, Patricia and David plan a more permanent flight from the yacht and the societal structure it represents.

Patricia and David's attempted journey to Mandeville is one of the more resonant episodes in *Mosquitoes*, mainly because it represents a pronounced change in tone and form. In this section of the novel, Faulkner playfully invokes literary naturalism, with its emphasis on the struggle between internal human will and the external forces of nature that promote determinism. As June Howard explains in *Form and History in American Literary Naturalism*, naturalist writers such as Stephen Crane, Theodore Dreiser, and Jack London draw significant parallels between the order of nature and human social order structured in terms of class stratification. Consequently, for Howard, characters in naturalist novels "are thwarted by nature and . . . by the 'second nature' of social forces" (44). This feature of literary naturalism holds true for Faulkner's use of the form as well. Seeking to escape the confines of the *Nausikaa*, the ill-fated lovers enter a primeval setting, a thick swamp full of trees "heavy and ancient with moss" that seem to engulf them (*M* 169). Early on, Patricia and David revel in the natural world as a place of possibility, for it offers them the hope of transcending the boundaries of social distinction. But this journey quickly becomes more harrowing than liberating. Having lost any sense of direction, Patricia and David must contend with the debilitating heat of the swamp and the maddening swarms of mosquitoes that maintain persistent attacks. Consequently, what begins with the hope of freedom and movement quickly turns to the despair of oppression and stagnation that the swamp imposes. This ironic and self-conscious expedition into naturalistic territory is made all the more evident by one of the scenes that Faulkner uses to halt Patricia and David's adventure in the swamp. Several members of the yachting party embark on one of the smaller boats in an absurd mission to tow the *Nausikaa* away from the sandbar. This scene ironically alludes to Crane's "The Open Boat," as these "castaways" enact with hyperbole a futile struggle against the forces of nature that seem to conspire against them. In no real danger of peril, however, this "open boat" adrift in the water merely stands in comic relief to the more earnest struggle for survival occupying Patricia and David.

Ultimately, the mode of naturalism used to convey Patricia and David's journey stresses the futility of their effort to erase the boundaries of social division and thus exposes the power of class as a determinant of stratification. True to the established form of the novel, Faulkner uses ironic juxtaposition of scenes so that the journey unfolds in a narrative of constant interruption. Not only does Faulkner interject the parody of "The Open Boat," but he also repeatedly returns the focus to the *Nausikaa*, usually for more of the patented repartee among the yachting party that has by now become a staple of the novel. In this juxtaposition, we find a politics of form at work, as the very structure of the novel responds to the social conflict under representation and negotiation. The continued interruption of Patricia and David's journey denies it progressive validity and thus prevents these characters from achieving their goal of reaching Mandeville and, symbolically at least, transcending rigid social distinctions. The constant return to the *Nausikaa* has the aesthetic effect of reaffirming the prevailing social structure represented in the form of the yacht. Like the journey of the *Nausikaa*, initially conceived as a flight from societal constraints, Patricia and David's attempt to reach Mandeville winds up ironically representing and reinforcing the very constraints they seek to escape. In this instance, what Arnold identifies as Faulkner's sense of "the antithetical freedom inherent in movement and change" (282) is apparent in terms of class relations: what appears to be a journey beyond class distinction is, in the end, an inevitable return to it.

In this brand of naturalism, the forces of nature act to reinstate social boundaries. For one, the heat and mosquitoes take their toll on Patricia to the point that David must continually serve her, literally giving the shirt off his back in the line of duty. Moreover, as Arnold observes, "David is ultimately reduced to the level of an animal: like a horse or a mule he carries Patricia on his back" (295). Compounding David's role as beast of burden, Patricia expresses her gratitude by assigning monetary value to what would surely be viewed as a labor of love if these characters were on par socially. "I'd like to do something for you. Pay you back in some way," she says to David, just before the sound of the boat that will rescue them signals the end of this journey and their relationship (*M* 213). The forces of the natural world have compelled Patricia to reassert her class prerogative over David by producing intense longing for the relative comfort of the *Nausikaa* and the boundaries that its form mimics and enforces. Accordingly, Patricia takes firm control of the financial negotiations with the captain of the rescue boat, directing David to pay with her money and thus further relegating him to servile status. Patricia and David's ill-fated attempt to transcend differences rooted in class illustrates social stratification as a force that works ideologically to promote hegemony by appearing to be the "natural" order of things.

For this reason and others, Faulkner's second novel is a text at odds with itself, due in large part to its moment in cultural history. On one level, *Mosquitoes* is quite prescient in its critique of modernist formal excess and solipsism and its avant-garde impulses, thus anticipating the fundamental shift in cultural attitudes and aesthetic ideology that would preoccupy the literary establishment of the thirties. Though of a different genre, Faulkner's *Mosquitoes* prefigures works such as Cowley's *Exile's Return* and Edmund Wilson's *Axel's Castle*, staging a biting cultural critique of the expatriate bohemianism celebrated and cultivated among artists and intellectuals of the "lost generation." Like his artist Gordon, Faulkner probes beneath the veneer of frivolity, social masquerade, and hedonism to reveal the depths of despair that would soon rise painfully to the surface of the individual consciousness and that of the society at large. Moreover, Faulkner, in his own way, acknowledges the importance of social relations in producing art. A fundamental aesthetic principle expressed in the novel is that art must speak with vibrancy of the artist's interaction with life or else suffer the sterility and stasis that come from isolation.

Despite these aspects of the novel that find common ground with the wellspring of literary radicalism stirring in American culture at the time, the scope of *Mosquitoes* extends only so far. While Faulkner charts the boundaries of class difference and the limitations that they impose, his second novel finally accepts these divisions as "natural," remaining closed to alternative visions of social structure. For this reason, the artist's interaction with life remains an uneasy prospect. This condition is evident as Fairchild and Gordon take to the streets of New Orleans in the epilogue—an episode that owes much to the *Walpurgisnight* section of Joyce's *Ulysses*. The gritty and visceral descriptions of street life are tempered by lyrical, stream of consciousness interludes that frantically flow in the artists' minds as they try to fortify themselves against social reality with the shield of abstraction. In the mania of this episode, the tensions between competing aesthetic ideologies—those of formalism and social realism—reach full crescendo. Amid such tumult, there is a noticeable urge to restore order, stemming from the formalist aesthetic principle that a novel divided against itself cannot stand. In this light, the final image of Talliaferro, a club-wielding aesthete intent on asserting his prerogative, signals a desperate attempt to impose narrative closure on an unwieldy novel unhinged by aesthetic and ideological tension. On another level, however, this image reads as a fitting and prescient call to arms for the literary class war looming on the cultural horizon. As Talliaferro's futile display of power suggests, the forces of cultural conflict would prove not only disruptive but also resistant to overt acts of containment, no matter how urgent and forceful. It was an understanding of emerging cultural politics that would continue to inform Faulkner's literary production, as illustrated by the novel that is for many his signature work.

The Sound and the Fury is both a disturbing and a disturbed novel. In the voluminous scholarship devoted to the work that Faulkner often cited as his most cherished, a prevalent theme addressed by critics is the pain of loss—the profound material, familial, and psychological dispossession that the Compsons suffer during a tragic decline. Scholars have examined this theme from a range of perspectives, focusing on the novel's similarities to Greek tragedy, evidence of emotional trauma and despair in the characters, gender issues arising from the representation of Caddy Compson in absentia, and the elusive pursuit of meaning resulting from the complex and at times confounding linguistic play under the framework of an experimental narrative structure heavily influenced by European modernism.[3] Within this diverse body of scholarship, the sectional quality of the text has remained a consistent topic of discussion centered on whether the individual parts effectively form an organic whole or, in the end, remain as alienated from one another as members of the Compson family. Conrad Aiken's defense of Faulkner in the late thirties insists on unity, describing the novel's "massive four-part symphonic structure" and proclaiming its status as an "indubitable masterpiece" (142). In his introduction to *The Portable Faulkner*, Malcolm Cowley argues for an overarching integrity in spite of textual instability, declaring the novel "superb as a whole" (xxv). Cowley equivocally claims that "we can't be sure that the four sections of the novel are presented in the most effective order; at any rate, we can't fully understand the first section until we read the three that follow" (xxv). Olga Vickery goes even further than Cowley, contending that the four parts of the novel "appear quite unrelated" (29). Subsequent accounts cast this condition in more ominous and vexing terms. Eric Sundquist, for example, sees labyrinthine dimensions to the four sections that render "the psychology of the novel as a form of containing consciousness" (9). In Donald M. Kartiganer's estimation, this condition manifests as a kind of formal mania, as the novel "struggles, with all the signs of its struggles showing, toward wholeness." Nevertheless, Kartiganer insists that "the four sections remain isolated, as each imagined order cancels out the one that precedes it" (*Fragile* 5, 7). As these interpretations and scores of others suggest, the endeavor to understand *The Sound and the Fury*, perhaps inevitably, has for the most part hinged on matters of form.

While yielding much insight, this approach can run the risk of diminishing the novel's contextual relations, perpetuating a longstanding tendency to treat it as the epitome of "art for art's sake." Such a reading casts the novel as the inspired creation of a virtuoso at the height of his powers. Along these lines, legend has the novel emerging from a heightened state of artistic vision similar to the rapture that Coleridge claimed to have experienced while writing "Kubla Khan" or springing suddenly from Faulkner in much the same way that Athena was born of Zeus. Notably, Faulkner himself was the primary source of this lore, as illustrated in two versions of an introduction he wrote for a 1933 reprint of *The Sound and the Fury*. Although this particular edition never came to pass, these versions of the introduction did, heavily influencing views of Faulkner's writing process.[4] In both documents, Faulkner recalls the genesis of *The Sound and the Fury*, confessing his feelings of alienation from the publishing world as a result of his regional roots and the repeated rejection of his previous novel, *Flags in the Dust*. For that novel, Faulkner had abandoned the derivative style and subject matter of *Soldier's Pay* and *Mosquitoes*, turning instead to his "postage stamp of native soil" as inspiration for the founding of Yoknapatawpha. Despite Faulkner's considerable regional and emotional investment in this family saga set during the Civil War, he was not initially able to attract much interest from publishers. Ultimately, however, after more rejections and substantial cuts, the novel was published in 1929 as *Sartoris*.

According to Faulkner, this outcome was bittersweet, creating in him a deep-seated resentment of the literary marketplace as well as a renewed commitment to notions of artistic integrity and appreciation of aesthetic value. Rather than stalling his creative drive, Faulkner claims, the despair of rejection reinvigorated him as an artist. With the burdens of the marketplace lifted, Faulkner recalls, "It suddenly seemed as if a door had clapped silently and forever between me and all publishers' addresses and booklists and I said to myself, Now I can write. Now I can just write" ("An Introduction" 158–59). By this reckoning, Faulkner was able to retreat gladly to the realm of the solitary artist, where he could revel in his craft rather than bow to the pressure to churn out cultural commodities. Experiencing a kind of rapture, he could write the Benjy section in the throes of "that ecstasy, that eager and joyous faith and anticipation of surprise which yet unmarred sheets beneath my hand held inviolate and unfailing" (160). With metaphorical reference to a Roman who bestows loving kisses on his beloved Tyrrhenian vase, Faulkner exhibits a text fetish, describing his intense affection for his novel as an ideal form. This "creation story" and critical accounts influenced by it have embossed *The Sound and the Fury* with what John T. Matthews appropriately calls a "mythical aura," which conveys the false impression that the novel exists "with no apparent connections to its history" (*Sound* 23). For this reason, treatments of the novel in relation to external influences have remained in the minority, leaving much work left to be done in placing *The Sound and the Fury* in historical and cultural context.

Although my interest, like that of many other critics, is on the theme of dispossession and elements of form, I want to use this emphasis to expose connections between *The Sound and the Fury* and the emerging literary class war, demonstrating Faulkner's continued participation, un-recognized though it might have been, in an ideological avant-garde im-mediately responsive to cultural politics and, as such, attuned to social and economic factors signaling the onset of a crisis. In terms of thematic content and formal structure, *The Sound and the Fury* mediates aesthetic ideologies active in its cultural context and, in so doing, explores and comments on related social, economic, and political conditions. As we have seen, the aesthetic ideologies that would enter into open conflict, in theory, and unacknowledged negotiation, in practice, during the literary class war in many respects produce the internal contradictions and dis-rupted form of *Mosquitoes*. In my view, this pattern extends as well to *The Sound and the Fury*, albeit in a less explicit manner consistent with the fact that this novel is far less self-conscious with regard to aesthetics than *Mosquitoes*. Attention to this component reveals how *The Sound and the Fury* works ideologically to critique a socioeconomic order rooted in capitalism and to expose obstacles to collective identity and imposed central planning arising from efforts to temper the social ills of capitalism by reforming classical liberalism. As these elements of *The Sound and the Fury* confirm, Faulkner's turn away from the literary marketplace fails to provide a satisfactory means of escape from society, in spite of his insistence to the contrary. Instead, Faulkner's attempt to close the door between artistic and capitalist modes of production results in a literary form that is, as Adorno instructs, indelibly shaped by the very system the author claims to have rejected.

Opposition to capitalist excess was one of the few issues on which sworn enemies in the literary class war would be able to find common ground, even though they reached it from different paths. As the writings of the Southern Agrarians attest, cultural conservatives viewed capitalism as a totalizing force that threatened individual liberty with mass industrialization and cheapened the value of art by reducing it to the level of commodity. Advocates of social realism perceived capitalism as a brutal system that fostered competition and injustice, encouraging exploitation of the working class by a privileged ruling class. In response to capitalist hegemony, cultural conservatives stressed the values of humanism and the techniques of high modernism to maintain artistic integrity and a sense of autonomy, while ardent leftists urged a comprehensive view of society to expose the cruelties of capitalism. *The Sound and the Fury* moves on a spectrum between each aesthetic ideology, as the modernist form established at the outset gradually gives way to the more panoramic social perspective that Faulkner seems compelled to explore. From this standpoint, the four sections display variations in form that highlight the vital role of cultural politics in the novel's production and, more specifically, its pointed diagnosis of troubling symptoms developing in American society.

Faithful to the Shakespearean allusion, *The Sound and the Fury* begins with a tale told by an idiot. The act of reading the Benjy section is perhaps one of the more disconcerting experiences to be found in literature. Among the numerous questions that inevitably confront the unsuspecting reader who enters the world according to Benjy Compson is certainly the very basic: What exactly am I reading? The Benjy section is a study in paradoxes. For one, the simple style—short, declarative sentences, child-like in construction—is at odds with the complexity of form achieved through stream of consciousness and abrupt shifts in time and setting, all working to destabilize the reader accustomed to linear narrative structure. This section exhibits classic traits of modernism, as the shards of perception that form its world seem resistant to a more overarching social vision and yield the aesthetic effect of abolishing the constraints of standard time. Thus the Benjy section would seem to be the achievement of Faulkner's stated desire to create autonomous art by distancing himself and his work from the demands of social reality.

In many respects, the Benjy section is antisocial, constructed from the observations of a man-child alienated from family and society and thus unable to comprehend or participate in the larger network of familial and social relations that he occupies. André Bleikasten emphasizes Benjy's isolation, asserting that he embodies the profound agony that comes with dispossession. In structuralist terms, Bleikasten argues that Benjy's "idiolect . . . forms a closed system, a strictly private code, designed to suggest the functioning of a strictly limited consciousness" (*Most* 68). And within this system, Bleikasten continues, Benjy is reduced to a primitive existence, representing "humanity at its most elemental and most archaic, the zero degree of consciousness" (71). The only time Benjy is able to bridge the distance inherent in his isolation is when he loses something or someone, given that "most scenes in which [Benjy] is directly implicated are scenes of loss" (75). In this regard, I would agree with Bleikasten's interpretation: the Benjy section does enact a sort of primal scene of dispossession in the novel. But I would cast a wider net in order to transcend an inherent limitation of the structuralist/psychoanalytic approach. An examination of Benjy's individual psyche has the effect of obscuring the social implications of his response to dispossession when placed in a broader familial and social context. In my view, the Benjy section is best understood in terms of a social psychology inscribed in the form. This perspective reveals that the modernist technique in Benjy's narrative resists and, at times, represses a broader perspective and, in so doing, engenders a return of the repressed that sets the novel on an exploratory path into matters of social reality.

Benjy's relationship to the land illuminates this feature of his section. In the course of his narrative, Benjy experiences dispossession through various means: he loses his name (Maury, after his uncle) due to his inability to bear it with the kind of distinction desired by Mrs. Compson; he loses his means of sexual prowess after an incident with a young woman passing by the Compson house leads to his castration; and, most profoundly, he loses Caddy, whose resistance to social codes oppressive of female sexuality forces her finally to flee under a cloak of scandal fashioned by her mother. The experiences of dispossession seem to converge in the form of the pasture originally designated as Benjy's inheritance but later sold to pay for Quentin's abbreviated Harvard education. For Benjy, the golf course is, in Lacanian terms, a symbolic order—a closed system of signifiers that introduces him to the inherent connection between language and loss. While the golf course promises to be a place where Benjy can have his "Caddy" and his "balls," as it were, the elusive nature of the signifier in each instance only reinforces the loss of the signified. Peering through the gate and whimpering, Benjy is what Lacan terms a barred subject (141–42). He is literally denied access to the golf course and figuratively precluded from assuming a stable place in the symbolic order, leaving him at the mercy of signifiers that playfully define him in terms of what he lacks. As a result, the temptation to isolate Benjy from both the symbolic order and the broader social one is great indeed. As a barred subject, Benjy seems incapable of revealing much about the social reality that exists beyond the line of demarcation drawn by the gate and, on a personal level, by the boundaries that mark his stream of consciousness flow.

On the contrary, Benjy's primitive state affords him the opportunity to initiate the more expansive social vision that develops in *The Sound and the Fury*. Taken in isolation, for example, Benjy's fixation on the pasture–turned–golf course may seem no more than an arbitrary effect of his arrested development. However, expanding the scope of this concern exposes how Benjy's relationship to this parcel of land yields profound insight into a dominant ideology that shapes the Compsons' familial and social identity by defining social status in terms of property ownership. In fact, the considerable "investment" that Benjy has in the land originally intended for him calls to mind the relationship between owner and private property as defined by Marx. In this arrangement, landed property becomes a variant form of the person who owns it and thus takes on elements of shared identity. The association is so strong that the land becomes, in effect, "the inorganic body of its lord" (*Economic* 114). Employing this theory, the pasture figures as an extension of Benjy that was suddenly cut off, making it a source of such intense pain and longing that he is repeatedly drawn back to it. Consequently, the sale of Benjy's promised land is another form of castration—a symbolic and material dispossession that aligns Benjy with the overbearing sense of loss that the Compsons are suffering in terms of diminished wealth and social status. In this regard, Benjy is more of a Compson than Mrs. Compson would like to admit.

Benjy's intense desire to return to the dispossessed land is evident throughout his section, as virtually all roads lead him to the fence that bars him entry. Early in the Benjy section, for example, there is a typical series of rapid time shifts indicated by italics and connected by repetition, the Compson family carriage in this instance providing the unifying detail. Seeking solace, Benjy recalls a time from childhood when Caddy comforted him by saying, "You're not a poor baby. Are you. Are you" (*SF* 9). This memory leads to a brief vision of the carriage house and the family carriage recently fixed with a new wheel; another abrupt shift returns us to the present time of the section as T.P. prepares to drive Mrs. Compson to town in the now dilapidated carriage. For Mrs. Compson, hiding behind her veil, the ride to town in the carriage is like a funeral procession—a ritual display of the Compsons' fall from social distinction acted out in full view of society. As Benjy records, the procession also offers Mrs. Compson the chance to issue her two most common refrains in response to the family's decline: " 'It's a judgment on me.' Mother said. 'But I'll be gone too, soon' " (13). These statements, which provide ample evidence of Mrs. Compson's martyr complex, prompt in Benjy a memory of walking into the barn with Luster. The scene is punctuated by dispossession, illustrated by the harsh words that Benjy recollects: "*You ain't got no pony to ride now, Luster said*" (13). Significantly, Luster's taunting provokes Benjy to run for the golf course, as if the land holds the key to emotional and material recovery. In retrospect, Benjy's move serves as a poignant harbinger of the response dispossessed Americans would have after the economic crash, acting on an instinctual drive to go "back to the land," in spite of the illogical and impractical prospect of recovering a sense of wholeness from doing so.

In many respects, the juxtaposition of scenes and rapid shifts in time and memory are exemplary of psychological realism and its antisocial bent. Not only are these apparently random thoughts, but they are those of a man who has not progressed beyond the understanding of a child. Still, the associative pattern woven into these scenes does suggest that Benjy is able to read the outward signs that point to his family's diminished means and thus to understand their meaning in a broader social context. Consider how Caddy's mention of "poor baby"—a sympathetic sign of affection rather than a reference to material poverty—nevertheless leads Benjy to recall the carriage in a finer state, showing that he measures current conditions against a more prosperous time for the Compson family. Moreover, the impending ride through town in the failing carriage—an outward sign of the Compson decline—and Mrs. Compson's declarations that the family's plight is the effect of divine judgment lead Benjy to recall what he has lost as a result of this adverse change in family fortunes. For Benjy, the loss of the pony must figure in the loss of the land, to which he instinctively returns in search of recovery. In a Lacanian sense, the dispossessed property has undergone sublimation; it has become an elusive object of desire that promises a sense of wholeness but, alas, never delivers. Benjy is, in effect, the ground zero, the primal scene, of this paradoxical desire shared by the Compson brothers, who reproduce their own frustrated desire by longing to recover what they never truly possessed in the first place.

Benjy's affinity for the land is, of course, linked closely to his longing for Caddy's return. After all, it is ostensibly the call of "caddie" from the golfers on the course that lures Benjy to the fence. The association of Caddy to the land is reinforced by images that represent her in terms of nature. For instance, Benjy repeatedly likens Caddy's smell to trees and honeysuckle. Moreover, the ur-image of the text, Caddy's mud-stained drawers, is one that stresses her affinity with the earth. One episode in particular shows just how closely Benjy associates his sister with the sold property. After Benjy once again makes a path for the golf course, Luster admonishes him and suggests that he play near the creek instead. This suggestion leads Benjy to recall a childhood memory of playing in that spot at a time when the Compsons still owned the adjoining pasture. Benjy remembers Caddy's rebellious insistence on playing in the water, despite Versh's reminder that she was not allowed to do so. The confrontation with Versh prompted a threat from Caddy to run away and proved traumatic for Benjy, who remembers Caddy "all wet and muddy behind" (*SF* 18) as she reassured him that she would not leave. Once again, Benjy recalls, "Caddy smelled like trees in the rain" (18). This memory causes Benjy to head for the fence, where he surveys the golf course and cries out with longing. Limiting this episode to Benjy's psyche renders this memory a process of free association: faced with the loss of Caddy, Benjy makes tangible connections to the smell of trees and the golf course in an effort to recover his sister in some variant form. Notwithstanding this subjective response, the fractured form of the novel allows a glimpse of how Benjy's action is interpreted in a broader social context. While peering through the fence and crying is a way for Benjy to express his longing for Caddy's return, Luster perceives this action in a different way: "*He still think they own this pasture, Luster said*" (22). In this instance, the form of the text meant to render Benjy's individual psyche lays bare the social realm he occupies. For Luster, Benjy's wailing cannot exist in and of itself as merely the illogical workings of an arrested mind but instead must involve broader implications. That is to say, Benjy's expression of pain must exist as part of a greater Compson agony rooted in material dispossession. No matter what, Benjy's wailing cannot escape its social significance. This scene further establishes a pattern of conflict in which the modernist form of the text, approximating Benjy's internal thought process, fails to contain an underlying social vision that emerges from his perceptions of the external world.

The Benjy section is a fitting introduction to *The Sound and the Fury* because it establishes dispossession, the American dream turned to nightmare, as a central theme in the novel, if not *the* central theme. In many ways, Benjy signals what is to come, within the novel and beyond its pages, making Roskus's assessment ring all the more true: "He know lot more than folks thinks" (*SF* 36). The analogy to a pointer dog that Roskus uses to illustrate Benjy's clairvoyance is an apt one, considering how his section functions in the novel and how the novel functions in its historical and cultural context. Much like a montage sequence in film, Benjy's section evolves through juxtaposition of scenes that challenge preconceived notions of narrative structure. Although this form contributes to a sense of insulated chaos, vivid impressions of the exterior world that Benjy observes and recalls and toward which the novel progressively reaches surface repeatedly. Through Benjy's eyes, it is difficult to approach full comprehension but not impossible to gain a tangible sense that the Compsons are a family in decline. The Benjy section points the way toward better understanding of the Compson curse noted by Roskus when he says quite simply, "Taint no luck on this place" (33). The Compson curse is deeply rooted in class and coincides, as numerous critics have noted, with the changes taking place in a larger social order in flux. Marx offers us insight into the transition that determines the change in Compson fortunes when he points out that the "disposal of landed property and transformation of the land into a commodity is the final ruin of the old aristocracy and the complete triumph of the aristocracy of money" (*Economic* 113). By essentially merging the sale of the property with the loss of Caddy in the Benjy section, Faulkner opens the way for elaboration of this relationship in the Quentin section.

The progression of the novel from Benjy's section to Quentin's is, in a strict chronological sense, actually a regression, given that Quentin's narrative precedes Benjy's by eighteen years. Although the Quentin section spans only one day in linear time—June 2, 1910—the scope of Quentin's interior monologue is as wide as Benjy's and frequently as disjointed, unfolding in a narrative form evocative of what philosophers, psychologists, and artists around the turn of the century were envisioning as the "specious present." As Stephen Kern explains in *The Culture of Time and Space, 1880–1918,* this concept, introduced by the philosopher E. R. Clay and borrowed and adapted by others, arose from efforts to "expand the traditional sharp-edged present temporally to include part of the immediate past and future" (81). Kern cites an array of disciplines and forms of cultural expression concerned with this conception of time, noting in addition to the writing of philosophers the innovative theories of psychoanalysts, the painting of Futurists, and the formal experimentation practiced by modernist novelists who "used various techniques to fan out their sequential narratives into a 'continuous' or 'prolonged' present," especially during instances of heightened emotion or anxiety (82). Kern's cultural history makes it possible to comprehend Faulkner's awareness of temporal perception as a defining feature of modernity in the novel's historical frame. Like Joyce, Woolf, Stein, and Proust, Faulkner employs this "specious present" to illustrate the pain of loss invariably marked by the passage of time and, in so doing, points toward signal developments in American society and culture.

For Quentin, temporal perception brings his separation from Caddy and feeds his intense longing to be reunited with her. Manifesting as tormented and tormenting desire, Quentin's sense of loss is a direct result of Caddy's sexual awakening. Owing in large measure to Caddy's maturity, Quentin feels dispossessed of the "pure" sister whom he feels bound by honor to protect and preserve. As numerous critics have observed, this sense of obligation is far from noble, considering its roots in psychological dysfunction as well as a patriarchal southern ideology that, as Wilbur J. Cash explains, figures white women in terms of a reductive virgin/whore dichotomy (89). Quentin is governed by the same sort of thinking that drives Mrs. Compson to wear black as a means of mourning her daughter's lost "innocence." Mrs. Compson is steeped in the patriarchal ideology that Cash delineates, as demonstrated by her belief in the maxim learned during her Bascomb upbringing: "that a woman is either a lady or not" (*SF* 118). Caddy's sexual encounter with Dalton Ames immediately places her on the negative side of the equation, amounting to her death as far as Mrs. Compson is concerned. While Mrs. Compson dons the clothes of mourning in response to Caddy's sexual development, Quentin goes so far as to imagine committing incest as a way of asserting control over his sister. In addition, Quentin goes the way of the cavalier, defending Caddy's virtue—and indeed that of Woman in general—by trying to be what his college buddy Spoade calls the "champion of dames" (191). But Quentin's interference has the opposite of its intended effect. Although he is successful in breaking up Caddy and Dalton, he is also largely responsible for Caddy's heightened promiscuity in reaction to the loss of her first love. Quentin thus contributes to his own dispossession by driving his beloved sister away. He is left, then, to measure his loss against the constant march of time, which haunts him to the point of exercising self-negation through suicide.

Quentin's obsession with time is one of the most obvious motifs in the section devoted to him. For Quentin, time is an external determining force whose very progression brings disruption and destabilization of the familiar simply because it brings change. Time is the outward measure of the Compson decline, extending from the past when the family boasted prominent statesmen to the present when its members are plagued by diminished material means and debilitating neuroses. Early in his narrative, Quentin displays this neurotic edge as he professes to be at the point of hopeless self-reliance, which he describes in this way: "It's not when you realise that nothing can help you—religion, pride, anything— it's when you realise that you don't need any aid" (*SF* 91). This profession of individualism is supported by the insular form of Quentin's section but undermined by the external social forces that shape Quentin's experiences and exacerbate his fear of time. After all, time is the mechanism that enables Caddy's maturity and thus her burgeoning, and quite natural, sexual desire. Through the changes in Caddy, time acts on Quentin with contradictory force, luring him out of his self-contained existence as he attempts to recover the sister he wants to preserve and then driving him to retreat in failure to the inner recesses of his mind in search of some semblance of familiarity and order. As elusive to Quentin as she is to Benjy, Caddy becomes, in his view, the embodiment of time and a social order transformed by modernity to the point that "all stable things had become shadowy paradoxical" (194).

Quentin interprets Caddy's transition from "purity" to "defilement" in terms that reflect his opposition to a dominant ideology rooted in capitalism. In this regard, Quentin shows clear signs of the "rape complex" that Cash defines as an extension of the virgin/whore dichotomy. For southern men, Cash explains, the "pure" woman embodies established social order, while threats to that order are cast in terms of sexual assault (114–17). This mode of representation was common in defenses of the South during Reconstruction and extending through the rise of industrialism in the New South. Particularly vivid examples can be found in the poetry and prose of the Southern Agrarians, as they draw on sexual imagery, symbolism, and metaphor to describe the defilement of southern values of honor and social grace by the assault of crass and materialistic northern industrialism. Along the same lines, Quentin views Caddy's sexual maturity as a process of defilement that reduces her from "purity" and "innocence" to a form of capital or a traded commodity. Caddy's association with the land underscores this point, for she becomes in Quentin's way of thinking like the "pristine" parcel that is tarnished once it enters the marketplace for exchange. Philip J. Hanson makes the keen observation that *The Sound and the Fury* expresses "anxiety over a traditionalist Southern socioeconomic system in the process of disintegrating, a system which had long regarded itself as opposed—and superior—to capitalist marketplace values" (4). Thus, for Hanson, Quentin's response to Caddy is informed by the logic of anticapitalism evident in a southern dominant class ideologically resistant to modes of capitalist production. This motivation adds another dimension to Quentin's despair over Caddy's involvement with Dalton, the nomadic drummer fond of sporting silk shirts to signify his conspicuous consumption. It is important to note that the resistance to capitalism apparent in Quentin's section, and in much of the entire novel, can be aligned as well with the critique of capitalism growing ever more pronounced in American society, especially in the realm of cultural politics, as the twenties roared on excessively toward what some warned would be a devastating crash.

Enacting his brand of capitalist critique, Quentin draws frequent connections between Caddy and capitalist modes of production and consumption. For instance, he perceives the virtual arrangement of Caddy's marriage to Sydney Herbert Head in terms of economic exchange. Through the engagement, Caddy is commodified as Herbert offers the Compsons entry into the market-driven economy in return for the family's blessing of his marriage proposal. The brand new car Herbert gives to Caddy signals the potential for consumption, while the job he promises to Jason in his bank promises means to capital. Mrs. Compson is especially impressed by the added value Herbert can bestow on the diminished Compson name, writing to Quentin that "Herbert has spoiled us all to death" (*SF* 107). Having successfully wooed Caddy, Mrs. Compson, and Jason, Herbert sets his sights on gaining the upper hand with Quentin, treating him as a rival for Caddy's affections. In the scene involving Herbert and Quentin in the Compson parlor, Faulkner opposes Quentin's sense of honor to Herbert's unscrupulousness. Like the "robber barons," Herbert is driven by acquisitive impulses, whether his possessive instinct fixes on expensive Havana cigars or on Caddy. For Herbert, the bottom line is all that matters; he will do whatever it takes—from cheating at Harvard to paying off Quentin for his blessing—to possess what he desires. "Call it a loan then just shut your eyes and you'll be fifty" (126), says Herbert, trying to persuade Quentin to accept money, in effect, as payment for his sister.

The offer of cold, hard cash from Herbert is an affront to Quentin's tragically noble sensibilities and prompts his understanding of Caddy not only as a sexual object but also a commodity assigned an exchange value determined by Herbert's market savvy. Honor bound, Quentin is determined not to participate in the mode of exchange Herbert represents. Quentin's refusal strikes Herbert as highly impractical, rendering Quentin, in Herbert's words, a "half-baked Galahad of a brother" (*SF* 126). Herbert, who has "been out in the world now for ten years" (125), has learned not only to accept the crass ways of the marketplace but also to profit from them. Quentin, by contrast, experiences the growing sense that his internal system of beliefs is at odds with an external socioeconomic order adversely transformed by capitalist values and traceable in Caddy's path from virgin to sexual commodity. Adding insult to injury, Caddy even speaks the logic of the marketplace when she rejects Quentin's idea that they run away together—a counterproposal that he offers in an effort to prevent her from marrying Herbert. In response to Quentin, Caddy displays Herbert's brand of pragmatism, pointing out to him the flaw in his plan when it comes to the bottom line: "*On what on your school money the money they sold the pasture for so you could go to Harvard dont you see you've got to finish now if you dont finish he'll have nothing*" (142). While Quentin is concerned with protecting Caddy's virtue, as he defines it, Caddy thinks in economic terms. Mindful of a familial ledger, she stresses the importance of achieving the return on Mr. Compson's sizeable investment so that Quentin might prosper and provide compensation for Benjy's lost inheritance. Opposed firmly to such values, Quentin is left with his outmoded sense of honor to strike out in futility at the likes of Dalton Ames, Sydney Herbert Head, and Gerald Bland, all of whom signal for Quentin acceptance of a crass and often brutal socioeconomic order in which the once distinguishing characteristics of honor and class can be discarded or purchased outright like commodities on a market open for exchange.

The conflict between Quentin's internal system of values and those prevailing in a transformed social order produces a loss of meaning that, in turn, leads to paralysis and isolation. For Quentin, concepts once considered stable have now become unstable, causing confusion not unlike Benjy's when he confronts the conundrum of "Caddy" versus "caddie."

But Quentin's dilemma occurs in a more explicitly social context. After all, he is far more capable than Benjy of engaging the world around
him, though he is ultimately no more successful at achieving a comfortable existence in it. Clearly, *The Sound and the Fury* comprehends this
breakdown of meaning largely in terms of class anxiety, a recognition
that registers at the level of form. While the mere mention of his sister's
name sends Benjy into fits, Quentin seems especially troubled by the word
"gentleman," which causes manic disruptions in the thought process, rendered by Faulkner through disrupted form. A case in point is when Shreve
comments in an offhand manner, "God, I'm glad I'm not a gentleman"
(*SF* 116), prompting this rapid-fire series of thoughts in Quentin:

> He [Shreve] went on, nursing a book, a little shapeless, fatly intent. *The street*
> *lamps* do you think so because one of our forefathers was a governor and three
> were generals and Mother's weren't any live man is better than any dead man
> but no live or dead man is very much better than any other live or dead man
> *Done in Mother's mind though. Finished. Finished. Then we were all poisoned*
> you are confusing sin and morality women dont do that your mother is thinking
> of morality whether it be sin or not has not occurred to her. (116)

On one level, these thoughts are shards of a shattering mind; however, on
another level, this fractured form makes it possible to put the destabilized
concept of "gentleman" in a specific familial context with broader social
implications. For Quentin, the devalued meaning of the term is expressed
as a process of genealogical defilement. The memory of prominent Compson forefathers—gentleman all, in Quentin's view—is tainted by "inferior" Bascomb blood, by egalitarian principles, and, most egregiously, by
the blight of Caddy's sexual exploits. In this respect, the dispossession of
the "pure" Caddy, an idealized form of the actual Caddy, also constitutes
a loss of both the familial and the social role that Quentin feels compelled
to assume. With no "lady" to preserve and to protect, how is Quentin to
be a "gentleman"?

Stripped of his social role in any stable form, Quentin is reduced to futile performance, enacting a hopeless parody of gentlemanly deportment.

This social masking is apparent in his recollection of Deacon, a black man who defers to Quentin at a Cambridge train depot with strategic assurances of "Yes, suh, young marster" (*SF* 111). But this social masking only serves to heighten the force of the egalitarian message Deacon wants to deliver as part of his tale of political conversion from Republican to Democrat: "I draw no petty social lines. A man to me is a man, wherever I find him" (114). This refusal to accept the orthodoxy of rigid social stratification is a reminder to Quentin of his inability to assume the role of gentleman in the transformed social order now surrounding him. Quentin thus endures a ghostlike existence, living as the embodiment of a fading social concept that lacks resonance outside the confines of his own mind. This ambiguousness not only destabilizes Quentin's social identity but also raises the prospect of a complete role reversal—a condition apparent when Quentin encounters the young boys swimming in the river, one of whom says to another, "You said he [Quentin] talks like a colored man" (137).

The prospect of role reversal is punctuated in the episode involving the lost girl whom Quentin meets in the bakery. For Quentin, the little girl is a stand-in for Caddy, as his greeting of "Hello, sister" (*SF* 143) makes abundantly clear. Betraying an ideology of racial purity, Quentin views the girl as the tainted Caddy, the darkness of her skin a visible mark of defilement. Walking with the little girl, Quentin notices her "unwinking eyes like two currants floating motionless in a cup of weak coffee. Land of the kike home of the wop" (144). This xenophobic fear of a "pure" land defiled by foreign elements calls to mind the commodified Compson pasture and, by way of symbolic association, the sexually active Caddy. Quentin's encounter with the lost girl serves as a humiliating commentary, exposing the perverse ideological underpinnings of his gentlemanly code. Initially, Quentin feels the urge to protect the lost girl, presumably out of a sense of honor and duty. As he walks with her, though, his obsession with defilement resurfaces in a recollection of "dirty" girls from childhood. First, Quentin remembers when Caddy walked into the Compson barn to find him and a girl named Natalie *"dancing sitting down"* (156), as Natalie explained it to Caddy. After the incident, Quentin recalls, he got into an argument with Caddy and performed a ritualistic defilement: *"I wiped mud from my legs and smeared it on her wet hard turning body"* (157). Faulkner renders the conflation of past and present in typical modernist form, using italics to indicate shifts in time. The form adds to the aesthetic effect of objectifying the lost girl, as she is manipulated by Quentin's associative thought process. Nevertheless, Quentin cannot construct the definitive interpretation. Instead of viewing Quentin as a benevolent gentleman come to her rescue, the girl's brother takes him for a child molester. This charge elicits hysterical laughter from Quentin, who clearly recognizes the irony of his being cast as a sexual predator rather than in his self-appointed role as guardian of feminine virtue. Adding insult to injury, Quentin must now measure himself against the lost girl's brother, who is the very sort of protector Quentin wants so desperately to be.

Quentin's encounter with the lost girl's family and subsequently with the law demonstrates that he has difficulty comprehending a perspective that is foreign to the internal and increasingly outmoded system of beliefs rooted firmly in his regional and class upbringing. Unable to see things from a different perspective, Quentin does not recognize that what is for him an act of noblesse oblige is for the lost girl's family a form of exploitation. In short, he fails to comprehend the social implications of his thoughts and actions. In the eyes of the law, Quentin's motivation seems suspect, despite the fact that there is not ample evidence to convict him on the charge of child molestation. Ironically, Quentin is forced to buy his way out of the predicament, not unlike what Herbert Head would do in such a quandary. Near the end of Quentin's narrative, this episode extends *The Sound and the Fury* outward, as Quentin encounters a rapidly changing social order governed by values that he cannot tolerate. Quentin's answer to this social reality rooted in the values of the marketplace is to make a final trade with no hope of return. Amid the stream of thoughts flowing through Quentin's final moments, he professes, "I have sold Benjy's pasture and I can be dead in Harvard. . . . Harvard is such a fine sound forty acres is no high price for a fine sound. A fine dead sound we will swap Benjy's pasture for a fine dead sound" (*SF* 200). This internal surrender in the face of the harsh external forces acting on him draws a clear line of distinction between Quentin's section and the one to follow, for Jason Compson's insatiable greed is vastly different from his brother's impotent nobility and self-serving self-sacrifice. Significantly, the death of Quentin marks as well Faulkner's shift from the stream of consciousness mode. Jason's section unfolds in a straightforward form reflective of his pragmatic attention to the bottom line and expressive of his desire to prosper in the marketplace, despite his continually frustrated efforts to do so.

Much happens in the time span that separates Quentin's section from Jason's. The period between June 2, 1910, and April 6, 1928, encapsu-lates no less than World War I and a subsequent expansion of the Ameri-can economy driven largely by burgeoning mass production and con-sumption. In the historical present of Jason's narrative, capitalism stands triumphant, the culmination of a period ranging from roughly 1890 when an expanding mercantile economy with an industrial base substantially redefined America's socioeconomic order. William Leach describes the consequent effect of a cultural revolution that was apparent by the late 1920s: "A new commercial aesthetic had flowered, a formidable group of cultural and economic intermediaries had emerged, and an elaborate institutional circuitry had evolved, together creating the first culture of its kind that answered entirely to the purposes of the capitalist system and that seemed to establish and legitimate business dominance. Corporate business now orchestrated the myths of America, and it was through busi-ness . . . that the American dream had found its most dependable ally" (377). Leach contends that the dominant myth to emerge from this new order cast America as the Land of Desire, thriving on the idea of each indi-vidual subject as "an insatiable desiring machine or as an animal governed by an infinity of desires" (385). Fundamental elements of classical liber-alism such as individual liberty and self-reliance were thus translated into agents of consumption. It was this condition that made the frustration and suffering attending the Great Depression so acute, with Americans having honed the desire to consume but no longer possessing the means to gain fulfillment. Although the ideological components of this myth would seem to serve capitalism well, they are not without drawbacks. As Leach explains, this "capitalist concept of self, the consumer concept of the self . . . is a broker's view of people" that encourages speculation and irrationality and discourages social responsibility (385). Faulkner exposes the ideological effects of this myth on the individual by creating in Jason Compson IV a palpable subject whose intensely tormented nature is, by and large, a product of the social and economic forces that shape his experiences. In terms of the form and content in the Jason section, Faulkner expands the social vision of *The Sound and the Fury* to encompass the swift and comprehensive transformation coinciding in the text and its historical context. Through ill-conceived and executed speculation, Jason ironically scores a variant form of material return, exposing the harmful detritus of the capitalist dream factory and demonstrating Faulkner's often visionary take on matters of social and economic concern.

Like his brothers Benjy and Quentin, Jason is, in many respects, governed by a desire made all the more intense by his inability to satisfy it. Also like his brothers, Jason suffers his individual losses within the context of the collective Compson decline and the socioeconomic conditions that serve as contributing factors. While Benjy's and Quentin's efforts to repossess an idealized Caddy, and thus to "profit" from the recovery, occur on a symbolic level, Jason's are literal. For Jason, as for his brothers, Caddy is most directly associated with dispossession. As a desiring subject of capitalism, Jason relates to Caddy in terms of strict cost-benefit—the degree to which Jason is responsive to Caddy is roughly equal to the likelihood that he stands to reap material gain for his trouble. The prime example of this form of sibling exchange is the job in the northern bank that Herbert promises to Jason. This position, as stated above, would offer Jason access to capital in the burgeoning economy of consumption and credit. On a higher plane, though, the job offers hope that the Compson decline will desist, with Jason learning the ways of the world and presumably restoring the family to a place of prominence in the new order at least comparable to the one it enjoyed in the old. But the Compson curse strikes again when the job prospect fails, leaving Jason to negotiate the consequences of a tragic loss to match Benjy's and Quentin's and, ultimately, to seek revenge against his sister. After swindling Caddy out of a hundred dollars paid to him in return for seeing her daughter, Quentin, Jason feels a sense that the ledger has been balanced. "I reckon you'll know now that you cant beat me out of a job and get away with it" (*SF* 236), Jason says in his mind to Caddy, as he passes by her in the carriage while holding up baby Quentin and fulfilling with cruelly literal intention his promise to let Caddy "see" her child.

The failed job prospect is even more painful for Jason, considering that he sees himself as the Compson most capable of thriving in the dog-eat-dog world of the marketplace. From an early age, Jason is the budding entrepreneur of the family. At one point, Quentin recalls Jason's plan to profit from selling flour out of the family barrel—a prophetic scheme in light of Jason's obsessive preoccupation with keeping the flour barrel full once he becomes head of the household. Notwithstanding his familial re-sponsibilities, Jason is guided by an individualistic profit motive. Offering his thoughts on money, for example, Jason claims that it "has no value; it's just the way you spend it" (*SF* 223). This privileging of exchange value leads Jason to conclude that money "don't belong to anybody, so why try to hoard it. It just belongs to the man who can get it and keep it" (223). In this instance, Jason discloses a response to money as a pure object of desire, illustrating Marx's theory that "*money*, since it has the *property* of purchasing everything, of appropriating objects to itself, is, therefore, the *object par excellence*" (*Economic* 189). Later, feeling frustrated by his secondary role in the feed store, Jason lashes out at his circumstances and his boss's lack of profit motive: "What the hell chance has a man got, tied down in a town like this and to a business like this. Why I could take his business in one year and fix him so he'd never have to work again, only he'd give it all away to the church or something" (*SF* 263). Jason thus reveals himself as a creature of acquisition, driven mainly by the desire to profit and consume. This commentary is indicative of his dilemma in a socioeconomic order governed by capitalism: while he accepts and understands, to some degree, the highly competitive rules of the game, his lack of access to capital leaves him feeling powerless and ultimately determined by forces beyond his control. Through Jason's dispossession and his intensely conflicted nature, Faulkner offers up an indictment of a system that cruelly stimulates desires likely never to be fulfilled and, in turn, can foster a climate of irrational speculation.

Jason's lack of productive capability contributes to his impulsive and unwise financial decisions—for instance, his withdrawal of the thousand-dollar investment in the feed store to purchase a new car and his misguided speculation on the stock market to gain purchasing power. In Jason's mind, the market is, on the one hand, the primary mechanism of the new order responsible for his lack of economic opportunity and the diminishment of his power and privilege. But, on the other hand, it also offers him the means to rectify that predicament. For this reason, Jason's market philosophy is governed less by financial common sense than by a resolve to retaliate against a perceived socioeconomic determinism: "Well, I just want to hit them one time and get my money back. I don't want a killing. . . . I just want my money back that these dam jews have gotten with all their guaranteed inside dope. Then I'm through; they can kiss my foot for every other red cent of mine they get" (*SF* 270).

Jason's section is peppered with anti-Semitic references, which in tandem reveal a conspiracy theory bred of frustration and feelings of powerlessness. For Jason, Jews embody the "foreign" elements that have taken control and redefined the socioeconomic order so that it is unrecognizable to "true" Americans: "Well, I reckon those eastern jews have got to live too. But I'll be damned if it hasn't come to a pretty pass when any dam foreigner that cant make a living in the country where God put him, can come to this one and take money right out of America's pockets" (*SF* 221). Jason's anti-Semitic sentiments are in line with a prevalent ideology that emerged in the interwar years. In *Antisemitism in America*, Leonard Dinnerstein points out that World War I had left Americans fed up with internationalism and "frightened that foreigners would corrupt the nation's values and traditions" (78). Consequently, many Americans agreed with the 1920 presidential candidate Warren G. Harding's call for a return to "normalcy." Dinnerstein notes that this return "meant remaking the United States into what it symbolized in the minds of old stock Americans" (78). The element of false consciousness in this ideology is revealed in the common perceptions of Wall Street that it inspired. Increasingly, those who felt disenfranchised in the new economy of consumption, in which financial institutions were gaining increasing power, imagined a Semitic takeover of Wall Street. Gordon Thomas and Max Morgan-Witts, in *The Day the Bubble Burst,* note that market volatility resulted in heightened talk of "shylocking" and "Jewish-style deals," despite the fact that this conspiracy theory defied reality. In actuality, by the end of the 1920s, "Wall Street was still three-quarters white Protestant, a WASP enclave in a city where nine tenths of the population were Catholic, Jewish, or black" (59). Though the specifics of Jason's resentful market philosophy are objectionable, based as they are in notions of racial superiority and xenophobia, his sense of being determined by unpredictable market forces exposes a fundamental component of the dominant capitalist ideology. Moreover, despite Jason's irrationality and often exaggerated sense of doom, he is able to issue a remarkably prescient warning, as we can see from the privileged view of hindsight. After receiving a market advisory via telegram that reads, "The market will be unstable, with a general downward tendency," Jason fires back a prophetic response: "Market just on point of blowing its head off" (*SF* 282).

John T. Matthews argues that Jason's conspiracy theories, which are rooted in an interwar nativism, highlight the basic "logic" of a reactionary ideology: "If blood descent determines who belongs to America (and whom America belongs to), then the family gains primacy as the ultimate ground of national identity" ("Whose" 71). Indicatively, Jason's raging against the capitalist machine leads him to moments of self-fashioning within the family that are heavily influenced by forces active outside it. Set against the backdrop of American society, this condition makes developments and relations in the Compson family socially and politically symbolic. Jason's expressions of populist affinity with the "common man" and strong statements of class resentment are instructive cases in point. Noting that hill farmers are in the predicament of producing a crop for speculators to "whipsaw on the market," Jason poses a rhetorical question to show sympathy: "Do you think the farmer gets anything out of it except a red neck and a hump in his back?" (*SF* 219). Later, Jason widens the scope of his conspiracy theory with a populist edge: "Only be damned if it doesn't look like a company as big and rich as the Western Union could get a market report out on time. Half as quick as they'll get a wire to you saying Your account closed out. But what the hell do they care about the people. They're hand in glove with that New York crowd. Anybody can see that" (261). However, this paranoid sympathy for the powerless is less a matter of sincerity than a means of claiming oppressed status in the Compson household for his own advantage. On one level, Jason views the family as yet another mechanism of the deterministic forces apparently intent on dispossessing him. Feeling exploited, he fashions himself the working-class Compson. When Mrs. Compson confides that Jason is the only member of the family who "isn't a reproach to me," he responds, "I never had time to be. I never had time to go to Harvard or drink myself into the ground. I had to work" (207). The sale of the pasture for Quentin's education is obviously a sore point for Jason, who says in reference to his father that "I never heard of him offering to sell anything to send me to Harvard" (227). Not only that, but Jason recognizes that the "loss" on this "investment" has only added to the family's diminished social status, recognizing that it is more fodder for the town's suspicion that "the whole family's crazy" (268).

The decline of the Compson family, suspicions of town gossip about the family's mental instability, the menial tasks associated with his job, and a steady rain of bad news from the stock market—all of these factors remind Jason of his inability to satisfy the desire for wealth, status, and success that the new socioeconomic order has inspired in him. Jason seeks to compensate for his diminished capacity by exerting harsh control in the domestic sphere to regain a sense of stability and order. This move has the effect of once again aligning the familial and the national, further rendering the Compson family a symbolic political stage. Acting out, Jason harps on the opportunities denied him and the sacrifices he has made and continues to make in order to provide for the family; this provision is underscored by Jason's common refrain to the family and servants that he is the only one "man enough to keep that flour barrel full" (*SF* 238–39). Because of his role as provider, Jason feels justified in lording over the household and employing deception and cruelty in an attempt to gain material and emotional compensation for his tremendous sacrifices. Jason's scheme to steal the money that Caddy sends to her daughter is a case in point. He tries to reconcile the moral deficiency of his actions by imagining that cashing the actual checks and spending money on Loraine, while allowing Mrs. Compson to perform a ritualistic burning of fake checks, achieves worthy ends: offering his mother some level of comfort and reimbursing him for the failed job prospect in Herbert's bank and his sacrifices to the cause of family preservation.

Jason's compensatory moves to be lord of the manor and to orchestrate the familial economy are further illustrated by his relationship with Caddy's daughter, Quentin. For Jason, Quentin is the embodiment of the familial and socioeconomic forces that have rendered him powerless. Associating care for Quentin with the failed job prospect, Jason says with noticeable irony that "instead of me having to go way up north for a job they sent the job down here to me" (*SF* 225). Because Jason's desire to control Quentin proceeds from his lack of power and agency in a fluid marketplace defined by laissez-faire speculation, his efforts to exert that control mimic more stratified arrangements such as tenancy and centralized economic planning. Accordingly, when Caddy tells Quentin to expect money in the mail, Quentin visits Jason at the feed store to demand what is rightfully hers. "It's mine. She sent it to me. I will see it. I will" (244), Quentin insists, as she grabs for the money order that Jason keeps from her. Jason immediately thwarts this attempted "insurrection" by imposing what amounts to a share agreement—as "lord," he will collect the full "profit" and then dole out a small percentage to the "tenant." But the attempt to regulate Quentin through this system ultimately instills in her an urge to mount resistance, making her in at least one respect much like Uncle Jason. Quentin's rebelliousness in pursuit of individual liberty and self-reliance leads Jason to reaffirm his initial assessment of his niece: "Like I say once a bitch always a bitch" (305).

Although Jason's remark is a unifying detail that lends a formal element of closure to his section, Quentin is a force not so easily contained. Consequently, the familial power struggle between uncle and niece extends throughout the final section of the novel as well. Staging her ultimate rebellion against Jason's established domestic order, Quentin lays claim to the lock box full of the entire sum that her uncle has appropriated. When Jason reports this "theft," the sheriff's suspicion is directed toward Jason, an indicator of his reputation for unscrupulousness in the community. "My house has been robbed," Jason implores before asking, "Are you going to make any effort to recover my property, or not?" (*SF* 351). The sheriff's refusal to pursue Quentin effectively denies a communal sanctioning of the domestic order that Jason has tried to maintain. In the end, Quentin becomes yet another accomplice in the vast, seemingly cosmic conspiracy to dispossess him: "Of his niece he did not think at all, nor of the arbitrary valuation of the money. Neither of them had had entity or individuality for him for ten years: together they merely symbolised the job in the bank of which he had been deprived before he ever got it" (354). As objectified reminders of the financial success apparently destined to remain just beyond his reach, his niece and the money prove every bit as elusive for Jason as Caddy is for his brothers.

That the struggle for power and profit between Jason and his niece plays out against a communal backdrop in the final section of the novel is significant. The aforementioned exchange between Jason and the sheriff is an instance of how a communal perspective enters the novel in the final section, which aspires toward a different and broader vantage point on the same saga of loss. Even more demonstrative in this regard is the impassioned sermon by Rev. Shegog, witnessed by a visibly moved Dilsey and a characteristically whimpering Benjy. The narrator stresses the idea that the sermon is not an expression of Shegog as an individual but of the community speaking as one. At the beginning of Shegog's sermon, for example, the narrator discloses that "the voice consumed him, until he was nothing and they were nothing and there was not even a voice but instead their hearts were speaking to one another in chanting measures beyond the need for words" (*SF* 340). There is a populist theology at work in the sermon, as Shegog imagines a negation of distinctions rooted in material wealth: "Wus a rich man: whar he now, O breddren? Wus a po man: whar he now, O sistuhn?" (341). The minister's vision of Calvary fixes on "de thief en de murderer en de least of dese" (342), showing an affinity for the outcast and downtrodden. The brutality of the crucifixion paradoxically brings new life—the resurrection, which Shegog describes in revolutionary terms as a victory of the "arisen dead whut got de blood and de rickilickshun of de Lamb!" (343). The sermon serves as a fitting parallel to Quentin's uprising against Jason, infusing her act of familial rebellion with broader social significance. For, as the novel increasingly lays bare, the inner turmoil of the Compson family is bound to the outer turmoil of social reality. This dynamic corresponds as well to the relationship between the form of the novel and the contextual forces informing its production. Encompassing a broad range of form, *The Sound and the Fury* moves, as the literary establishment soon would, from emphasis on insular narrative structure and formal experimentation toward the struggle to represent tensions between individual and collective identity informed by the rhetoric of class struggle and the insight of social commentary.

The shift in point of view, tone, and form that Faulkner employs in the final section—the "Dilsey section," as it has been called, for lack of a better term—has attracted much critical attention. This discussion has centered mostly on the extent to which the third-person narrator, in striving for greater objectivity, fills in the numerous blanks left by the Compson brothers. Launching this debate, Olga Vickery identifies in the novel a "progressive revelation or rather clarification of the plot" before asserting, "The objective nature of the fourth section precludes the use of any single level of apprehension, and accordingly it provokes the most complex response" (31, 31–32). Disputing Vickery, Margaret Blanchard counters that the narrator is neither omniscient nor objective but rather "an extremely acute and articulate observer" (124). Noting that the transition from the third to the fourth section has been likened to "an emergence from confining voice into clear sight," Stephen M. Ross adds, "We escape from the novel's solipsistic monologues into highly visual description where objects and, most important, people can now be seen—if not objectively at least with striking clarity" (37). Matthews adds a qualification to the interpretation of objectivity as well, stressing "the narrator's confinement to particular circumstances and ways of seeing and saying" (*Sound* 78–79). Taking an altogether different tack, however, Kartiganer contends that nowhere in the final section do we see "the ability of the human imagination to render persuasively the order of things. Instead there is the sense of motion without meaning, of voices in separate rooms talking to no one: the sound and fury that fails to signify" (*Fragile* 21). Similarly, Noel Polk defines the novel's movement as being "more and more consciously and self-consciously 'narrated' " and thus driving toward "a complete breakdown in the representation of words, and so in the capacity of words themselves to convey meaning" (133). In my view, the concluding section is not objective but comprehensive, revealing a method in the madness by marking the culmination of the progressively expanding social vision established fleetingly in the Benjy section.

Whether or not the final section delivers the "whole" story, the more comprehensive view afforded by the narrator does capture a social order entering a state of flux, signaled by the familial uprising of Quentin and the rhetorical one of Rev. Shegog. Each of these challenges to existing social order raises the possibility of redistributed power and wealth, of a fluid socioeconomic system in which individual liberty extends to all who are able to claim it—even "de least of dese," to repeat the minister's phrase. The force of this upheaval is compounded by yet another representative uprising, staged when Luster changes the course of the carriage around the town square in the novel's concluding scene. Luster's move is so intolerable to Jason because of the frightening bellows it elicits from Benjy, making the Compsons once again a public spectacle. It also represents an open challenge to Jason that exposes once again his tenuous hold on the Compson familial economy through a form of centralized authority. Refusing to be led astray again by someone in his charge, Jason feels urgently compelled to reassert his command by grasping the reins, literally and figuratively. But forcing Luster to redirect the carriage so that "cornice and façade flowed smoothly once more from left to right, post and tree, window and doorway and signboard each in its ordered place" (*SF* 371) is merely an aesthetic show of control for Jason. This display of power stands completely at odds with the material reality of Quentin's destabilizing great escape and its symbolic value in the context of Jason's failure to harness the forces of the marketplace to his advantage. That Jason regains control of the carriage is, in the final analysis, not much compensation for the fact that in virtually all other pursuits, his reach painfully exceeds his grasp. On the symbolic stage, for example, the force of Quentin's individual liberty emerges triumphant over Jason's attempts to break her by applying the reins of manipulation. In the end, Jason's compulsion to restore order by wielding power, like Talliaferro's in *Mosquitoes*, is an impotent expression of frustrated desire and chronic anxiety in the face of social upheaval. The resulting condition of instability is framed in narrative terms by the ineffectual attempt to impose closure on a form that inherently resists such a desperate act of containment.

On the spectrum marked by aesthetic ideologies that would drive the literary class war, *The Sound and the Fury* moves closer to the concerns of social realism than traditional readings of the text would allow, particularly those that hold forth the novel as an exemplar of modernist orthodoxy and autonomy. Undergoing a thorough revision in form, the novel moves from the shards of meaning found in Benjy's stream of consciousness toward a collective point of view in the final section. The expansive vision that emerges through the course of the novel captures not only the forces of social upheaval as well as the consequent longing and even compulsion for restored order. Both *Mosquitoes* and *The Sound and the Fury* testify to Faulkner's insight into cultural politics and his foresight in matters of social, economic, and political consequence. Taking into account this dimension of Faulkner offers a way to redeem a much-maligned apprentice novel and to reevaluate a masterpiece in terms of an integrated artistic and social value determined at the level of form.

With the onset of the Depression, the relations between text and context in Faulkner remained dynamic and constitutive. With the nation facing heightened instability in the years after the crash that Jason Compson had predicted, the desire for strong leadership and the temptation to consolidate power were considerable. Various forms of cultural expression produced in the early thirties explored this phenomenon. Faulkner's fiction was no exception, showing fascination with ambitious characters who have designs on absolute power in the context of mounting concerns over the potential rise of homegrown fascism in Depression America.

CHAPTER THREE

Power by Design

Faulkner and the Specter of Fascism

WITH THE ECONOMY in disarray and the social order potentially in jeopardy, Americans in the early years of the Depression understandably entertained visions of strong leadership to restore the nation's
prosperity and purpose. Reading this development ominously, a steady
stream of articles and books from some of the nation's foremost intellectuals reflected on the potential rise of a dictator figure playing on fear
itself in order to manipulate a desperate populace and to accomplish the
rise of fascism in America. The ironic title of Sinclair Lewis's provocative
novel *It Can't Happen Here* (1935), a fictional rendering of authoritarian
signs appearing on America's political landscape, issued a statement that
the intellectual community responded to in both the affirmative and the
negative. Raymond Gram Swing's *The Forerunners of American Fascism*

(1935) and Lawrence Dennis's *The Coming American Fascism* (1936) marked opposite points on the spectrum of concern over the possibility that fascism might surface in the United States. In his book, Swing gives voice to the fear that fascism would arrive under cloak, emerging as a threat veiled in the institutions and traditions of American democracy. Dennis, by contrast, predicts that an overt show of force would signal the American incarnation of the fascist state, and his book expresses a longing for a system of consolidated power and economic planning that would maintain private ownership and market principles under the rubric of a corporate state. Taken together, these works represent the dialectical forces active in a Depression culture that maintained both fear and fascination in response to the notion of a great dictator achieving absolute power by design in the midst of economic strife and social unrest.

Despite the emergence of organizations such as the German-American Bund and William Dudley Pelley's "Silver Shirts," taking their cues from the Nazi Party in Germany, fascism in America remained for the most part a specter—an elusive signifier far more often assigned than claimed in the rhetorical tactics of political and cultural discourse. Such was the case with Faulkner, whose violent fictional content and perceived lack of social consciousness prompted the literary critic Maxwell Geismar to conclude with egregious parenthetical maneuvering that "it is in the larger tradition of reversionary, neo-pagan, and neurotic discontent (from which Fascism stems) that much of Faulkner's writing must be placed" (152). For writers and critics aligned with the aesthetic ideology of social realism, the charge of fascism served as a means of marginalizing authors who appeared too enamored of formal experimentation and the individualism inherent in the cultivation of "pure" form. Based largely on Faulkner's modernist formal practices, he could be associated with, say, Ezra Pound and thus figured as an opponent of the enterprise to integrate art and social reality. Also a factor, as Robert Brinkmeyer convincingly argues, was a "prevailing democratic revival that saw regionalism, not democracy, as the seedbed of fascism" (92). In this context, Brinkmeyer adds, Faulkner's southern traditionalism "left him open to the charge of fascism" (92).[1]

On such tenuous grounds, Geismar's attempt to link Faulkner and fascism now stands exposed as a product of its time, a cry of wolf lacking the substance that has led to evaluations of other notable figures linked to modernism whose connections to fascism could be seen as more explicit—Pound, T. S. Eliot, Wyndham Lewis, and Paul de Man, to name a few.[2]

A clear case of political posturing, Geismar's remark nevertheless serves as a point of departure for mapping tangible and compelling intersections between Faulkner's fiction and the preoccupation with fascism in the thirties. The tools of ideological analysis are especially suited to such an endeavor, but the temptation to fall into a reductive pattern of inquiry looms large. For this reason, it is important to stress at the outset that my objective is not to document or to discern Faulkner's ideological position relative to fascism as a basis for actual political rule—for instance, how Faulkner himself felt about Mussolini's rise to power in Italy or Hitler's Third Reich. Rather, my intention is to explore how the thematic content and formal structure of Faulkner's fiction implicated his texts in the discourse around fascism in the cultural context of the Depression. This discursive formation is easiest to document in terms of cultural history, especially works of popular culture to which Faulkner's fiction has striking connections.

Michael Denning identifies traits common to cultural representations of fascism in the thirties that are useful for approaching Faulkner in this regard. Denning's overview seeks to define an "aesthetic of anti-fascism" (375) as exemplified in the work of Orson Welles during the latter half of the thirties and the first half of the forties. Although Denning approaches fascism from the standpoint of leftist opposition, his characteristics nevertheless can be applied more generally to establish categories of cultural forms that evoke what he calls "the rhetoric of fascism and anti-fascism" (375). These characteristics generally include the following: (1) the gangster theory of fascism; (2) the celebration of power for the sake of power; and (3) the prominent feature of characters cut from the mold of the "great dictator" or "gigantic hero/villains" (375–76). To these I would add a fourth characteristic: representations of violence, particularly mob

violence and lynching, stemming from appeals to notions of racial and
national purity. Fixed on relevant aspects of Faulkner's *Sanctuary*, *Light
in August*, "Dry September," and *Absalom, Absalom!* the critical lens
forged from these traits brings into focus how the discourse around fascism functioned as a constitutive force in relation to Faulkner's literary
production. This influence is measurable in terms of stylistic components,
thematic elements, and aspects of character development that contribute
to an overall sense of form. Viewed in this context, these elements serve as
determinants of aesthetic value and as ideological inscriptions that con-
nect Faulkner to the cultural history of Depression America's encounter
with the specter of fascism.

William Faulkner's engagement with the discourse around fascism began
with his most controversial novel, *Sanctuary*, published in 1931. By the
time the sensational and provocative tale of gangster Popeye Pumphrey,
college coed Temple Drake, and stoic attorney Horace Benbow appeared
in print, large numbers of Americans were feeling the devastating effects
of the Depression and, consequently, were becoming increasingly impa-
tient with what was perceived as a lackluster and even uncaring response
to the crisis from the Hoover administration. The ineffectual effort to
reverse the tide of economic depression between the stock market crash
of 1929 and the election of FDR in 1932 created a sense of frustration
and skepticism that led many Americans to reevaluate the nation's basic institutions and founding principles. Works of popular culture aided
this collective enterprise substantially—perhaps none more so than the
rash of gangster sagas that became wildly popular during the transition
from the Roaring Twenties to the Great Depression. The public consumed
these stories in the form of novels such as Dashiell Hammett's *Red Harvest* (1929) and *The Maltese Falcon* (1931), W. R. Burnett's *Little Caesar* (1929), Armitage Trail's *Scarface* (1930), and Paul Cain's *Fast One*
(1932); however, film became the primary medium for providing a seemingly insatiable public with the exploits of gangsters and the lurid underworld they inhabited. Andrew Bergman notes that after the release, in

1930, of the classic gangster film *Little Caesar*—adapted from Burnett's novel and starring Edward G. Robinson and Douglas Fairbanks Jr.—fifty more such films followed before the end of 1931 (3). In many respects, the gangster was the ideal cultural icon for the early years of the Depression, embodying the intense desperation and steely determination to survive that many Americans felt in their everyday lives. While the gangster films reflected the hard times, they also functioned as protective devices for the great American success story and other cherished myths that seemed to be in danger of extinction. As Bergman explains, "The outlaw cycle represented not so much a mass desertion of the law as a clinging to past forms of achievement. That only gangsters could make upward mobility believable tells much about how legitimate institutions had failed—but that mobility was still at the core of what Americans held to be the American dream" (7). At the same time gangster films performed this important social function, they staged protofascist cultural fantasies of authoritative leaders who took decisive action in the face of adversity and an endangered rule of law. This cultural context illumines Faulkner's *Sanctuary* as a text influenced at various levels by a contemporaneous fixation on gangsters resulting from frustrated social, political, and economic desires.

Connections between *Sanctuary* and the gangster theory of fascism represented in *Little Caesar* and the copycat films that it inspired arose from Faulkner's determination to attract a mainstream audience by tapping into a vibrant trend in popular culture. Of course, it was this element of topicality that for a long time relegated *Sanctuary* to inferior status in the Faulkner canon. Based on distinctions between "high" and "low" art and between what Faulkner claimed to write for craft and merely for cash, the novel gained the reputation of being a mere financial venture. The longstanding perception of *Sanctuary*'s inferiority was based in large part on Faulkner's own assessment of the novel in an introduction to the 1932 Modern Library reprint. Riddled with inaccuracies and trademark embellishments, the introduction is yet another illustration of Faulkner's disregard for facts when constructing the events of his life and work. Still, as Sondra Guttman observes, the introduction is useful because it "represents an important moment of self-presentation in Faulkner" (16). Indeed, this moment yields much in the way of Faulkner's response to forces active in the cultural context.

One immediately striking feature of the introduction is Faulkner's construction of *Sanctuary* as a mass commodity—above all, a work of art in the age of mechanical reproduction, to apply Walter Benjamin's often cited phrase. Faulkner claims to think of the book as "a cheap idea, because it was deliberately conceived to make money" (vi) and thus dispossessed of what Benjamin calls "aura"—that singular alluring quality of an original work inevitably diminished by the process of reproduction. For Faulkner, the aura of *The Sound and the Fury* could remain intact "because I had done it for pleasure. I believed then that I would never be published again. I had stopped thinking of myself in publishing terms" (vi). But *Sanctuary* was clearly a different matter—a work conceived from and tarnished by acquisitive ulterior motives and attention to consumer desires and demands. Accordingly, Faulkner goes on to explain how the publication of *Sartoris* altered his self-perception and gave life to *Sanctuary*:

> I began to think of myself again as a printed object. I began to think of books in terms of possible money. I decided I might just as well make some of it myself. I took a little time out, and speculated what a person in Mississippi would believe to be current trends, chose what I thought was the right answer and invented the most horrific tale I could imagine and wrote it in about three weeks and sent it to [Random House editor Harrison] Smith, who had done *The Sound and the Fury* and who wrote me immediately, "Good God, I can't publish this. We'd both be in jail." (vi)

Here Faulkner acknowledges the commodification of *Sanctuary* and alludes to its topical quality—a work produced in tune with its cultural milieu and designed for mass consumption rather than fashioned as a singular work of "pure" art, as he proclaims of *The Sound and the Fury*. With his ear on the track, Faulkner clearly detected the lurid interest in the underworld contributing to the enormous popularity of *Little Caesar* and the subsequent wave of gangster films appearing in the same year as *Sanctuary*. Constructed as a work of popular culture, Faulkner's novel bears as much relation to this genre of film as to contemporaneous works of literature. After all, it was *Sanctuary* that first attracted Hollywood's attention to Faulkner and initiated his storied relationship with the film industry. Presumably, Hollywood executives at the time recognized what influential critics would later seek to downplay: Faulkner's keen awareness of the "current trends" and his ability to exploit them, as his sensational gangster tale demonstrates. That awareness goes far in explaining why Faulkner is "the most cinematic of novelists" (Kawin 5).

Like the gangster films popular in the early years of the Depression, *Sanctuary* features an enigmatic figure capable of eliciting both the fear and fascination that the Depression public found so captivating in outlaws. Faulkner introduces his gangster, Popeye, with a vivid use of imagery, creating a visual frame that evokes the discovery shot in film. Drinking from a stream, Horace Benbow, the gentlemanly attorney who comes to embody the conscience of the novel, sees his own image broken by ripples in the water, which captures as well "the shattered reflection of Popeye's straw hat" (*S* 4). This fractured form is quickly reassembled, however, when Horace looks up from the water and beholds Popeye with clarity: "He saw, facing him across the spring, a man of under size, his hands in his coat pockets, a cigarette slanted from his chin. His suit was black, with a tight, high-waisted coat. His trousers were rolled once and caked with mud above mud-caked shoes. His face had a queer, bloodless color, as though seen by electric light; against the sunny silence, in his slanted straw hat and his slightly akimbo arms, he had that vicious depthless quality of stamped tin" (4). Popeye strikes a classic gangster pose reminiscent of, say, *Little Caesar*'s Caesar Enrico Bandello, who shares in common with Popeye a small frame packed with remarkable ambition and ruthlessness, particularly when it comes to carrying out his designs on absolute power. Through mythical allusion, Faulkner establishes Popeye as the sinister guide poised on the bank of the Styx to shatter Horace's narcissistic contemplation and to lure him into the murky depths of the underworld. And there is clearly more than the width of a stream separating these two men, as Faulkner subsequently takes great pains to divide Horace and Popeye along class lines to delineate the struggle for viability and power staged in the remainder of the novel. As Lawrence Hanley observes, Popeye is a character "who belongs to the popular fiction and film genres of the period that metaphorically equated America's urban working classes with crime and disorder" (257).

In *Sanctuary*, as in the gangster films, the characters embody social concepts that imbue their conflicts and relations with ideological significance. Horace represents the logic of the dominant class, as his frequent appeals to ethos make clear. Philosophically, Horace lives by the mantra that he speaks to the falsely accused Lee Goodwin in an effort to convince him to reveal Popeye's presence at the scene of Tommy's murder: "You've got the law, justice, civilization" (*S* 132). From his enlightened perspective, Horace keeps a close watch for signs of societal collapse, ever wary of civilization's fragility and the possibility that it might descend further into incivility, chaos, and even anarchy. Goodwin shares Horace's belief in civilization, though his faith is much more practical, based on a sense that the rule of law demands that his innocence alone will prevent his wrongful conviction. While Horace and Goodwin represent faith in the justice system, Temple Drake embodies that system for Horace and subsequently for the Jefferson lynch mob that forms in defense of her "honor."

Opposed to Horace's concept of civilization, Popeye represents the element of disorder, for he despises the lofty notions valued by Horace and the rule of law trusted by Goodwin. Not only does Popeye refuse to accept the principles that Horace valorizes, but he is also determined to destroy them in favor of the fundamental precept of gangster naturalism that might makes right. The primary vehicle of this destruction is rape, a point made clear when Popeye's brutal violation of Temple yields a range of destabilizing effects. For Horace and the mob, the bodily violation of Temple signifies the vulnerability of the body politic and a crisis in the system of law and order. A familiar patriarchal construct surfaces here: the men contest the terms of civilization and justice on a field of representation embodied by Temple.[3] With these characters poised in a representative light against the backdrop of a volatile social order, *Sanctuary* probes the intense and often violent nature of power relations and thus becomes implicated in the cultural politics shaped by the gangster films that introduced protofascist images and themes into American popular culture.

A fundamental component of the gangster theory of fascism is that the lead gangster prefigures the fascist dictator. In the case of *Little Caesar*, for example, Rico methodically carries out his designs on power, moving up the ranks of the Vettori mob family in Chicago and enhancing his reputation as a ruthless and ambitious criminal. Like the fascist dictator, Rico relies heavily on appearances in order to amplify his power—a feat made all the more difficult by his slight stature. The higher he rises, though, the more Rico knows he must foster an aesthetic that conveys a sense of his rightful authority as a means of further consolidating power and achieving absolute control over the Chicago syndicate. By assuming a sort of legendary status, in the underworld and in the society at large, Rico attempts to impose a sense of structure on an underworld that is inherently unstructured, given its ethos of gangster naturalism. In *Sanctuary*, a similar aesthetic surrounds Popeye, for it is constructed largely from anecdotal evidence of his intense capacity for ruthlessness and cruelty and his legendary marksmanship. For example, when Horace implores Goodwin to pin Tommy's murder on Popeye, Goodwin refuses because "I've seen him light matches with a pistol at twenty feet. Why, damn it all, I'd never get back here from the courtroom the day I testified that" (*S* 132). The aesthetic constructed from lore empowers Popeye to the point that he is equally feared in his presence and his absence—an important condition of Popeye's design on power. In contrast to Rico in *Little Caesar*, Popeye remains for the most part a sinister and shadowy figure lurking at the margins of action and continually posing the menacing threat that violence will erupt upon his arrival. However, like Rico, Popeye relies on aesthetic means to wield power and thus to maintain order through fear, manipulation, and the ever-present threat of violence.

While the gangster theory of fascism focuses understandably on the lust for power in defining the individualistic gangster as a prototype for the fascist dictator, this theory places significant emphasis on the violent criminal methods employed to affect the social formation of the underworld in response to conditions in the society as a whole. As noted above, critical reception of Faulkner tended to concentrate on the violent nature of his work; frequently, *Sanctuary* was cited as evidence of this disturbing Faulknerian emphasis. But *Sanctuary* was certainly not alone in attracting the notice of critics troubled by representations of violence and criminal activity and the readily apparent social implications of such representations. In fact, the gangster films appearing in the cultural context of Faulkner's novel drew similar responses. Not surprisingly, much of this concern came from politicians and civic organizations disturbed by the gangster films' apparent glorification of violence and mayhem in defiance of law and order. In response to this considerable public pressure, the Motion Picture Producers and Distributors of America (MPPDA) crafted a code intended to regulate depictions of criminal activity and violence in contemporary film. The code stipulated that breaking the law must "never be presented in such a way as to throw sympathy with the crime as against law and justice or to inspire others with a desire for imitation" (qtd. in Bergman 5).

Other aspects of the code focused specifically on representations of murder and brutal crime, emphasizing in both instances that the depictions should not display vivid detail that might inspire copycat crimes. In another telling section of the code, the MPPDA declared, "Revenge in modern times shall not be justified" (qtd. in Bergman 5). Concerns over potential imitation and depictions of vengeance betray the dominant ideology that shaped these codes. This regulatory effort was motivated, at base, by the desire to prevent the sort of chaos that these films represented from playing out in the streets and presumably ushering in a restructured social order. Bergman offers a concise and cogent explanation of this social dynamic: "It was a jittery society that felt compelled to denounce, and filled theatres to watch, outlaw protagonists" (6). Faulkner's *Sanctuary* is noticeably responsive to this paradoxical arrangement, which pits the consumer desire for representations of underworld mayhem against the anxieties of a dominant ideology intent on regulating these representations in the interest of preserving established social order.

One of the more noticeable instances of this negotiation in *Sanctuary* is the portrayal of violence as a palpable force lurking always beneath the surface of apparent calm and waiting at any moment to erupt. This representation is accomplished quite remarkably through the depiction of Temple, who attracts a menacing male gaze with virtually every appearance she makes in the novel. When Temple first arrives on the scene, for instance, she is described from the perspective of leering town boys who often showed up for dances and "watched her enter the gymnasium upon black collegiate arms and vanish in a swirling glitter upon a glittering swirl of music," her darting stare appearing "cool, predatory and discreet" (*S* 29). Even Temple's name is the focus of this gaze, as revealed later by Gowan Stevens when he chides her for trying to appear beyond the pale of the town boys who look at her longingly. Berating Temple, Gowan says, "Think you can play around all week with any badger-trimmed hick that owns a ford, and fool me on Saturday, don't you? Dont think I didn't see your name where it's written on that lavatory wall" (38).

Significantly, these two gazes in such close textual proximity serve to construct Temple alternatively as "lady" and "whore," the binary opposition standard in the ideology of "pure" southern womanhood to which Temple, like Caddy Compson before her, is subjected. Like Caddy's dirty drawers, the inscription on the bathroom wall is a harbinger—in this case, of the horrific sexual violation that is to come. For now, though, the constitutive male gaze subjects Temple to an oppressive gender ideology at the same time it foregrounds social class by juxtaposing the town boys and Gowan as the agents of the gaze. It is important to note the correspondence of the alternative forms of Temple's character ("lady" and "whore") to the ideological conflict present in a dominant class that professed its integrity while fearfully contemplating a sordid "fall" into the lower ranks or, much worse, a brutal violation (i.e., revolt) stemming from class hostility. As the embodiment of the justice system, Temple represents the concerns of a dominant class that relies on the perceived viability of this system in the interest of its own perpetuity. From this standpoint, representations of violence in the novel—most of them related somehow to Popeye's violation of Temple—can be read as constituting and constituted by the same class anxieties evident in the gangster films and the response to them from the "jittery society" (Bergman 6). This conflicted response came from fans as well as the censorial forces that remained fearful of the images these films projected into popular consciousness.

The locus of violence in *Sanctuary* is the volatile relationship between Popeye and Temple, culminating in the novel's infamous signature episode: Popeye's raping of Temple with a corncob. The rising action preceding this brutal act compounds its eventual impact, as Faulkner charts what Horace later calls "a logical pattern to evil" (*S* 221) with chilling certitude. From the very first moment that Temple encounters Popeye, there is a sense of foreboding—aimed from Popeye's eyes, the male gaze intensifies, infused with a sinister quality not readily apparent in the description of the attentive town boys. A note of class difference is immediately injected into the exchange, as Temple asks Popeye to give her and Gowan a ride back to town in the wake of their car accident. When Temple offers payment to a reluctant Popeye, he reacts angrily and says to Gowan, "Make your whore lay off me, Jack" (49). The word choice is telling, for it signals to Temple and Gowan that their understanding of Popeye as servile and inferior is subject to reversal in this underworld setting—the dilapidated old Frenchman's Bend plantation, a base of operation for bootlegging. Suggesting the demise of social distinctions familiar to Temple and Gowan, the fallen plantation also serves as an ominous backdrop for the violent encounter set to unfold. The description of the estate reveals that "nowhere was any sign of husbandry—plow or tool; in no direction was a planted field in sight—only a gaunt weather-stained ruin in a somber grove through which the breeze drew with a sad, murmurous sound" (41). This barren image calls to mind Benjamin's observation that the fascist aesthetic requires a lack of productivity so that it might replace nature with violence (680). Such is the case in this setting, as the presence of Temple stimulates (in every sense of the word) the production of violence that ultimately Popeye will harvest, fittingly enough, in the corn crib.

The volatility resulting from Temple's presence on the estate is immediately apparent. When she enters the room where the bootleggers and Gowan have gathered, the tension becomes palpable. First, Van, a drunken lout, grabs her by the wrist and invites her to sit on his lap, urging Tommy to make room with a directive that acknowledges social disparity: "Move down, Tommy. . . . Aint you got no manners, you mat-faced bastard?" (*S* 65). Van's unwelcome advances mobilize Gowan: he stands ready, at least from his perspective, to defend Temple's honor. Ironically, Gowan finds himself defending something he has earlier called into question, suggesting that his defense is less about protecting Temple per se than about pronouncing and preserving the class distinction ideologically encoded in his stand. Instead of Gowan, though, Goodwin assumes the mantle of defending Temple, stepping in hastily to defuse the potential conflict. That Goodwin has to defend Temple highlights Gowan's inability not only to protect Temple but also to articulate his need to protect Temple, much less to do so in actuality. Reminiscent of Quentin Compson, that failed gentleman and protector of feminine honor, an extremely intoxicated Gowan can manage only to utter fragments of the chivalric code he tries to invoke. Angered by Van's refusal to leave Temple alone, Gowan says, "—ginia gentleman; I dont give a—" (68). Later, after the conflict has escalated, Goodwin attempts to intervene once again, but Gowan resists: " 'Got proteck. . . . . . .' Gowan muttered ' . . . girl. 'Ginia gem. . . . . . . gemman got proteck. . . . . . .' " (73). Like the barren estate, Gowan and his code of honor are rendered unproductive and ultimately powerless, a condition punctuated by Gowan's severe beating at the hands of Van and the emasculation that it apparently accomplishes: "[Gowan's] hair was broken about his face, long as a girl's" (73). By contrast, it is Popeye who holds the power here. Significantly, the invocation of his name and his legendary marksmanship immediately precedes the brutal beating of Gowan. The violent attack on Gowan comes so swiftly that it registers only in absence, once it is "gone like a furious gust of black wind, leaving a peaceful vacuum" (72). The dark and tempestuous image conveys the sudden force of violence, creating a sense of displacement stemming from the absence of vivid detail—a distancing effect magnified in the infamous rape scene.

For obvious reasons, the rape of Temple Drake lends itself to interpretations based in psychoanalytic theory.[4] As in the case of *The Sound and the Fury*, however, there is much insight to be gained from extending the examination from the interior to the exterior—in terms of the rape scene, then, to consider its profound social implications. As suggested above, the abandoned plantation offers a setting in which class divisions active in the broader social order are subject to reversal, owing mainly to the power that Popeye exerts in defining this underworld milieu. However, Popeye's vision does not ensure complete acquiescence, for Goodwin and Ruby appear resistant to the restructuring that Popeye seeks to bring about through threatened and actual violence. Out of moral conviction and an apparent desire for peace and stability—a stark contrast to Gowan's nominal chivalry—Goodwin does attempt to protect, and thus essentially to preserve, Temple in response to the threat posed by Popeye. Though tinged with noticeable hostility, Ruby's repeated acknowledgment of Temple's social status essentially confirms the hierarchy that Popeye seeks to destroy. And the rape is the signature act of destruction, representing Popeye's brutal violation of Temple and the social formation that she embodies.

The rape scene begins with Temple confined to the corn crib by Goodwin. She remains under the watchful eye of Tommy, presumably to give her protection from Van's clutches and from Popeye's menacing presence. However, instead of providing safety, the crib functions in the manner of Foucault's Panopticon, a confining space in which Temple becomes a spectacle for yet another incarnation of the voyeuristic gaze that has fixed on her from the outset of the novel.[5] Ironically, it is her appointed protector who first directs the gaze with "a diffident, groping, hungry fire" as he begins "to rub his hands slowly on his shanks, rocking a little from side to side" (*S* 101). But Popeye assumes control of the gaze once he descends ominously into the corn crib from the top floor of the barn, standing before Temple and "thrust[ing] his chin out in a series of jerks" in a highly sexualized gesture (101). The phallic imagery compounds the sexual tension, as Temple eyes Popeye and spots "the pistol behind him, against his flank, wisping thinly along his leg"; next, we are told, Popeye "waggled the pistol slightly and put it back in his coat, then he walked toward her" (101). The potency signified by the phallic imagery stands in opposition to the reality of Popeye's sexual impotency. This feature of Popeye's character is a variation on a familiar theme in the gangster genre. In *Little Caesar*, for example, Rico takes what amounts to a vow of celibacy, choosing instead to channel all his energy toward ambition. A common trope, desexualizing the gangster serves to channel all energy toward his will to power, thus maintaining a healthy balance between fear and fascination for the audience to behold. In *Sanctuary*, however, Popeye's impotency feeds a sexual deviancy apparent in his use of the corncob to rape Temple and his voyeuristic employment of Red as a stud. Instead of offering a source of identification and unity, Popeye's response to sexual frustration contributes to his alienation, clearly marking him as aberrant and Other in his propensity to commit violent acts.

In constructing the rape scene, Faulkner generally anticipates a post-production-code technique, resisting the sort of graphic depiction that leaves little to the imagination. But I would argue that this mode of representation suggests not so much a censorial compulsion as an interest in collectivizing the violation of Temple from the perspective of an expansive social vision. Unlike the vivid descriptions at other points in the novel—the "discovery shot" of Popeye cited above, for instance—the rape of Temple is recounted with an absence of particulars. Still, the scene conveys Popeye's predatory nature and Temple's sheer vulnerability, which is underscored by her futile cry for help to Pap, the blind and deaf old man seated nearby. The violence is displaced primarily through Faulkner's use of pronouns with increasingly remote antecedents, a formal decision that places distance between the brutal action and the characters involved:

> Moving, he made no sound at all. . . . She could hear silence in a thick rustling as he moved toward her through it, thrusting it aside and she began to say Something is going to happen to me. She was saying it to the old man with yellow clots for eyes. "Something is happening to me!" she screamed at him. . . . "I told you it was!" she screamed, voiding the words like hot silent bubbles into the bright silence about them until he turned his head and the two phlegm-clots above her where she lay tossing and thrashing on the rough, sunny boards. "I told you! I told you all the time!" (*S* 102)

Emphasis shifts here from the personal violation that Temple feels ("Something is happening to me!") to an admonishment delivered via second person ("I told you!"). Ostensibly, Temple's outrage is directed at the old man, but the direct address also works to project the displaced violence outward to the realm of shared experience. This projection underscores the representative component of the violation, as it registers on a range from the personal to the social through the remainder of the novel. The impact of the rape is felt most immediately, of course, by Temple, whose posttraumatic stress is evident in her facial expression, which is described from Ruby's point of view as being "like a small, dead-colored mask drawn past her on a string and then away" (104). Taken by the gangster Popeye to the shyster city of Memphis, Temple will eventually come to call her captor "daddy" (231), the symbolic replacement of Judge Drake indicating the culmination of Popeye's design on power. In turn, the abduction of Temple and the unfolding mystery of her violation traced by Horace pose the threat of disruption in a social order growing increasingly skeptical of traditional means of ensuring stability and preserving justice.

The social implications of the rape foreground the novel's concern with an endangered rule of law, thus establishing another intersection between *Sanctuary* and the gangster theory of fascism. Bergman explains one of the more subversive views projected in the gangster films of the early thirties:

"What was negative and despairing surfaced in their treatment of the law. A viable state commands a viable law, and the law depicted, at its best, was never more than something to beat. At its worst, it scarcely seemed to exist" (13). Gangster films such as *Little Caesar* and *The Public Enemy*, which was released in 1931 with James Cagney in the lead role, exposed a central paradox of the Depression: that the only means of satisfying the demand for success dictated by the American dream appeared to be outside the rule of law. In particular, public officials and agents of law enforcement in these films come across as ineffectual or corrupt, often constructing bureaucratic obstacles to the very justice they are entrusted to uphold. For instance, *City Streets* (1931), starring Gary Cooper, casts law enforcement officers as the thugs, transferring the redemptive value to the outlaws. Such depictions reflect the lack of confidence that Americans held in the established system of order and, in turn, the admiration they had for the gangsters' decisive action in maintaining a code of justice in the underworld, violent though it was. As Bergman points out, the "endorsement of the power of the mob reflected an intense desire for authority and an impatience with indecision and obstacles—obstacles which got defined as the law" (114). By extolling the virtues of the outlaw over the law, the gangster films of 1930–1932 offer incisive social commentary that seem to sanction a radical restructuring of society in response to the frustrations of economic depression and ineffectual leadership from government officials and institutions. In representing the dynamic conflict between the established rule of law and the challenge posed by the ethos of gangster naturalism, *Sanctuary* bears certain similarities to its novelistic and cinematic counterparts but also features telling variations that resonate with ideological significance and ultimately register the novel's dissent from the often radical social commentary expressed in the gangster novels and films.

What *Sanctuary* does share in common with the gangster films is an acknowledgment that the institutional means of dispensing justice are not merely fallible but inherently flawed and prone to corruption. Consider, for example, the depictions of public officials and agents of the law in the novel. Eustace Graham, the district attorney in Jefferson, is portrayed as a political opportunist who is more concerned with advancing his career in the Goodwin murder trial than seeing that justice is done. Horace sets the tone of Graham's portrayal, referring to him as "damn little squirt" (*S* 185) when Narcissa mentions his name. Horace then charges that it was Graham who had Ruby and her child evicted from the hotel for "public effect, political capital" (185). Confirmation of Horace's charges, which must be taken with a grain of salt in light of the impending trial, can be found in Graham's willingness to compromise the ethical standards assigned to his public office when Narcissa pays him a visit. When she inquires about Horace's chances for a victory in the trial, Graham says without much prodding, "This is purely confidential. I am violating my oath of office; I wont have to tell you that. But it may save you worry to know that he hasn't a chance in the world" (263). Graham's opportunism is further on display during the trial when he employs unethical maneuvers to gain favor with the jury and to manipulate public opinion. A case in point is Graham's irrelevant reference to Ruby and Goodwin's unmarried status—a tactic designed to undermine her testimony (269–70).

Compounding this troubling depiction of public officials is the presence of Senator Clarence Snopes, a character whose perpetual lack of cleanliness serves as an obvious metaphor for his questionable political modus operandi. Senator Snopes abides by a sort of libertarian belief that "a man aint no more than human, and what he does aint nobody's business but his" (*S* 187), a belief that invariably sets his private desires at odds with the sworn duties of his public office but nevertheless affords him the necessary cover to deny his remarkable hypocrisy. Critical of Eustace Graham's abuse of his office for political gain, Senator Snopes clearly exhibits his own opportunistic bent in using the information he gains about Temple's whereabouts in Memphis to his advantage. In his various dealings, the senator confirms the self-assessment that he offers to Horace when he first encounters him on the train: "I aint hidebound in no sense, as you'll find out when you know me better" (206). Senator Snopes and Eustace Graham would have been at home in *Little Caesar, The Secret Six, City*

Streets, or the numerous other gangster films that depicted public officials in an unflattering light and thus reflected common perceptions in society of a justice system crippled by apparently inherent graft and corruption. They would have fit comfortably as well in the rash of 1932 productions about "shyster lawyers and shyster politicians," which Bergman defines as a subgenre of the gangster films (23). With Eustace Graham, Faulkner anticipates characters in films such as *Lawyer Man* and *The Mouthpiece*, and with Senator Snopes, those in films such as *The Dark Horse*, *The Phantom President*, and *Washington Masquerade*.[6]

But *Sanctuary* differs in a key respect from the gangster films with their harsh and comprehensive indictments of failing social and political institutions. While the gangster films offer the protofascist ethos of gangster naturalism as a decisive alternative to the ineffectiveness of a corrupt legislative and judicial system, *Sanctuary* resists such an endorsement by locating the conscience of the novel—albeit a conscience in crisis—in the character of Horace Benbow rather than in Popeye, the gangster. This move stands in contrast to the popular trend of telling the story from the gangster's point of view established by Burnett in the novel *Little Caesar* and continued in the film adaptation. In *Sanctuary*, it is Horace, after all, who professes with sincerity that "I cannot stand idly by and see injustice—" (*S* 119). The long dash here leaves ample space for the numerous manifestations of injustice that Horace will stand idly by and witness, as his faith in law and civilization is shattered through the course of his quest to find Temple and prevent Goodwin's false conviction. For the most part, Horace wages this pursuit of justice on a conceptual plane, existing above what he deems the "free Democratico-Protestant atmosphere of Yoknapatawpha" (128) that is prone to the corrupt practices of Eustace Graham and Senator Snopes. In this regard, Horace is like Cicero, whom he invokes when Ruby offers him sexual favors in return for legal services rendered in defense of Goodwin. "O tempora! O mores! O hell!" cries Horace in disbelief that Ruby assumes his service to stem from base self-interest rather than a commitment to justice and to the preservation of "the harmony of things" (275). Ruby's frank offer of compensation

and Horace's appalled rejection of it underscore the inherent conflict between Horace's idealistic perceptions of the law and the corrupt system
he must negotiate to vindicate Goodwin. To achieve this goal, Horace
knows that he must solve the mystery that centers on Temple Drake—a
mystery that forces him, as it turns out, into the role of sleuth in search
of clues that stand to reveal the details of the crime and the harsh conditions of social reality that his conceptual frame of mind has heretofore
prevented him from recognizing.

In the first leg of his quest to find Temple, Horace pays a visit to the
university post office, where he experiences an instance of mistaken identity, at least as far as his vocation is concerned. Wary of Horace's inquiry
as to Temple's whereabouts, the postal clerk asks, "Are you another detective?" (*S* 171). Horace offers a muddled response, finally insisting, "It
doesn't matter" (171). On the contrary, Horace's foray into the detective
business is quite significant because it represents, as a story within the
story, Faulkner's homage to the popular hard-boiled detective fiction—a
close relative of the gangster stories—and because of the social and ideological function that the traditional detective story has performed. From
the perspective of Marxist cultural theory, as Dennis Porter explains, this
popular genre "involves the celebration of the repressive state apparatus
or at least of that important element of it formed by the police" (121).
However, what is lacking in this formula, Porter adds, is any acknowledgment of fallibility in the law—so much so, in fact, that "the law itself
is never put on trial" (122). The agent of this infallible apparatus is, of
course, the detective, whose investigation "represents in its way the exercise of lucid power over an identified enemy of society" (125). In this
respect, the detective serves as a stabilizing force, offering reassurance to
the established order that the only logical outcome of any internal threat is
that it will be detected, exposed, and incarcerated. For the dominant class,
then, the detective story is entertaining to the extent that it is reassuring—
that is to say, insofar as the familiar formal conventions of the story signal
the foregone conclusion that any disruption caused by the crime will give
way to a restored order once it is solved.

If, as Porter suggests, the traditional detective story "adapts itself easily to the changing objects of popular anxiety" (127), then it is not surprising at all that Faulkner's extended allusion to the genre is imbued with irony. In his comparison of *Sanctuary* to the hard-boiled detective fiction popular as the twenties gave way to the thirties, Eric J. Sundquist, following Andre Malraux, points out the fundamental inadequacy of Horace Benbow as a detective "who is powerless to prevent gross misapplications of justice and incapable of revealing why such evil as the novel continually dwells on should occur" (50).[7] Not only that, but Faulkner also breaks virtually all the rules by subverting key narrative conventions of the traditional detective story. For example, Faulkner depicts the crime and makes little effort to hide the perpetrator, except from Horace, whose entrapment in dramatic irony highlights his failure as an agent of the law—first as a "detective" and then as a lawyer. Furthermore, Faulkner features the trial prominently in the novel, a component missing from the traditional detective story, with the notable exception of Agatha Christie's "Witness for the Prosecution." Traditional detective fiction resists description of the criminal's life outside the circumstances of the crime and generally concludes with the exposure of the criminal, leaving the brand of punishment to the reader's imagination. On both counts, Faulkner is guilty of infractions, which occur at the end of the novel in the misplaced exposition that recounts Popeye's upbringing before revealing his apprehension by the law and, finally, his execution.

These subversions of convention represent in narrative terms the system's chronic failure to perform as expected and enable the novel "to induce in the reader nervous terror rather than aesthetic submission," as Clifton Fadiman keenly observed in an early response to *Sanctuary* (106). Although Horace sets out to solve the crime, what he discovers instead is that he is powerless—impotent, really—when it comes to performing the desired social functions of the "detective"/lawyer, an agent with heightened powers of surveillance and a reassuring sign of established order. Instead, what Horace comes to discover in the course of his investigation is that the noble concepts he cherishes no longer seem to apply in a system now apparently guided by Popeye's codes of gangster naturalism. Jay Watson aptly describes this outcome as a reversal: "Foucault's Panopticon is turned inside-out: the outlaw becomes its silent overseer, while the official representatives of law and the law-abiding are reduced to inmates, the inspected. Popeye has beaten the law at its own game" (63).

The success of Popeye's effort to subvert the justice system and disrupt the established order is apparent in the trial of Lee Goodwin. Presumably a means of seeking justice in the case of Tommy's murder, the trial becomes instead a spectacle of social disruption. While Goodwin is the nominal defendant, Horace's sensibility stands trial as well, his grand notions of law and civilization facing harsh scrutiny before standing first exposed and then essentially convicted as obsolete. The trial intensifies the dramatic irony on display during Horace's search for Temple and, more to the point, during his visit to Memphis when Temple's account of the murder and rape forces him, at last, to acknowledge the power of evil that the other characters—and indeed the entire novel—have taken for granted all along. The conflation of Little Belle and Temple in a nausea-inducing vision of the rape that overwhelms Horace, complete with the sound of shuffling corn shucks, is a psychosomatic overture to the destruction of his refined sensibility that will occur through the course of the trial.

The element of irony is skillfully enhanced by the distance that Faulkner constructs between Horace and the participants in the trial, a distance measured in terms of class. From the very outset, Horace misinterprets the events of the trial, exposing a difference between his expectations rooted in class ideology and what actually transpires. Clearly, Horace lacks Eustace Graham's understanding of audience. Graham's allusion to the fact that Ruby and Goodwin are not married—a statement punctuated by Ruby's cradling of their child in her lap—demonstrates the district attorney's awareness that Goodwin is being tried by the court and, more important, by the court of public opinion. In Horace's conceptual view, however, the letter of the law, with its foundation in the noble cause of justice, is the ultimate determinant. Consequently, he misreads Graham's ploy as a sign of desperation. "Dont you see your case is won?" he assures Ruby. "That they are reduced to trying to impugn the character of your witness?" (*S* 270). Horace operates on the faulty assumption that the ethos of the trial—and, by extension, of the community—accepts as given his honor-bound sense of character informed by a class-specific system of values revealed in his remark to Ruby that "God is foolish at times, but at least He's a gentleman" (280). Insulated by confidence in this divine authority, Horace feels no compulsion to acknowledge the observers of the trial as any more than a mass of humanity, which he perceives with increasing objectification: "Above the seat-backs Horace could see their heads—bald heads, gray heads, shaggy heads and heads trimmed to recent feather-edge above sun-baked necks, oiled heads above urban collars and here and there a sunbonnet or a flowered hat" (281).

From his abstracted perspective, Horace initially holds fast to the belief that the justice system is, after all, his world—a place that offers certain protection from and powerful opposition to Popeye's underworld of graft, corruption, and evil. Confident in the conceptual integrity of the justice system, Horace cannot yet tap into Ruby's "deep reserve of foreboding" (*S* 270), which signals to her and to the reader the weakness of Horace's initial reassurance that he still knows the ways of his world: "You may know more about making whiskey or love than I do, but I know more about criminal procedure than you, remember" (270). As the trial proceeds, Horace does develop his own sense of foreboding, coinciding with the arrival of Temple and prompting his epiphanic admission, "I know what I'll find before I find it," which signals denouement in the narrative arc (282). Adding insult to injury, Graham supplants Horace as the caretaker of justice, albeit a vigilante justice cloaked in rhetoric of chivalry that professes to honor "that most sacred thing in life: womanhood" and pledges to exchange paternal safety for Temple's story: "Let these good men, these fathers and husbands, hear what you have to say and right your wrong for you" (284–85). Rendered impotent first by his conceptual sensibility and now by the painful recognition of its limitations, Horace is left to stand idly by and see injustice prevail in the cruel form of Temple's perjury. Representing the end of "civilization," as Horace envisions it, this destruction of the Temple, so to speak, marks submission to Popeye's design. But it also stems from a tacit alliance with the mass of observers who now share, as a result of the perjury, a "collective breath" (286) that will fan the flames eventually consuming the falsely convicted Goodwin in a frenzy of vigilantism.

In the original text of *Sanctuary*, Faulkner represents this alliance more explicitly in terms of class. Upon Temple's arrival at the courthouse, Horace experiences a revelation: "He realised now that it was too late, that he could not have summoned her; realised again that furious homogeneity of the middle classes when opposed to the proletariat from which it so recently sprung and by which it is so often threatened" (*SO* 260). Kevin Railey convincingly asserts the usefulness of this original passage for comprehending the larger significance of Temple's perjury. For Railey, the earlier version helps to define the cooperation between Judge Drake and Eustace Graham, resulting in the perjured testimony, as representative of a shifting social formation—a consolidation of power between segments of the middle class that essentially excludes other classes. Horace's sense of abandonment in response to this shift leads Railey to conclude that "even though the Jefferson society in this book can be associated with the bourgeois, middle class, the novel's narrative perspective—Horace's perspective—has more to do with that of an aristocratic paternalist" (70). The language in the original version illuminates a level of class anxiety not as specifically expressed in the revised text but nevertheless active. What is particularly striking is the emphasis on collective mobilization that develops in the conclusion of the trial, as rendered in the revised edition: "The room sighed . . ." and "the heads turned as one" (*S* 286, 288). This narrative perspective conflates the crisis in the rule of law and the unification of the middle and lower classes represented by the tacit agreement between Judge Drake and Eustace Graham and the consequent mobilization of the masses that it inspires.

Had Faulkner ended *Sanctuary* with Goodwin's immolation, or even with Horace's dejected and defeated return to Kinston, then it would have come much closer to the sentiment commonly on display in the gangster novels and films of 1929–32: that desperate times require desperate measures, even to the point of adopting the basic power principle that might makes right illuminated by the gangster theory of fascism. For the duration of the novel, Popeye's brutal crime precludes the level of sympathy for the devil that enticed moviegoers to cheer Edward G. Robinson's Rico in *Little Caesar* and James Cagney's Tommy Powers in *The Public Enemy* as heroes in alternative pursuit of the American dream. On first inspection, the final section of *Sanctuary*, which reads in large part as Popeye's psychosocial history, might seem an attempt to lend him at least some level of sympathy by explaining his pathological nature as largely a product of his cruel upbringing. Sundquist does well to note the tenor of social realism on display in the final section, which calls to mind Dreiser and Crane in casting Popeye as "rather a compendium of naturalistic doom" (48). For Sundquist, though, Faulkner's foray into naturalism ultimately serves the cause of critique, revealing the limitations of naturalism as a literary form and philosophical system and eventually "exposing the moral void of psychoanalysis and social science, the conspicuous fields of inquiry that bring naturalism into the twentieth century and conspire to make justice a subject of pathological study" (49). It is worth noting, however, that these limitations and failures are more apparent in retrospect than they likely would have been in the cultural context of the novel, especially given the emergence of social realism as a revitalized literary form. Moreover, the gangster films display a visible sociological curiosity in depicting the outlaws as products of environmental factors. Wary of the growing controversy that would result in the production codes, for instance, the producers of *The Public Enemy* championed the film as essentially a case study designed to explore the social conditions that could produce a man like Tommy Powers (Bergman 10–13). Filmmakers figured that if they could sell their products as attempts to explain the criminal mind, then they could skirt the charge of celebrating violence, mayhem, and social disruption.

In this cultural context, the cold ethos of gangster naturalism offered a troubling model for constructing social order. However, naturalism employed in the service of sociological insight could be viewed as a re-assuring form capable of tracing "a logical pattern to evil" (*S* 221) for those in power feeling unsettled by the social implications of the gang-ster craze. Invoking naturalism in the curious final section of the novel, Faulkner attempts an aesthetic act of containment rooted in the desire to impose order on a social system rendered chaotic and unstable. What can be termed the radical center of the novel, extending basically from the rape scene to the aftermath of the trial, goes far in contemplating the possibility of a radically revised social structure, but only in terms of the threat posed by Popeye as a source of disruption and brutality, as the rape of Temple dictates. The association of social transformation with protofascist themes leaves the novel closed to alternatives beyond the established social order, such as it is. Because contemporary social conditions and the popular form of the gangster story were resistant to favorable representations of the justice system, Faulkner, like the gang-ster figures, had to circumvent the letter of the law, in a sense, to ren-der an aesthetic containment. Accordingly, the final section of the revised *Sanctuary* demonstrates resistance to the laws of narrative convention, featuring exposition as afterthought and a drastic alteration in form and tone yielded by Faulkner's shift into a naturalistic mode of social realism. This shift conveys the sense of a higher law inscribed in Faulkner's text apparently capable of "explaining" Popeye's motivation while girding the fallible justice system so as to render his conviction and execution as logi-cal conditions of "natural" order. In this respect, *Sanctuary* might be read as "a profoundly conservative document" (Sundquist 59), sending com-forting signals of restored order to those made uneasy by the destabilizing implications of the gangster craze.

As in *Mosquitoes*, however, this representation exposes a dominant ideology insistent on equating "natural" order with conditions favorable to its own continued viability. With Popeye convicted, a turn of events cast more in terms of submission than apprehension, the deputy assigned to guard the gangster remarks, "It's them thugs like that that have made justice a laughing-stock, until even when we get a conviction, everybody knows it wont hold" (*S* 312). Significantly, the publicly staged execution of Popeye proves the guard wrong and, on a social level, appears to signal restoration of the old order. With this move, Faulkner could prevent the sort of controversy surrounding Howard Hawks's celebrated gangster film, *Scarface* (1932). Betraying the ideological imperative of aesthetic containment, the New York censor board, after viewing the film's first cut, demanded and received a new ending in which the gangster figure is hanged according to the rule of law and a change in the title—the revised version was released to theaters, quite tellingly, as *Shame of a Nation* (Bergman 14). From this standpoint, the "natural" chain of events leading to Popeye's execution and the sheriff's final words to him—"I'll fix it for you" (*S* 316)—offer some reassurance to an apprehensive dominant class wary of social upheaval. But this containment is, at best, a quick fix, for the final words of the novel immediately comprehend "the embrace of the season of rain and death" (317) manifested in the numerous representations of mob violence that establish further connections between Faulkner's texts and the discourse around fascism active in the Depression.

By 1932 the wave of gangster films had diminished to a slow trickle. At this point, the protofascist themes evident in this cycle gave way to more explicit ones in a series of films that appeared from 1933 to 1937, reflecting an ongoing fascination in American culture with mob mentality and vigilante justice. While gangsters were still featured in films, they were now depicted more often than not as insidious figures intent on disrupting the rule of law. Simply put, the gangsters of post-1932 Hollywood were more like Faulkner's Popeye Pumphrey than Edward G. Robinson's Rico Bandello or James Cagney's Tommy Powers. In place of the gangster, representations of an unruly public now simultaneously reflected the longing for decisive action in the vacuum of ineffectual leadership as well as the need for civil restraint to prevent revolution.

On the issue of mob rule, these cultural forms remained responsive to contemporary politics, running the gamut from endorsement to ambivalence to condemnation. In some instances, vigilante justice was presented as a viable and necessary alternative in desperate times; more often, however, it served as the crux of the cautionary tale. It is no coincidence that favorable depictions of vigilantism coincided with the recognition that just replacing Hoover with FDR would not end the Depression, while condemnations emerged virtually in lockstep with the cohesive social and political formations of the New Deal and the Popular Front. For example, in the latter half of the thirties, with Popular Front antifascism at its zenith, Orson Welles delved into the nature of mob mentality with his 1937 Mercury Theater production of Shakespeare's *Julius Caesar*, which preceded a less welcome staging of mass hysteria prompted by his infamous radio broadcast of *War of the Worlds* the following year. Hollywood joined in the exploration of mob mentality as well, producing a series of lynching films: *Black Fury* (1935), *Fury* (1936), *Black Legion* (1937), and *They Won't Forget* (1937). For Welles and Hollywood filmmakers, representations of mob violence were part of an overriding concern with the rise of fascism playing out on the international stage. From a domestic standpoint, forms of cultural expression stressed the Popular Front's insistence that fascism and racism were virtually synonymous, as illustrated by the heinous practice of lynching still active primarily in Faulkner's South and influential in the culture as an issue that defined social consciousness. By engaging in graphic depictions of lynching and consistently projecting mob mentality as a destructive, though sometimes inevitable, force opposed to the causes of justice and reasonable reform, Faulkner's fiction advanced a major trend in cultural production apparent in the work of Orson Welles and in Hollywood's treatments of lynching.

Offering a useful historical perspective, Stewart E. Tolnay and E. M. Beck refer to the five decades from the end of Reconstruction through the Great Depression as the "era of lynching." During that period, Tolnay and Beck document, an estimated 2,462 African American men, women, and children were lynched by mobs in the South. Although instances of lynching occurred prior to 1880, "radical racism and mob violence peaked during the 1890s in a surge of terrorism that did not dissipate until well into the twentieth century" (17). Lynching surfaced as a major source of concern in the thirties due to increases in documented cases in 1933 and 1935. Drafted by NAACP lawyers, an antilynching bill was presented to Congress in 1934. However, FDR refused to lend public support to the bill for fear of alienating southern lawmakers whose votes were needed for advancement of the New Deal. In 1935 a filibuster led by southern lawmakers stalled the progress of the antilynching legislation.

In this context, producers of Hollywood's lynching films set out to probe a chronic social ill in graphic terms. Despite such intentions, however, they obscured the historical and social reality of lynching by blatantly discounting race as a contributing factor, focusing instead on lynching mainly through the prism of class conflict. Forged predominantly from the ranks of the working class, the lynch mobs in these films are comprised of people portrayed as inherently ignorant, chaotic, and unruly. At a time when the harsh conditions of the Depression invited social protest among the scores of unemployed, such depictions sent the unmistakable signal that the masses were incapable of governing and therefore needed to be governed by a social system that could restrain them. Or, as Bergman remarks, these films "argued from authoritative benevolence to the irrationality of the governed" (122). Consequently, these representations functioned ideologically to promote fear of mass mobilization stemming intrinsically from the working class and to naturalize the legitimacy and authority of the existing social system favorable to the dominant class. Understood in this cultural context, Faulkner's representations of mob violence and vigilante justice can be read as responsive to this ideological formation and thus active in an ongoing political struggle through means of cultural expression.

The lynching of Lee Goodwin in *Sanctuary* offers an instructive case in point for exploring this dimension of Faulkner's fiction. As we have seen, the depiction of Goodwin's trial features a clear line of distinction drawn between Horace Benbow and the mass of townspeople gathered to observe the spectacle. That this distinction is decidedly social in nature is illustrated by Horace's condescending tendency to see the spectators in court not as peers but rather as an objectified mass. This perception is evident much earlier in the novel, too, as the display of Tommy's corpse attracts a crowd to the town square and especially to the music stores, where "a throng stood all day, listening," as if in a trance, to "ballads simple in melody and theme, of bereavement and retribution and repentance" (*S* 112). This easily manipulated crowd later supplies both a pool of jurors to falsely convict Goodwin in court and a mob of executioners to sentence him to death under the improvisational codes of vigilante justice.

District Attorney Eustace Graham, a product of the working class, reads as a skillful manipulator of the "throng" comprised of his social ilk. Graham's working-class roots are explained in great detail, with the narrator noting that "the town remembered him as driving wagons and trucks for grocery stores" and that he was a waiter in the commons (*S* 262). The recounting of Graham's biography casts him initially as a self-made man, rising up from his humble origins and gaining an allowable amount of respect: "He graduated well, though without distinction" (262). But the rhetoric of the self-made man is quickly undermined by the revelation that Graham's rise was supported in large measure by questionable poker tactics. The poker anecdote establishes Graham as a speculator, a corrupt figure with little regard for rules of order. Displaying this trait, Eustace incites mob violence explicitly, proclaiming in open court the gynecologist's supposed claim that the rape is "no longer a matter for the hangman, but for a bonfire of gasoline" (284). Graham's base appeal to mob rule is represented as a perversion of the civilized rule of law that Horace valorizes. Worth noting as well are the undertones of class difference girding this opposition: while Graham may wield power over the masses from which he rose, he lacks Horace's gentlemanly reverence for the law and thus appears incapable of bearing the duties of his office in a manner that promotes individual and civic responsibility as well as peace and stability in the social order. Eventually, Graham's incendiary call for vigilante justice leads to the formation of a mob from the ranks of townspeople who seem gullible and irrational by nature. Confirming this inclination, the jury's false conviction of Goodwin after only eight minutes of deliberation suggests the abandonment of reason and rational judgment. The hasty verdict signals the start of a violent storm of social disruption forming since the disclosure of the rape.

Represented from Horace's point of view, the lynching unfolds in the form of an apocalyptic vision for an apprehensive dominant class. Still reeling from the verdict, Horace encounters "a shifting mass filling the street, and the bleak, shallow yard above which the square and slotted bulk of the jail loomed" (*S* 293). In the way of reassurance, the sheriff applies his interpretive powers to the form of this mass movement: "When a mob means business, it dont take that much time and talk. And it dont go about its business where every man can see it" (293). From the perspectives of the sheriff and Horace, the incarnation of the mob appears at first "quite orderly" (293). However, such appearances are deceiving, for only a bit of agitation is needed to bring about chaos. Anticipating a common convention of the lynching films, the agitation in this case comes largely from outsiders who question the resolve of the community to achieve justice by whatever means necessary. The outsiders' instigation also highlights the fickle nature of the townspeople and their misguided motivations. Clearly, this mob-in-progress is bent on avenging the rape rather than the murder, acting out of a sense of chivalry that parodies and perverts the gentlemanly codes of conduct associated with Horace. Referring to Temple, one of the men gathered in the street says, "I saw her. She was some baby. Jeez. I wouldn't have used no cob" (294). According to this line of reasoning, the crime was not that Temple was raped but that she was not raped "properly." This twisted motivation for anger and revenge, echoed later by the Kinston carriage driver who is described mainly in terms of his fall in the ranks of social distinction, underscores the depravity of the class-specific mob mentality now unleashed.

The description of the lynching conveys a dominant impression of civil unrest consistent with the ascendance of vigilantism in Jefferson. As the mob forms, Horace sees the hotel proprietor running in the street toward the fire consuming Goodwin. Swept up by the chaotic wave, the hotel proprietor embodies a social order in disarray; having abandoned his post, he appears to Horace as "ludicrous; a broad man with his trousers clutched before him and his braces dangling beneath his nightshirt, a tousled fringe of hair standing wildly about his bald head" (*S* 295). Contributing further to this sense of chaos and absurdity are the vivid sensory images registered from Horace's point of view: "Against the flames black figures showed, antic; he could hear panting shouts; through a fleeting gap he saw a man turn and run, a mass of flames, still carrying a five-gallon coal oil can which exploded with a rocket-like glare while he carried it running" (296). Once in the fray, Horace bears direct witness to the immolation of Goodwin in a "blazing mass" (296), a phrase that signifies both the fire and the mob that sets it with a vengeance. The repetition of the word "mass" occurs throughout the scene and reinforces the mob mentality on display as originating from the masses. The rampage of violence that Horace witnesses exacerbates his impotence as an agent of the law; consequently, Horace stands in contrast to the virile mob that rapes Goodwin with a corncob as part of its ritualistic torture. Faced with this chaotic scene, Horace is struck by a profound silence, which strangely insulates him from the mob and from his surroundings: "Horace couldn't hear them. He couldn't hear the man who had got burned screaming" (296). The powerful aesthetic effects yielded by this episode make for a close encounter with mob mentality that must have been especially unsettling for contemporary readers fearful of actual mob violence and the social disruption it would engender. But the impact of these aesthetic effects must have strengthened as well the case for maintaining order in response to the threat vividly depicted—a maneuver that prefigures a key component of the lynching films produced later in the decade.

The lynching depicted in Fritz Lang's *Fury*, for instance, bears striking resemblance to that of Lee Goodwin in *Sanctuary*. Whether or not Faulkner's novel had any direct bearing on Lang's film, the similarities demonstrate at the very least shared aesthetic features largely constituted by ideological forces active in the cultural context. Like Goodwin, Joe, the protagonist of *Fury*, initially places his trust in the rule of law, declaring to his racketeering brother that "times have changed. The people are against you monkeys now." After a year of working hard to save money, Joe sets out to marry his fiancée, but he runs into trouble in a small town when flimsy circumstantial evidence makes him the prime suspect in the kidnapping of a prominent citizen's daughter. Rushing to judgment, the townspeople convict Joe in the court of public opinion, according to the rumormill logic expressed by a woman who insists that "in this country people don't land in jail unless they're guilty." Dawson, a Eustace Graham–like manipulator, fans the flames by declaring to a gathering of citizens, "An attack on a girl hits us ordinary people where we live, and we're gonna see that politics don't cut any ice." Dawson is aided by an outside agitator who eggs on the townspeople by questioning their commitment to justice. In response to the frenzied call, "Let's have some fun," the mob storms the jail and sets it ablaze with Joe left inside. With an array of disturbing images, the scene parallels the immolation of Goodwin. At one point, there is a shot of Joe's urgent and futile attempt to free himself through a barred window, the flames rising up to engulf him. The film then falls silent as it intersperses shots of Joe and vivid close-up shots of wild faces in the mob, a technique reminiscent of Faulkner's description of the fire consuming Goodwin as "soundless: a voice of fury like in a dream, roaring silently out of a peaceful void" (*S* 296). Both Faulkner's novel and Lang's film depict the lynching of white men—a choice that foregrounds class instead of race as a primary factor. The mobs in *Sanctuary* and *Fury* are comprised largely from the ranks of the lower classes and coalesce in response to the violation of a young woman of higher social status. Unable to perform the role of "gentlemen" as socially scripted, though, the men comprising these mobs lash out with indiscriminate violence in the service of misguided justice. Capturing the implications of vigilantism represented in both works, the governor in *Fury* says after the lynching, "The very spirit of government has been violated, the state disgraced in the eyes of the world by this brutal outburst of lust for vengeance."

Sanctuary and *Fury* both depict this lust as class specific. In the hands of people like Eustace Graham and Dawson, assumes the logic, the cause of justice is almost certain to evolve into the chaos of mob rule. This line of reasoning exposes lynching and these representations of it as agents of desire. Specifically, they function as cultural expressions of the social desire to maintain established order by conveying impressions of the masses as inherently volatile and in need of restraint by a resurgent rule of law meant to fill the vacuum of authority. In *Fury*, oddly enough, it is not only the incensed DA who champions this resurgence but also the victim. Having somehow escaped the jailhouse fire, a jaded Joe plots his revenge for the attempted lynching in compliance with the justice system: "They'll hang for it according to the law which says if you kill somebody, you gotta be killed yourself. . . . They'll get a legal sentence and a legal death." Giving new meaning to the legal concept of habeas corpus, Joe makes a grand entrance into the courtroom during the trial of twenty-two citizens indicted for the lynching. Thus a trial corrupted by ambitious reporters, evidence mailed anonymously from Joe to the DA, numerous instances of perjury committed by the citizens, and a climactic swooning confession ends with a variation on the sidebar: a kiss between Joe and his fiancée in front of the presiding judge's bench. Though much less compelling, the ending of *Fury* hearkens back to the final section of *Sanctuary* by offering reassurances that the spirit of the law, as defined by the dominant class, prevails, even as the letter of the law fails miserably.

Faulkner's treatment of mob violence in *Sanctuary* demonstrates his indirect engagement of the discourse around fascism primarily through thematic association. *Light in August*, however, constitutes a much more explicit treatment of fascism and further indicates Faulkner's use of lynching to represent and negotiate the politics of social upheaval. Although my primary concern is with Faulkner's fictional representations of lynching, it is important to consider as well a disturbing public pronouncement that Faulkner apparently made on the subject not too long before he began *Light in August*. In "Faulkner on Lynching," Neil R. McMillen and Noel Polk examine a letter to the editor of the Memphis *Commercial Appeal* dated February 15, 1931, and signed, "William Falkner." McMillen and Polk make a strong case for the authenticity of Faulkner's authorship of the letter, noting that "it is astonishing for the baldness of the racial attitudes it expresses, its virtual defense of lynching as an instrument of justice" (3). Indeed, the letter concludes on a disturbing note, given Faulkner's approach to mob mentality and lynching in his fiction:

> I hold no brief for lynching. No balanced man will deny that mob violence serves nothing, just as he will not deny that a lot of our natural and logical jurisprudence serves nothing either. It just happens that we—mobber and mobbee—live in this age. We will muddle through, and die in our beds, the deserving and the fortunate among us. Of course, with the population what it is, there are some of us that won't. Some will die rich, and some will die on cross-ties soaked with gasoline, to make a holiday. But there is one curious thing about mobs. Like our juries, they have a way of being right. (qtd. in McMillen and Polk 6)

That such expressions could come from the man who would sit down just a few months later to write *Light in August* and who would later expose the hollow ignorance and brutality of mob rule in "Dry September" is confounding. But Faulkner was in this regard a product of the time, with his fictional and personal voices entering into intense conflict, as they often did, over a profound social issue that was "anything but settled" (13).

When Faulkner focuses on the practice of lynching in *Light in August*, one of the most graphic and violent episodes in all of his fiction emerges: the death of Joe Christmas at the hands of Percy Grimm. A militant nationalist, Grimm materializes seemingly out of nowhere to perform this swift and brutal act of vigilantism and then disappears just as suddenly as he arrived, once the deed is done. From a formal standpoint, Percy Grimm's addition to an already crowded cast of characters seems curious. On the one hand, his brief yet explosive appearance might be read as yet another in a series of disruptions that propel the story in fits and starts to its conclusion; on the other hand, it might be viewed as Faulkner's frustrated response to an unwieldy narrative that resists definitive conclusion. However, Percy Grimm makes much more sense as a character when considered in relation to the discourse around fascism developing in the cultural context of the novel. With Grimm cast as an inevitable product of the social disruption depicted in the text, Faulkner's novel anticipates cultural representations of fascism as a domestic possibility rather than a remote international phenomenon.

Light in August extends the frantic concern over imperiled social order reflected in *Sanctuary*, registering this concern similarly in the portrayal of key characters. As in *Sanctuary*, major characters in *Light in August* can be viewed as embodiments of disorder whose internal conflicts both reflect and affect the destabilized society they occupy. Lena Grove's disruptive contribution comes mainly in terms of her unorthodox approach to motherhood, particularly her inability to name the father of her child and her reluctance to name the child after he is born. Both of these deferrals challenge the conventions of a patriarchal order invested in naming and lineage as indicators of continuity and order. Aptly named, Joanna Burden adds the weight of historical conflict to a narrative obsessed with the workings of memory—especially the uneasy and often turbulent coexistence of past and present, a raw theme in *Light in August* that gains refinement in *Absalom, Absalom!* Home to Joanna, the Burden estate is a historical site of social conflict. The community and the estate have been forever at odds, "the descendants of both in their relationship to one another ghosts, with between them the phantom of the old spilled blood and the old horror and anger and fear" (*LA* 42). Ironically, though, it is the spilling of Joanna's blood that inspires a reconciliation of sorts, at least from the standpoint of the community. With the Burden estate in flames and Joanna nearly decapitated, the community can essentially redefine her in its own terms as a violated white woman; thus she becomes a powerful symbol of upheaval and the urgent need to reinforce existing social order. In the eyes of the community, Joe Christmas figures as the agent of this upheaval, confounding social expectations with his conflicted racial identity. In the transformation from internal to external conflict, Joe's racial uncertainty presents an irreconcilable contradiction for a social order largely dependent on the black-white racial binary for its structural integrity. Betraying this ideological impasse, the communal

voice representing Mottstown explains, "He never acted like either a nigger or a white man. That was it. That was what made the folks so mad"
(331).[8]

One of the immediate dangers of social disruption, as *Sanctuary* makes
clear, is that it creates a breeding ground for mob mentality. *Light in
August* is even more methodical than its predecessor in tracing, and then
retracing, this powerful social force as it moves through narrative pro-
gressions, regressions, and digressions toward the inevitable violence enacted by Percy Grimm in the zeal of vigilante agency. Once again, mob
mentality is distinctly associated with the lower ranks and marginalized
sectors of the social structure, as well as outside agitators. Accordingly,
among the crowd gathered at the Burden estate to watch the flames are
"the casual Yankees and the poor whites and even the southerners who
had lived for a while in the north" (*LA* 271). From the narrator's point
of view, these onlookers seem prehistoric, staring at the fire "with that
same dull and static amaze which they had brought down from the old
fetid caves where knowing began, as though, like death, they had never
seen fire before" (272). Motivated apparently by primeval instinct, they
"canvass about for someone to crucify," acting on the belief that Joanna's
burning body "cried out for vengeance" (272, 273). Similar in form, the
mob that takes shape later in Mottstown, after the initial apprehension
of Joe Christmas, is heralded by Doc Hines, a vocal, if not respected, advocate of lynching the convict. Situating the Hineses in the social order,
the narrator explains that they "appeared to live in filthy poverty and
complete idleness, Hines, as far as the town knew, not having done any
work, steady work, in twentyfive years" (322). But now with a new sense
of purpose, he joins the growing throng composed of "the merchants, the
clerks, the idle, and the curious, with countrymen in overalls predomi-
nating" (326). Despite the appeal from the Mottstown sheriff to "respect
the law" (335), Hightower's subsequent ruminations, which are inspired
by the distant church music he hears through his window, signal ensuing
mob rule: "Pleasure, ecstasy, they cannot seem to bear: their escape from
it is in violence . . . the violence identical and apparently inescapable. And

so why should not their religion drive them to crucifixion of themselves and one another?" (347). In the end, of course, it is not religion per se but rather the quasi-religious fervor of nationalism that inspires what Hightower insists on deeming a "crucifixion" but what is to the mob clearly a lynching.

The lynching takes place in chapter 19, a crucial section of the novel in which two new characters arrive on the scene surprisingly late in the game—Grimm, as we have seen, but also Gavin Stevens, Jefferson's district attorney. Stevens shares much in common with Horace Benbow: as a lawyer-gentleman, Stevens occupies the same stratum of the social order as Benbow. Even though Stevens is much more adept at mingling with the masses on the town square, he exhibits the same tendency as Benbow to apply a conceptual perspective to pressing events of the day. The sequence in which Stevens ruminates on the yin-yang nature of Joe Christmas's black and white blood is a case in point. From a passive and remote stance, Stevens is content to observe and interpret people and events, while Percy Grimm means to alter them through decisive action. This juxtaposition of passive contemplation and assertive agency, of impotency and potency, is reinforced by an abrupt shift in emphasis from Stevens to Grimm, reflecting the changing dynamic of power in the social order. From either a narrative or a social standpoint, then, it is the absence of Stevens that enables the presence of Grimm and the vigilantism he inspires and manipulates.

Although Grimm seems to spring ex nihilo from the text, his relationship to impending developments in the cultural context is rife with intriguing connections. The characterization of Percy Grimm suggests that Faulkner was at the cusp of a movement to explore through various forms of cultural expression the potential rise of homegrown fascism in America. Again, film offers a particularly instructive means of illuminating this aspect of Faulkner's novel. Within a year of *Light in August*'s publication, Hollywood released two films that translated the international rise of fascism into national terms. First, *Mussolini Speaks* (1933), produced by Columbia Pictures and featuring the familiar narrative voice of

Lowell Thomas, offered Americans an unapologetically favorable view of Mussolini's fascist program in Italy. Referencing the economic crisis in America, the film documents the three stages of Mussolini's response to what Thomas calls a "similar" crisis in Italy: (1) restoration of order to society; (2) renewed economic prosperity and modernization; and (3) militaristic expansion inspired by appeals to racial purity and national identity. One segment of the film features a reenactment of the march on the Italian Parliament by Mussolini's brigade of uniformed Black Shirts. At the end of the film, the staying power of this force is suggested by shots of paramilitary camps filled with loyal Italian youth training for future service as Black Shirts. The tone of the film is laudatory, casting Mussolini in a favorable light as a strong, effective leader and a model worthy of emulation in America.

More explicit than *Mussolini Speaks*, *Gabriel over the White House* (1933) dramatizes the evolution of Judson C. Hammond, president of the United States, from a democratic leader into a fascist-style dictator. Produced by William Randolph Hearst's Cosmopolitan Studios, the film is transparent in its attempt to endorse the need for consolidating power in the hands of a strong leader in response to socioeconomic crisis. However, much like fascist political systems, the film spirals inevitably toward violence in its frenzied celebration of power. At one point, the Green Jackets, a deputized legion of zealous paramilitary agents, rounds up a large group of gangsters whose immigrant roots are underscored; the legion executes them on Ellis Island against a silhouette conspicuously featuring the Statue of Liberty. Operating under the assumption that desperate times require desperate measures, *Gabriel over the White House* and *Mussolini Speaks* transform the protofascist fantasies inscribed in the gangster films into explicitly political forms that imagine an American fascism sprouting from fields made barren by uninspired and ineffectual leadership.

By the time these films prompted large audiences to contemplate the potential rise of fascism in America, Faulkner had already offered something of a sneak preview in the form of Percy Grimm's limited engagement. Grimm's ideology of nationalism and racial purity is a major factor that aligns him with fascism and thus expands the novel's provincial setting to encompass issues of national and international import. As the narrator explains, the loyalty that Grimm holds for his concept of nation is "as bright and weightless and martial as his insignatory brass: a sublime and implicit faith in physical courage and blind obedience, and a belief that the white race is superior to any and all other races and that the American is superior to all white races and that the American uniform is superior to all men, and that all that would ever be required of him in payment for this belief, this privilege, would be his own life" (*LA* 427). Grimm and his band of paramilitary special deputies, clad in khaki shirts, act on a mandate to "preserve order," invoking powers reminiscent of a police state to accomplish their mission (427). Betraying his undemocratic inclination, Grimm dismisses the will of the people, insisting unequivocally that "there won't be any need for them even to talk" and then imposing a sort of martial law (427). In this move, Grimm calls to mind President Hammond in *Gabriel over the White House.* Faced with a crisis, Hammond dispenses with the inconvenience of pluralism by dissolving the Congress and imposing his own rule under the auspices of military power.

Despite Grimm's lack of respect for the vox populi, he commands a substantial following based on that intangible and mysterious charisma essential to powerful fascist leaders. It was this style of leadership, for instance, that led many to brand charismatic figures such as Father Coughlin, the "radio priest," and Huey Long as fascists. Likewise, as Yoknapatawpha's answer to Il Duce, Grimm is able to broaden his appeal, because "without knowing they were thinking it, the town had suddenly accepted Grimm with respect and perhaps a little awe and a deal of actual faith and confidence, as though somehow his vision and patriotism and pride in the town, the occasion had been quicker and truer than theirs" (*LA* 432). True to the form of fascism, though, any sense of common purpose is consumed by the egotism of the leader. The pursuit of Joe Christmas by Grimm and his militia/mob quickly evolves into a violent display of Grimm's individual lust for power. Unsatisfied with Joe's death

at the hands of an impromptu firing squad, Grimm is compelled to perform castration—an exclamation point to the lynching so gruesome that
even his faithful followers cannot bear to watch. Robyn Wiegman dis-
cusses the social significance of castration as part of the lynching ritual:
"In severing the black man's penis from his body, either as a narrative account or a material act, the mob aggressively denies the patriarchal sign
and symbol of the masculine, interrupting the privilege of the phallus and
thereby reclaiming, through the perversity of dismemberment, the black
male's (masculine) potentiality for citizenship" (83). The nature of Joe's
"blackness" remains, of course, the source of much critical debate. Joe
represents the unimaginable for Grimm, steeped as he is in the ideology
of national and racial purity essential to fascism. For this reason, Grimm
is compelled by ideology to erase Joe's existence from the social order
through the ritual of lynching as public spectacle. The sexualized component of Grimm's action conveys the intensity of his lust for power and
thus establishes him further as a harbinger of homegrown fascism.

When asked about Percy Grimm many years after the publication of
Light in August, Faulkner seemed to marvel at his own prescience, insisting that "I wrote that book in 1932 before I'd ever heard of Hitler's
Storm Troopers, what he [Grimm] was was a Nazi Storm Trooper, but
then I'd never heard of one then" (Blotner and Gwynn 41). Whether or
not Faulkner knew of Nazis in particular, the depiction of Percy Grimm
suggests that he was familiar enough with the discourse around fascism
to manage a palpable literary representation of how fascism might surface on the American political landscape. It is important to stress that
Faulkner's exploration of fascism through the character of Percy Grimm
differs from those in *Mussolini Speaks* and *Gabriel over the White House*
in that it occurs as part of a far more complex work. Moreover, far from
celebrating Grimm, Faulkner fashions him as the culmination of multiple forces that converge in the murder of Joanna Burden and the brutal
lynching of Joe Christmas as indicators of social disruption and urgent
reminders of the need to maintain order. Informed by dominant-class
anxiety, Faulkner's representation of Percy Grimm is useful in defining

the discourse around fascism more as a means of negotiating the politics of social upheaval than contemplating actual transformation to fascism as a political ideology and system.

Although the Percy Grimm section of *Light in August* shares many features in common with *Mussolini Speaks* and *Gabriel over the White House*, its ideological milieu is more consistent with that of films such as *This Day and Age* and *Wild Boys of the Road*, both released in 1933. These films project the chaos of mob rule, tempered in the end by a return to the status quo as the only viable alternative. This pattern occurs in *Light in August* as well, as the chaotic narrative structure and the horror of Percy Grimm give way in the end to the lighthearted tale recounted by the Tennessee traveling salesman. The style evokes the genre of Southwestern Humor and suggests in its heightened comfort level an attempt at aesthetic containment similar to the one enabled by the mode of naturalism in the concluding section of *Sanctuary*. Despite this sudden shift in tone and form, the perspective afforded by 1932 must have rendered Percy Grimm a timely and perhaps inevitable force to be reckoned with.

This pattern of representation is even more pronounced in Faulkner's "Dry September," a short story that explores the pathological nature of mob violence once again through the prism of lynching. Published in 1937, "Dry September" appeared in the same year that the cycle of lynching films initiated by *Black Fury* ran its course, with the release of *Black Legion* and *They Won't Forget*. The latter film is useful for situating Faulkner's story in a revealing cultural context. Directed by Mervyn Leroy, *They Won't Forget* was billed as an exposé of lynching meant to inspire decisive federal action to end the violence. Bergman explains how this transparent intention affected the final cut: "Like so many Warner efforts at public education, Leroy's film had the studied concern, depth, and texture of an editorial cartoon" (120). Like *Fury*, *They Won't Forget* obscures the racial dimension of lynching. Instead, the film highlights regional division: set in the South, it tells the story of a teacher originally from the North who is arrested for the murder of a student and victimized by an ambitious district attorney who stirs up sectional animosity in an effort to get a conviction and further his career. Pardoned by the governor, the teacher is then dragged from a train by an angry mob and lynched. Significantly, no one suffers consequences for this act of brutality, highlighting a disturbing and destabilizing absence of authority. In this regard, the film constructs a sort of social nightmare for the dominant class, playing on fear as a means of promoting the need for vigilant maintenance of the status quo.

Although not in the didactic vein of Leroy's *They Won't Forget*, Faulkner's "Dry September" performs a similar function, graphically illustrating mob mentality as a grassroots product of dissipated authority in a disrupted social order. The opening line of the story introduces the elements of chaos and destruction, describing atmospheric and social conditions conducive to explosive violence: "Through the bloody September twilight, aftermath of sixty-two rainless days, it had gone like a fire in dry grass—the rumor, the story, whatever it was" (CS 169). This climate informs the opening scene in the barbershop, which serves as a site of communal negotiation. Established here are the social forces entering into conflict in response to the ill-defined rumor that Will Mays, a black man, is guilty of sexually assaulting Minnie Cooper, a white woman. Hawkshaw, the proprietor, expresses the logic of established order, imploring the men in the shop to cast aside rumor and innuendo in favor of truth. But Hawkshaw's appeal only elicits derision from the other men, who accuse him of being a "niggerlover" (170) and a traitor to his heritage: "You better go back North where you came from. The South dont want your kind here" (171). As in *They Won't Forget*, the theme of sectional antagonism figures prominently. These followers coming under the spell of vigilante justice are only in need of an inspirational leader to guide them. McLendon gladly assumes this role, fanning the flames ignited in the exchange between Hawkshaw and the other men. Aiming a "hot, bold glance that swept the group," McLendon mobilizes the mob with the obligatory aid of an outside agitator and a firm ultimatum: "Well, . . . are you going to sit there and let a black son rape a white woman on the streets of Jefferson?" (171). Whether or not the incident actually occurred is of little consequence to McLendon, who favors the spectacle of power over the search for truth in the name of law and order. As a counterpoint to Hawkshaw, McLendon thus embodies the suspension of deliberation that accompanies vigilantism and propels the mob toward the lynching of Will Mays. Facing this condition, Hawkshaw, like Horace Benbow, is rendered powerless and inarticulate, declaring with futility, "I cant let—" (173). Though he joins the ranks of the mob with the hope of defusing it, Hawkshaw's weak declaration foreshadows his inevitable failure to prevent the lynching.

In contrast to Hollywood's lynching films and in spite of accusations that Faulkner was blind to social injustice in his region, his story delves into race as an essential component of the lynching, as the exchange in the barbershop makes abundantly clear. But, as in so much of Faulkner's fiction, race intersects with gender and class in this story to define the terms of a struggle for power raging in a transforming social order. As the narrator stresses, Minnie Cooper's reaction to the racially explosive rumor surrounding her and Will Mays is based on her sense of inadequacy in relation to gender and class assumptions prevailing in Jefferson. Minnie is depicted in many respects as the stereotypical "old maid," a woman whose life corresponds to the extended dry spell affecting the environment of the story. The narrator defines Minnie's diminishment explicitly in terms of her waning sexuality and her declining social status. Reared among "comfortable people," a youthful Minnie was able to exchange her "nervous body" and "hard vivacity" for the opportunity "to ride upon the crest of the town's social life as exemplified by the high school party and church social period of her contemporaries while still children enough to be unclassconscious" (CS 174). But this period ended with Minnie's cruel initiation into class consciousness, which registered, according to the narrator, in terms of a bodily transformation: "That was when her face began to wear that bright, haggard look" (174). Now Minnie is left to fill "empty and idle days" with fantasy, inspired by repeated visits to the movie theater in an attempt to forget that "men did not even follow her with their eyes anymore" (175).

From the narrator's point of view, Minnie's refusal to deny the rumor of Will Mays's advances is an attempt to represent herself to the community as a viable object of sexual desire and to reclaim some form of social status, albeit dubious at best. Given the nature of the accusation, it is not surprising that the prelude to the lynching conveys the power of mob mentality with unmistakable sexual overtones. Crowded in the car with Will Mays in tow, the mob experiences a sort of performance anxiety in anticipation of the lynching: "Where their bodies touched one another they seemed to sweat dryly, for no more moisture came" (*CS* 177). What is at first a "stumbling clump" (177) soon evolves into an orgy of violence. Even Hawkshaw succumbs to the frenzied attack on Will Mays, for we learn that "the barber struck him also" (178). The sexually charged energy invoked by the lynching extends as well to Minnie, imbuing her with the desired effect of awakening: "As she dressed for supper on that Saturday evening, her own flesh felt like fever. Her hands trembled among the hooks and eyes, and her eyes had a feverish look, and her hair swirled crisp and crackling under the comb. While she was still dressing the friends called for her and sat while she donned her sheerest underthings and stockings and a new voile dress" (180). In addition to the internal transformation, the lynching enables Minnie to regain the attention of the men in town. As Minnie sashays down the sidewalk in her new dress toward the movie theater, "even the young men lounging in the doorway tipped their hats and followed with their eyes the motion of her hips and legs when she passed" (181). But Minnie is ill prepared for the power of this transformation accomplished through violence and thus spirals into an inexplicable and frenzied laughter that registers the full volume of her awakened sexual energy. McLendon's energy, too, is spent by the lynching—a condition that extends the sexual reference to its logical conclusion. Having returned home from the lynching, McLendon sweats profusely, wiping his naked torso with his shirt and "panting" (183), as if in the aftermath of an intense sexual encounter.

Significantly, Faulkner resists a graphic depiction of the lynching, leaving the reader instead to conjure images of the violence exacted on Will Mays by McLendon and his mob. The choice to render the lynching offstage shifts the emphasis from the victim to Hawkshaw, whose

pronounced limp punctuates his impotence in relation to the lynch mob
led by the potent McLendon. Although the text indicates that Hawkshaw
"reached the highroad" (*CS* 179) after jumping from the car, it is clear
that he has done so only in literal terms. Hawkshaw's complicity, though
not total, strips him of the moral authority he displays at the beginning of
the story. The absence of such authority leaves a void, which is signified
in terms of silence and darkness in the final lines of the story: "There
was no movement, no sound, not even an insect. The dark world seemed
to lie stricken beneath the cold moon and the lidless stars" (183). The
aesthetic effect here draws attention to the lack of public authority that
enables the reign of vigilante justice to go largely unchecked and to extend
perhaps beyond the events of the narrative. In terms of the social order
represented in the story, this void is left by a nascent dominant class—a
condition reinforced formally and ideologically through point of view.
The explanation of Minnie's reaction to the rumor about her and Will
Mays, for instance, is clearly based on gender and class assumptions that
expose the narrator's complicity in a patriarchal social order. However,
like Horace Benbow, the narrator tries to maintain critical distance from
the action, interpreting—and likely misinterpreting—events in retrospect
rather than altering them in actuality. One implication is that the condition of a nascent dominant class is inherently volatile and highly conducive to the mob mentality and violence on display in the text. "Dry
September" thus parallels *They Won't Forget* in contemplating the social
nightmare of mob rule produced in a vacuum of dominant-class authority
that leaves society vulnerable to social upheaval and to ambitious designs
on absolute power. That was the case as well when Faulkner wrote *Absalom, Absalom!* and brought to life Thomas Sutpen to strike the pose
of the "great dictator" just as Popular Front antifascism evolved into a
powerful political and cultural formation.

In February 1936, eight months prior to the publication of Faulkner's *Absalom, Absalom!* the American Artists' Congress convened in New York
City to pledge opposition to the spread of fascism abroad and at home.

The organization was inspired in large measure by the American Writers' Congress, which had met in the previous year and had placed the struggle against fascism at the top of its agenda. The considerable energy that artists devoted to the cause of antifascism stemmed from a fundamental belief expressed cogently by Lewis Mumford in his stirring address to the Artists' Congress: "The irrepressible impulse of Art may upset the whole Fascist program" (64). The unity of artists on display in the congresses and in the numerous other organizations devoted to the cause of antifascism lent credence to Benjamin's conclusion that the fascist program to fuse aesthetics and politics would advance the politicization of art (681). This cultural enterprise was advanced mainly under the auspices of the Popular Front. Matthew Baigell and Julia Williams point out that "for the strategists of the Popular Front the central issue was the choice between war and fascism on the one hand, peace and democracy on the other. They chose to emphasize the fight against fascism rather than the fight against capitalism" (5). Adopting a less doctrinaire approach under the guise of the Popular Front, the Left sought to construct a broad alliance against an enemy manifested in the menacing forms of Hitler, Mussolini, and Franco, the "great dictator" figures who were strutting and fretting their hour upon the international stage. For this reason, the rigid categories professed in the literary class war, for instance, did not hold up under the tangible and immediate threat of fascism. Artists of various aesthetic and ideological inclinations were thus recruited for the cause, and many responded to the call through art and activism.

By the mid-1930s, with fascism on the march and the Popular Front mobilized in response, forms of cultural expression had generally discarded sympathetic depictions of fascism such as those in *Gabriel over the White House* and *Mussolini Speaks*. While representations of fascist-style figures still exhibited and attracted fear and fascination, mainstream culture could scarcely tolerate the portrayal of a dictator successfully achieving power by design, except as rising action leading to a certain demise. Still, as Denning comments, "The tale of the 'great dictator' haunted the Popular Front imagination" (376). This condition was on display in works such as Peter Blume's surrealist painting *The Eternal City* (1937), which features Mussolini's head springing from a classical vista, and Charlie Chaplin's classic 1940 film *The Great Dictator*. These works demonstrate how the Popular Front imagination tended to translate the terms of fascism for American audiences. Accordingly, "great dictator" figures tended to bear familiar traits associated with industrialist "robber barons" or racist and nationalist demagogues—a representational tactic that consolidated the natural enemies of the Left.

One of the artists most exemplary of this technique was Orson Welles, who emerged in the latter half of the thirties as a major force in the culture industry. From then until the late fifties, Welles engaged, reflected, and influenced the discourse around fascism. The result, as Denning explains, was that Welles's most prolific and provocative mode of narrative was the allegory of antifascism centered on the figure of the "great dictator." As Welles's work demonstrates, this genre incorporated myths of American capitalism and internalized anxieties over race and class associated with the politics of social upheaval. In the Depression, Welles's use of this form extended roughly from the Mercury Theater production of *Julius Caesar* in 1937 to the release of *Citizen Kane* in 1941 and found expression in various cultural forms. Consequently, his work from this period exhibits key aesthetic and ideological features of the antifascist allegory.

Many of these features are present in Faulkner's *Absalom, Absalom!*—specifically in the account of Thomas Sutpen and his design on power that results in the rise and fall of Sutpen's Hundred. As Brinkmeyer contends, Sutpen's character resonates with "echoes of the popular conception of the fascist dictator" (91). Cast in this role, Sutpen is the central figure in a story that fits the mold of the antifascist allegory. In many respects, Faulkner's novel looks forward to the cultural forms Welles would produce in subsequent years, even though the ideological and political implications are often divergent. Such an interpretation rests on the now commonplace assertion that *Absalom* is a novel concerned first and foremost with history. Indeed, *Absalom*'s complex narrative structure is in many ways an exploration of history as constructed and constructive, a constant presence "always reminding us never to forget" (*AA* 289), as

Shreve says to Quentin. In this respect, history is a life force driven by the dialectical relationship between past and present. Although *Absalom* is a novel about history, it is not necessarily a historical novel—at least in the sense that Georg Lukàcs defines the genre. Lukàcs cautions that setting alone does not confer on a text the status of authentic historical novel; on the contrary, many so-called historical novels reveal considerably less about the past than they do about the present—that is to say, the specific conditions of their production. In effect, such novels stage contemporary concerns with the trappings of history serving as props.[9] To some degree, *Absalom* falls into this category, as the story of Sutpen internalizes, represents, and indeed re-presents Depression anxieties and social desires active in the discourse around fascism and, more specifically, in the evolving allegory of antifascism as a cultural form.

Sutpen mirrors the "great dictator" figure first and foremost in terms of the enigmatic aura that renders him a source of fear and fascination from the moment he arrives in Jefferson. The first reference to him in the novel captures the charisma that will aid his design on power and make him a constant source of awe, intrigue, and animosity, even some forty years after his death, when his story again comes to life. Sutpen emerges in a visual image that evokes the arrival of a god in ancient mythology: "Out of quiet thunderclap he would abrupt (man-horse-demon) upon a scene peaceful and decorous as a schoolprize watercolor" (*AA* 4). In an image that calls to mind Blume's painting of Mussolini, Faulkner creates a juxtaposition here between figure and landscape that establishes Sutpen as a force of disruption capable of altering and encompassing the social canvas dramatically. And Sutpen exercises this capability immediately, with his arrival causing a ripple effect in the community, which is immediately mesmerized by his magical appeal. Soon after Sutpen's emergence on the scene, "the stranger's name went back and forth among the places of business and of idleness and among the residences in steady strophe and antistrophe: *Sutpen. Sutpen. Sutpen. Sutpen*" (24).

Like Welles's "great dictator" figures, and the actual ones, Sutpen wields influence through sheer power rather than thoughtful persuasion. So the townspeople "thought of ruthlessness rather than justice and of fear rather than respect, but not of pity or love" in relation to Sutpen (*AA* 32). As Rosa Coldfield discloses, albeit with considerable bias, there was certainly no love lost between Sutpen and the community when he marched into town to marry her sister, Ellen, and thus to stake a claim on legitimacy in the social hierarchy. Faced with this intrusion, the community views Sutpen as "a public enemy" (33). Even as they seek to incarcerate him, however, the community members are clearly under the Sutpen spell. Taking to the streets behind Sutpen, who is proudly clad in his familiar frock coat and beaver hat, the townspeople form a procession that ironically evokes the pied-piper mentality of a fascist parade. Despite the animosity, the show of resilience on Sutpen's part gains him a certain amount of legitimacy, which is conferred symbolically by the bond that General Compson and Mr. Coldfield post on his behalf. Sutpen is thus free to marry Ellen, to further his design on power, and to secure a position in the social order with the construction of Sutpen's Hundred, a fictive representation of planned society. Mr. Compson explains to Quentin the pleasure that Sutpen derived from his standing once his design had reached its apex: "He was not liked (which he evidently did not want anyway) but feared, which seemed to amuse, if not actually please, him" (57).

At this point, imagining Sutpen as a compatriot of Welles's Charles Foster Kane is not a difficult prospect. Both men are ruthless yet charismatic figures driven by the will to power toward an imperial vision that ultimately brings them isolation and despair. Indeed, the parallels between Sutpen's Hundred and Kane's Xanadu are numerous. Both visions betray their bearers as egotists exhibiting a fetish of infrastructure, which is informed by aesthetic and ideological influences. As Hitler and Mussolini demonstrated, an initial phase of the fascist program was to impress on the people a vision of restored order and renewed confidence through the repair and advancement of roads, bridges, and buildings. While such projects brought material improvements, they also provided structural support to the dictator's move to consolidate power by providing aesthetic and ideological reinforcements. It was this emphasis on infrastructure that led critics of the New Deal to lodge the fascist charge at FDR as well. For Sutpen, the fetish of infrastructure fixes on the large mansion he wants to construct as a display of his wealth and power and an added instrument of the mystique he wants to cultivate. The construction of the mansion is a vast project, taking more than two years to complete and attracting all the while a steady stream of onlookers intrigued by Sutpen's design. This design is so grand that the French architect must temper the "grim and castlelike magnificence at which Sutpen obviously aimed, since the place as Sutpen planned it would have been almost as large as Jefferson itself at the time" (*AA* 29).

Sutpen's Hundred not only rivals Jefferson in size but also revises its form, as the estate and its proprietor become significant determinants of a new social order. Even before his rise to power, Sutpen affects the conflict between stability and social unrest in Jefferson. After all, it is Sutpen's presence that inspires the "vigilance committee" to mob action and his defiance that forces the mob to disperse "like rats, scattered, departed about the country" (*AA* 44). However, by transforming the potential chaos of mob action into a progressive force to further his rise to power, Sutpen demonstrates his ability to achieve and his potential to maintain order. For the community, this capability is most apparent in Sutpen's relationship with his band of Haitian slaves. Repeatedly cast as a menacing threat, these slaves seem predisposed by nature to wreak havoc, at least as far as the community is concerned. This pattern is established when they are introduced in the novel as a "band of wild niggers like beasts half tamed to walk upright like men" who arrive on the scene "carrying in bloodless paradox the shovels and picks and axes of peaceful conquest" (4). Presumably this element of peace stems from Sutpen's proven ability to control the "wild" men in his charge and from the fear that he could unleash them on the community if he so chose.

In the tradition of the "great dictator," Sutpen accomplishes a controlling authority over his slaves in grassroots fashion by ritualistically joining their ranks in order to demonstrate the wide range and organic source of his power. For instance, he shares in the backbreaking work to carve Sutpen's Hundred out of the thick forest; the master and his slaves become caked with mud that obscures boundaries constructed in terms of racial difference and division of labor. Yet, as Sutpen's wrestling match with one of the slaves demonstrates, his purposeful descent into their ranks is less a show of solidarity than a means of consolidating and reinforcing his standing as a formidable master. Rosa Coldfield explains, "It seems that on certain occasions, perhaps at the end of the evening, the spectacle, as a grand finale or perhaps as a matter of sheer deadly forethought toward the retention of supremacy, domination, he would enter the ring with one of the negroes himself" (*AA* 21). Sutpen stages the wrestling matches to replay the conflict that first established him as a master of Haitian slaves and thus to reaffirm his position of dominance.

Although the details of Sutpen's personal history prior to his arrival in Yoknapatawpha are sketchy at best, Quentin does tell Shreve a detailed story handed down to him from General Compson and Mr. Compson about Sutpen's experiences on a sugar cane plantation during a slave revolt. With Sutpen, the plantation owner, and his family barricaded in the main house, Quentin narrates, a mob of slaves formed outside and prepared to take action. But Sutpen "just put the musket down and had someone unbar the door and then bar it behind him, and walked out into the darkness and subdued them" (*AA* 205). Quentin explains that Sutpen even showed the scars from the violent incident to General Compson as proof of his feat. Inscribed with this reference to the Haitian slave revolt, Sutpen's allure as a strong leader capable of maintaining order is amplified. In conjunction with the wrestling bouts, the self-inspired legend of Sutpen's heroism in Haiti strengthens his hand in the community, positioning him as a force of restraint between the "wild" band of slaves and the citizens of Jefferson frightened by their presence in the community—a presence that Sutpen himself engineered, of course.

Faulkner's representation of *Haitian* slaves is relevant both to the historical setting of Sutpen's story and to the interpretation of it as an allegory of antifascism. In the antebellum period framing much of Sutpen's story, Haiti was a palpable symbol with dual meaning: for the planter class in the South, it was a reminder of the potential for insurrection and violent retribution; for slaves and many abolitionists, it served as a source of inspiration in the fight for freedom. Given these associations, Faulkner's reference to Haiti in *Absalom* has attracted significant critical attention. Noting the Haitian influence on slave insurrections in America, Railey observes that Sutpen's arrival in Yoknapatawpha, in 1833, roughly coincides with the 1831 slave rebellion in Virginia led by Nat Turner. For Railey, the fear of Sutpen and the willingness on the part of community leaders to accommodate him stem from the "many historical precedents for the possibility of those like Sutpen leading a band of men, both white and black, against the citizens of Jefferson" (136). In quite a different reading, Richard Godden cites a major discrepancy in Faulkner's chronology, pointing out that in 1827, the year Sutpen supposedly quashed the slave rebellion, neither slaves nor French plantations actually existed in Haiti. Challenging scholars who call the discrepancy a mere error, Godden suggests an ulterior motive: "Faulkner's chronology creates an anachronism that rewrites one of the key facts of nineteenth-century black American history, in what looks suspiciously like an act of literary counterrevolution" (49). Such matters of historical representation, especially in a novel so clearly attuned to modes of recording the past, lend much insight into Faulkner's invocation of Haitian slave insurrection in *Absalom*. These readings hold it forth as a potent symbol of social upheaval and a source of considerable anxiety for a dominant class wary of revolutionary impulses.

But there are broader implications related to the cultural context of the novel's production and reception that should also be taken into account. In particular, the Popular Front's insistence on linking fascism and racism contributed to the ongoing resonance of the Haitian rebellion as a cultural narrative in America. The Haitian slave rebellion was transformed by African American activists into a metaphor for resistance to institutional forms of prejudice and the practice of lynching. In 1936 Orson Welles staged a Negro Theatre production of *MacBeth* in Harlem; the change in setting from Scotland to Haiti in the years following the rebellion rendered the play one of his earliest explorations of power and race, which were essential components of the discourse around fascism. On a related note, Welles's production was one of many forms of cultural expression concerned with Haiti. Others included *Black Jacobins*, a history of the Haitian Revolution by C. L. R. James; *Touissant L'Ouvreture*, a play also by James; *Haiti* and *Black Empire*, plays produced by the Federal Theatre's black companies; *Emporer of Haiti*, a play by Langston Hughes adapted into an opera, *Troubled Island*; and the proletarian historical novels *Drums at Dusk* and *Babouk* by Arna Bontemps and Guy Endore, respectively (Denning 396).[10] In the anxious thirties, as Denning observes, "The story of Haiti's black Jacobins was one of the few narratives in American popular culture that allowed the representation of black insurrection" (397). In this revealing cultural context, then, Faulkner's reference to Haiti would make Sutpen not so much a force of insurrection as an embodiment of the strong leadership deemed necessary to prevent insurrection.

As they unfold, the references to Haiti expose a bifurcated system of influence informed by the historical setting of Sutpen's story and the cultural context encompassing the novel's production and initial reception. This system is even more vividly on display in the parts of the Sutpen saga set during the Civil War. The war takes a heavy toll on Sutpen's Hundred, bringing hard times after a period of rapid expansion. But Rosa explains that she, Judith, and Clytie countered despair with hopeful thoughts of Sutpen's eventual homecoming, *"knowing that he would need us, knowing as we did (who knew him) that he would begin at once to salvage what was left of Sutpen's Hundred and restore it"* (AA 124). Rosa confirms to Quentin the fulfillment of her prediction upon Sutpen's return: *"We were right about what he would intend to do: that he would not even pause for breath before undertaking to restore his house and plantation as near as possible to what it had been"* (129). That Sutpen becomes a vibrant symbol of restoration and renewal in a period of devastating crisis has relevance to the Civil War setting in the novel, to the Depression, and particularly to the discourse around fascism. Along these lines, the desire for Sutpen's strong leadership derives from his promise to reconstruct order from the detritus of catastrophe—a feature of leadership that was as urgently appealing in the thirties as it was in the Civil War era.

Despite the hope that it inspires, Sutpen's return from battle is far from triumphant, of course. The internal and familial conflicts that come into relief against the historical backdrop of war and its tragic aftermath set in motion Sutpen's downfall and the ultimate failure of his design on power. Denning contends that the demise of Welles's Charles Foster Kane begins with "the loss of his magic" (390)—the mysterious aura that attracts fear, fascination, and, to some degree, sympathy for the devil. The loss of Sutpen's "magic" stems primarily from the intrusion of the past on the present, in particular the element of miscegenation that challenges the ideological underpinnings of Sutpen's authority. As we have seen, much of the Sutpen mystique derives from displays of power that blur the boundaries between master and slave, only to delineate them with reinforced clarity in the end. Yet Sutpen cannot obscure the inherent paradox between the ideology of racial purity that he invokes to achieve dominance and the actuality of miscegenation informing his material history and determining his ironic legacy. In describing this legacy, Shreve enumerates the deaths that expand Sutpen's story to tragic proportions, articulating an economy of race in which "it takes two niggers to get rid of one Sutpen" with a significant yet elusive remainder: "You've got one nigger left. One nigger Sutpen left. Of course you cant catch him and you dont always see him and you never will be able to use him. But you've got him there still. You still hear him sometimes. Dont you?" (*AA* 302). The howling figure of Jim Bond offers emphatic punctuation to the failure of Sutpen's design. Bond represents the blurring of a color line that Sutpen sought to maintain in theory, if not in practice, as a means of preserving his power. By the same token, Bond haunts the Jefferson social order, because he undermines the ideology of racial purity on which it relies for structural integrity.

The relevance of Faulkner's emphasis on miscegenation extends beyond the confines of the social system represented in the text, however. At a time when the eugenics movement was in flourish and lending substantial influence to the early stages of Hitler's "final solution," Sutpen's failure as a "great dictator" complicates and interrogates theories of racial purity and white supremacy essential to the aesthetic and ideological components of fascism. From this perspective, Sutpen's story reads as an allegory of antifascism every bit as attuned to its historical and cultural moment as those offered by Welles and others more conspicuously aligned with the Popular Front's antifascist crusade. It is most fitting, then, that three years after the publication of *Absalom*, Faulkner offered to donate the manuscript to raise funds for the Loyalist cause in the Spanish Civil War. Faulkner made the offer in a letter to Vincent Sheean and agreed to sign a statement of support to be issued by the League of American Writers on the issue of the Spanish conflict. In the letter, Faulkner wrote, "I most sincerely wish to go on record as being unalterably opposed to Franco and fascism, to all violations of the legal government and outrages against the people of Republican Spain" (qtd. in Blotner, *FAB* 2: 1030). This pledge of solidarity was worthy of the most ardent Popular Front advocate. Furthermore, it demonstrates Faulkner's sense of urgency with regard to the fascist threat and establishes that, while not a delegate or member, he had probably known about the League of American Writers from its inception in 1935.

While *Absalom*'s exploration of history and power offers glimpses of a more progressive Faulkner with respect to race, the novel nevertheless retains the sense of dominant-class anxiety informing earlier representations of fascist themes. As noted above, Faulkner's fiction and other forms of cultural expression tended to blend these themes with elements of class conflict active in the contemporary politics of social upheaval. The story of Thomas Sutpen in *Absalom* is certainly no exception. While Sutpen's story can be read as an antifascist allegory aligning Faulkner with a fundamental cultural enterprise of the Popular Front, there are noticeable class assumptions inscribed in the form of the text that limit the novel's progressive social vision. Although *Absalom* is for the most part the story of Thomas Sutpen, it is not, after all, Sutpen's story. The information that emerges about Sutpen must be gleaned from multiple—and sometimes competing—points of view. Sutpen is thus entirely a creature of narrative who springs to life "out of the rag-tag and bob-ends of old tales and talking" (*AA* 243) or, more specifically, out of the oral machinations of the narrators, Rosa Coldfield, Mr. Compson, Quentin, and Shreve. For all the power Sutpen amasses in Jefferson, he wields very little in the narrative structure of the text. Sutpen never speaks for himself, and so is completely defined by those who speak for him; in effect, these accounts are all the reader can really *know* of Sutpen. Informed by an ideology of the aesthetic, this elaborate narrative framework surrounding and shaping Sutpen is constructed mainly from a perspective that reinforces a sense of social order as envisioned by the dominant class. For this reason, the logic encompassing all points of view assumes that Sutpen's insatiable drive to accomplish his design must stem from his desire to rise far above his humble origins.

The birthplace of this desire is the plantation in Tidewater, Virginia, where Sutpen is shown the back door by a planter's house slave and thus given a harsh lesson in the ways of a world defined by social distinctions. Prior to this incident, Quentin imagines, Sutpen had no clear sense of class divisions; he assumed ownership and wealth to be arbitrary rewards. Quentin explains further that "it never occurred to [Sutpen] that any man should take any such blind accident as that [wealth] as authority or warrant to look down at others, any others. So he had hardly heard of such a world until he fell into it" (*AA* 180). As Richard C. Moreland explains, the slight Sutpen receives at the Tidewater plantation functions as a primal scene of class consciousness and awakens in him a furious determination to attain power through conflict (8–12). Quentin supplies Sutpen with an analogy that raises the specter of class warfare in reference to the Tidewater planter and his kind. Speaking to his father, the young Sutpen says, "If you were fixing to combat them that had the fine rifles, the first thing you would do would be to get yourself the nearest thing to a fine rifle you could borrow or steal or make, wouldn't it? . . . But this aint a question of rifles. So to combat them you have got to have what they have that made them do what he did. You got to have land and niggers and a fine house to combat them with. You see?" (*AA* 192). This element of class conflict lends a cautionary element to Sutpen's story as told by the cadre of narrators. Subject to the limitations of the form, Sutpen's actions and motivations are defined strictly in terms of a dominant social system that either absorbs, reveres, or repels him, depending on his ability to reflect its codes and values on a grand scale. The form of the text thus ensures that there is no alternative to this system and no space beyond the aesthetic containment for Sutpen to construct his own story.

From a structural standpoint, the story of Thomas Sutpen is to *Absalom* what the discourse around fascism was to the broad cultural narrative of social unrest in the thirties: a means of mediating disruptions in social order under the safety of aesthetic containment. Cultural production and the politics of social upheaval converged in the discourse around fascism, creating a set of visual and textual terms for representing power by design in artistic form as a means of negotiating the deployment of actual power at a time of national crisis. Faulkner was fluent in this language, speaking in a timely manner to concerns that raised the specter of fascism in America. While Faulkner could adopt multiple voices in this ongoing conversation, his accent remained for the most part consistent. And it was influenced in large measure by dominant-class anxieties that viewed the possibility of transformed social order, particularly the kind driven by the lower ranks of society, as inherently prone to chaos and violence. In many ways a product of the Depression, this component of Faulkner's fiction was immanently responsive to the overarching conflict between order and upheaval that registered in virtually all sectors of American life. This conflict was especially intense in rural America, where social and economic despair fanned the flames of unrest and prompted many, including Faulkner, to contemplate the prospect of agrarian revolution against the backdrop of an evolving New Deal welfare state.

CHAPTER FOUR

Revolution and Restraint

Faulkner's Ambivalent Agrarianism

THE DAMAGING EFFECTS of the Great Depression hit particularly hard in rural America, home to the small farmer and repository of many ideals that had been formed in the nation's infancy. At least since Thomas Jefferson's *Notes on the State of Virginia*, the yeoman farmer had remained one of the most enduring figures of strength and independence in the American mythos. But hard times in rural America, extending from the otherwise prosperous twenties through the destitute thirties, altered the symbolic value long attached to this cultural icon. During the Depression, the suffering of small landowners, tenants, and sharecroppers exposed the harsh realities of a market-driven agricultural economy with virtually no safety net. Striking at the heart of the country, the forces of nature, economics, and politics seemingly conspired to deprive small farmers of their livelihoods, breeding a sense of helplessness and frustration in farm families. Once a paragon of the productive work ethic, the yeoman farmer now became a gauge for measuring weakness and want, not only in terms of the economy but also with regard to the professed ideal of self-reliance—an essential component of agrarian and American identity and ideology.

Options for small farmers in such dire straits were limited. One response was to invoke the latent agrarian radicalism that had inspired uprisings against the British in the eighteenth century and had fueled the Populist movement in the late nineteenth century. John A. Simpson, president of the Farmers' Union, raised this prospect in an ominous letter to President Roosevelt written in 1933: "My candid opinion is that unless you call a special session of Congress . . . and start a revolution in government affairs there will be one started in the country" (qtd. in McElvaine 147). The threatening tone of Simpson's rhetoric reflected revolutionary sentiments stirring in rural America; the challenge for potential insurgents, however, came in identifying the enemy. The maze of financial institutions and transactions that defined the socioeconomic circumstances of the farmer in an age of credit contributed to a depersonalized atmosphere. Therefore, many in rural America found themselves in the same predicament as the angry, dispossessed tenant in John Steinbeck's *The Grapes of Wrath*. With all attempts to determine blame deflected to a faceless corporate entity, Steinbeck's tenant is left not with answers but with a loaded question, in every sense of the word. "Who can we shoot?" he asks a neighbor employed as a bulldozer driver sent to level homes for an agribusiness consortium (49).

Not only was the blame displaced, but also the farm families themselves, many of whom faced the same dim realities as the Joads in Steinbeck's novel. Families who had lived on the same plot of land for generations were dispossessed, disenfranchised, and uprooted, finally compelled to search elsewhere for means of survival—a harrowing experience for a segment of the American population that had placed great stock in cultivating deep roots. This tragic turn was documented by V. F. Calverton in his 1934 article "The Farmer Cocks His Rifle." Calverton traces the historical currents of social protest in rural America before describing present conditions in ominous terms: "Today, however, with land values at their nadir, and confronted with the impossibility of even meeting the costs of production, [the small farmer] has hung up his ploughshare and taken to his gun" (728). Wary of rural dissidence and the potential for the spread of social upheaval, government, law enforcement, and dominant-class hegemony mobilized to preserve the status quo. The forces of revolution and restraint thus converged in the plight of the small farmer, affecting rural America and, by extension, an American culture with deep ideological roots in agrarian soil.

With its expansive social vision, Faulkner's fiction of the Depression is responsive to this dialectical convergence, often expressing noticeable sympathy for the dispossessed and disenfranchised small farmers and sharecroppers and an acute awareness of the systematic oppression that compounds their suffering. However, his work also displays chronic anxiety over dissident impulses that could produce civil unrest and, in turn, fundamental changes in the existing social order. Added to this paradoxical mix is an increasing concern over the effects of New Deal policies and programs on the lives and landscape of rural America, establishing a pattern of scathing critique that Faulkner would aim at the federal welfare state as he defended classical liberalism's fundamental tenets of individual liberty and self-reliance for the remainder of his life as a writer and public figure. In my view, these dynamic influences imbue Faulkner's literary production with an ambivalent agrarianism in the context of competing ideological positions reflected in the "back to the land" movements, as discussed in chapter 1, that surfaced on the Right and the Left in response to the harsh circumstances of Depression life. Influenced by Faulkner's position in a dominant class threatened by social instability, this condition registers in a range of novels and stories spanning the Depression and manifests in terms of thematic content and formal tensions produced by competitive voices and perspectives vying for dominance. Acting as a disruptive and productive force in Faulkner's fiction, this ambivalent agrarianism affects the nature and level of social consciousness achieved in a given text and thus provides an instructive means of understanding how it relates to the cultural politics encompassing its production.

The first novel Faulkner published in the thirties was *As I Lay Dying*, the tragic and often darkly comic story of the Bundren family and their harrowing journey from country to town to lay the deceased wife and mother Addie Bundren to rest. While the ostensible purpose of the quest is Addie's burial, members of the Bundren family have underlying personal agendas as well. Anse longs for a set of dentures and, as we learn in the end, a replacement for Addie; Vardaman dreams of getting a toy train; Cash wants a record player; and Dewey Dell desperately needs "medicine" to terminate her unwanted pregnancy. In the confines of the Bundren family, a unifying collective purpose—or, to apply the parlance of social philosophy, a common good—is at odds with individual needs and desires that threaten to divide the family along the lines of competitive self-interest.[1] Though the Bundren family is the central focus of the novel, Faulkner offers frequent reminders—mostly observations from neighbors and onlookers—that the journey of the Bundrens is measured by the watchful eye of a rural community wary of the uncertainty that this death march signals. This concern extends as well to the form of the text, which displays tension resulting from the competing points of view and ideological perspectives inscribed in it. As in *The Sound and the Fury*, the modernist form of *As I Lay Dying* features an incisive social vision that emerges from the fractured subjective positions and experiences of individual characters to expose and comment on social, economic, and political issues active on a range that encompasses text and context.

A central issue represented and negotiated in *As I Lay Dying* is the potential for social upheaval that threatens to destabilize the foundation of rural community. This aspect of the novel is in many ways aligned with the historical moment of its production, as Joseph Blotner highlights in describing the moment Faulkner began the writing process: "On October 25, 1929, the day after panic broke out on Wall Street, he took one of these [onion] sheets, unscrewed the cap from his fountain pen, and wrote at the top in blue ink, 'As I Lay Dying.' Then he underlined it twice and wrote the date in the upper right-hand corner" (*FAB* 1: 633). Under the circumstances, the temptation to read the novel as an allegory of contemporary socioeconomic conditions is considerable. Such a reading might cast Addie, repeatedly described as a worn-out workhorse, in the role of an American economic system facing an imminent but as yet uncertain death, indicated by the curious first-person, past-progressive title. As a possibility, this allegorical reading suggests that while *As I Lay Dying* is undoubtedly a timeless novel, it is a timely one as well. Though the novel has "universal" qualities, such as an epic narrative structure that features a variation on the archetypal quest, it is also shaped by ideological responses to conditions that fueled the politics of social upheaval in rural America.

For the most part, *As I Lay Dying* is the story of the Bundren family told predominantly by the Bundren family. But, as Olga Vickery observes, the interjection of other points of view works to create a frame, granting distance for critical interpretation (50). Frequently, residents of the rural community enter the story to comment on the Bundrens' predicament, either commanding sections of their own or appearing in the sections narrated by members of the Bundren family. As André Bleikasten remarks, "Through their mingled voices the anonymous voice of the community is heard with its rules and values—an indisputable reference which, as always with Faulkner, emphasizes the opposition between social and individual, public and private" (*Faulkner's* 59). The communal frame functions, then, to situate the Bundrens in relation to the broader social order and against the various norms they violate along the journey. Early in the novel, for example, Tull reveals that Anse has relied frequently on the aid of the community to sustain his family: "Like most folks around here, I done help him so much already I cant quit now" (*AILD* 33). The perception of Anse as a communal charge is reinforced later when Tull recounts Uncle Billy's claim that God helps Anse for the same reason as his neighbors: "He's done it so long now He cant quit" (89). Although this history of assistance is widely known, Anse is too hypocritical to admit it to himself or anyone else. Accordingly, when Darl insists at one point in the journey that his father borrow a bucket to mix the cement for "setting" Cash's broken leg, Anse utters his common refrain: "I wouldn't be beholden, God knows" (206). Instead, he allows Darl to send Dewey Dell for help—a move that secures the assistance but allows Anse to persist in the delusion that he has not requested it. Anse's capacity for denial inspires a heightened sense of independence in Jewel, who has a steely determination to earn his keep and deny offerings of help in any form. When the Bundrens stop at Samson's farm, for instance, Jewel insists on paying for the feed that Samson offers to Jewel's prized horse. Jewel even projects his pride onto his stallion, echoing Anse when he points out to Samson that "I feed him a little extra and I don't want him beholden to no man" (116). Repeated throughout the novel, such scenes feature what was fast becoming a thematic staple in Depression culture, reflecting the resistance to dependency that resulted when Americans, deeply invested in the ideology of self-reliance, found themselves forced by circumstances to seek a helping hand. In depicting the social relations between the Bundrens and the surrounding community, Faulkner illustrates the complex negotiations ensuing between the proud but desperate victims of the Depression and communal networks of aid and thus assumes a position at the vanguard of cultural production.

In key respects, Faulkner's representation of this complex system of social exchange anticipates John Steinbeck's some nine years later. Faulkner's Bundrens are similar to Steinbeck's Joads in their determined effort—even to the point of denial and delusion—to preserve their dignity in the face of moving from a position of independence to dependence. In the truck stop scene in *The Grapes of Wrath*, for example, the Joads get a loaf of bread and some candy at a reduced price, thanks to the kindness of a server and her customers who recognize that the Joads desperately need help, as well as the illusion that they have not received any (196–209). Laying bare the ideology of self-reliance, time and again Faulkner shows the Bundrens' compulsion to obscure the reality of assistance through their own insistence—primarily expressed by Anse and Jewel but also by Cash's hyperactive work ethic—that they are getting by on their own. Moreover, Faulkner shows that the members of the community, like the server and truckers in Steinbeck's diner, recognize the family's need to maintain a sense of dignity rooted in independence, especially at their most vulnerable point. In the scene cited above, Samson invites the Bundrens to stay for dinner, but Anse clearly perceives the offer as a hand-out. Sensing Anse's reluctance, Samson stresses the social rather than the economic dimensions of the offer, pointing out to Anse that "when folks stops with us at meal time and wont come to the table, my wife takes it as an insult" (*AILD* 116). In this instance, Anse holds fast to his refusal, but later in the journey when the Bundrens' plight has worsened, he accepts a similar invitation from Armstid. Still unable to shoulder the burden of obligation himself, however, Anse transfers the "debt" to Addie: "It's for her sake I am taking the food. I got no team, no nothing. But she will be grateful to ere a one of you" (182). To a noticeable degree, *As I Lay Dying* interrogates the concept of self-reliance, exposing it as a creation of the Bundrens that is, all the more ironically, reliant on the community for its dubious viability.

Focusing on the Bundrens' dependence affords Faulkner the chance to probe the ideological complexity of relief and to engage in pointed social commentary and satire—most of it enabled by the characterization of Anse. Reminiscent of Jason Compson, Anse invokes the rhetoric of populism not to rail against the social and economic injustices suffered by the oppressed "common man" but rather to gain advantage for himself in the family and the community. In one of Anse's monologues, he insists, "It's a hard country on a man; it's hard" (*AILD* 110). What makes it so hard, Anse goes on to explain, is the systematic exploitation of poor farmers under capitalism: "Nowhere in this sinful world can a honest, hardworking man profit. It takes them that runs the stores in the towns, doing no sweating, living off them that sweats. It aint the hardworking man, the farmer" (110). While there is strength to be found in Anse's words, it derives from taking them out of context. For the self-serving and hypocritical nature of the messenger inevitably casts doubt on the credibility of his populist message. Prior to Anse's exhortation, Darl sets the stage, undermining the populist appeal in advance by exposing Anse's aversion to hard work: "I have never seen a sweat stain on his shirt. He was sick once from working in the sun when he was twenty-two years old, and he tells people that if he ever sweats, he will die. I suppose he believes it" (17). In contrast to the wholesome, industrious, and independent traits assigned to the idealized yeoman farmer, Anse comes across as a shifty and acquisitive "cracker" who is out to take full advantage of circumstances to gain profit—in the case of this journey to town, the new set of teeth that he mentions repeatedly and presumably the new bride whom he introduces sight unseen to the family in the final passage of the novel.

The relevance of Faulkner's depiction to the emerging cultural politics of rural dissidence can be measured by placing Anse next to one of his contemporaries—in particular, Jeeter Lester of Erskine Caldwell's *Tobacco Road*. Published two years after *As I Lay Dying*, Caldwell's novel casts Jeeter, like Anse, as the head of a family struggling to survive and turning on one another in the process. In many respects, Jeeter sings from the same sheet of music as Anse, aiming for high notes of populism in describing his woeful condition. In the opening chapter of the novel, with the family in a standoff over Lov's sack of turnips, Jeeter implores his son-in-law by citing a cosmic curse that has destroyed his means of sustenance: "What God made turnip-worms for, I can't make out. It appears to me like He just naturally has got it in good and heavy for a poor man. I worked all the fall last year digging up a patch of ground to grow turnips in, and then when they're getting about big enough to pull up and eat, along comes these damn-blasted green-gutted turnip-worms and bore clear to the middle of them. God is got it in good and heavy for the poor" (9–10). Any sympathy Jeeter might elicit with this lamentation becomes more difficult to sustain in light of subsequent revelations of Jeeter's past and present behavior. His stealing and hoarding Lov's turnips for himself and his history of sexual abuse are cases in point. A direct descendant of the ring-tailed roarer in Southwestern Humor—

Augustus Baldwin Longstreet's Ransy Sniffle from *Georgia Scenes*, for example—Jeeter stands as the embodiment of base desires and unmitigated self-interest, his malnourishment thus serving as a metaphor for his lack of moral integrity. These aspects of his character are repeatedly on display as he manipulates his family to improve his standing in the ongoing struggle to determine survival of the fittest.

While Faulkner draws on archetypal staples of classical tragedy and epic literature to chart the Bundrens' treacherous path, Caldwell is at great pains to put the plight of the Lesters in the context of explicit social and economic factors, invoking the nature-versus-nurture debate and tipping the scales decidedly toward the latter. Like Faulkner, Caldwell alludes to the genre of Southwestern Humor, creating a variation on the frame narrative. Caldwell's version of the frame mediates the tragicomic exploits of the Lesters with a narrator who becomes increasingly less objective in describing the family's plight from the standpoint of determinism. Consequently, we find passages in Caldwell's novel that we could scarcely imagine coming across in Faulkner's. For instance, at one point the narrator injects a scathing indictment of the Lesters' landlord, Captain John, citing his greed as the cause of his tenants' suffering: "Rather than attempt to show his tenants how to conform to the newer and more economical methods of modern agriculture, which he thought would have been impossible from the start, he sold the stock and implements and moved away. An intelligent employment of his land, stocks, and implements would have enabled Jeeter, and scores of others who had become dependent upon Captain John, to raise crops for food, and crops to be sold at a profit. Co-operative farming would have saved them all" (63). Such passages show Caldwell's hand as he revises the traditional frame narrative to provoke the kind of ethical quandary not inscribed in the original frontier sketches.

With the brutality of the sharecropping system highlighted, simply dismissing and disliking Jeeter becomes a more difficult prospect, as does responding to the grotesque comic elements that derive from Southwestern Humor. For if we find Jeeter and his family humorous, Caldwell forces us to do so rather uncomfortably. By adding complexity to his rural folk, Caldwell fleshes them out in a way that marks a noticeable departure from the flat characterization found in Southwestern Humor. With the safe distance from them suddenly removed, the characters of *Tobacco Road* stand as grotesque, in many respects, but also as human. A prime example can be found in the episode involving Bessie's car purchase—an updated version of the frontier horse-swapping tales that Faulkner draws on as well. Laughing at Bessie's naïveté and her garish display of religious fervor comes easy at first, but it presents an ethical dilemma once Caldwell brings us to the abrupt realization that we are laughing with the unscrupulous car dealers who have bilked Bessie for every cent to her name. In so doing, we become implicated in the brutal act of transforming the vehicle for Bessie's advancement, literally and figuratively, into the means of further deprivation.

In *As I Lay Dying*, placing blame at Anse's feet and laughing at his expense comes much easier. One reason is that Anse and his family are somewhat better off than the Lesters—Anse does, after all, still own his patch of land. While not living comfortably, the Bundrens have been able to get by, as suggested by the network of support discussed above. Also, the frame provided by the non-Bundren characters both cues and sanctions laughter, with Doctor Peabody's reaction to Cash's broken leg set in concrete serving as a prime example. Another reason is that Anse's role as the primary source renders indictments of the system dubious at best; his raging against the machine must always be taken with a grain of salt, given his obvious ulterior motives. A typically conflicted representation is thus on display, lending a complexity to Anse's character not found in those crafted to promote "back to the land" sentiments from the Left or the Right. This attitude is evident in the characterization of Anse by way of the kind of justice he envisions. Faulkner stops short of having Anse call for an immediate solution, preferring instead to have him stress a transcendent reversal of fortune. Referring to heaven, Anse explains, "Every man will be equal there and it will be taken from them that have and give to them that have not by the Lord" (*AILD* 110). Significantly,

Jeeter Lester echoes this faith in eternal justice in *Tobacco Road*, temper-
ing his Job-like anger at God with the assertion that "God, He'll put a
stop to it some of these days and make the rich give back all they've took
from the poor folks. God is going to treat us right" (10). Once again,
however, Jeeter's message finds in the authoritative and credible narrator
the kind of support that Anse's is lacking. Severely compromised by the
respective messengers, Anse's and Jeeter's declarations are clearly not in
line with the calls for immediate political transformation found in, say,
works of proletarian literature starting to appear on the cultural landscape. Tainted by ulterior motives, this shared vision occurs in the teleol-
ogy of a promised eternal justice through which the poor will finally gain
their just reward through the benevolent workings of a divine arbiter. For
those who could not wait for eternity, though, the option of revolution
seemed a much more productive course of action, as Faulkner palpably
signals in *As I Lay Dying*.

Faulkner represents the impulse toward revolution in the form of barn
burning, which captures the essence of social unrest in a defining and
historically resonant act. To comprehend the implications of this representation, at least some attention to its historical and social significance is
in order. In " 'Southern Violence' Reconsidered: Arson as Protest in Black-
Belt Georgia, 1865–1910," Albert C. Smith attempts to revise the understanding of violence in southern culture, stressing incidence of property
destruction as a means of calling into question longstanding emphasis on
personal acts of violence such as rape and homicide. Noting significant
cases of arson in Georgia, Smith asserts that "arson was violent, interracial protest, a form of revenge for racism and poverty that defined the
region's race relations" (528). While the racial component of Smith's argument is tangential, his secondary focus on intraracial acts of arson committed by those without property against those with substantial holdings
is relevant to Faulkner's treatment of barn burning. Of particular significance is Smith's finding that higher incidence of arson tended to coincide
with seasonal pressure points in agricultural production, such as plant-
ing and harvest, and with periods of economic depression (538). Also

significant is Smith's explanation of why barns, gins, and other institutions associated with agricultural production were prime targets: "By consistently destroying such property, these arsonists were attacking the very symbols of power and status that differentiated the propertied from the propertyless and sustained and perpetuated that inequality" (543). Consequently, mounting social unrest in the Great Depression would have certainly rekindled fears in the dominant class of arson and other forms of property destruction prevalent during the economic depressions and the rise in populism that marked the last two decades of the nineteenth century.[2]

Ostensibly, Darl's burning of Gillespie's barn in *As I Lay Dying* is an act of familial rebellion prompted by his need to bring about a swift and definitive end to the horrific death march of the Bundren family. At base, Darl's defiance is motivated by the indignity his mother has suffered—her body hauled on the back of a wagon through the countryside while emanating an increasingly more pungent odor and attracting a flock of ever-present buzzards circling overhead. However, as in *The Sound and the Fury*, what occurs in the family resonates with social and political implications that extend from text to context. Regardless of his motivation, Darl's act is subject to the interpretation of communal authority: in narrative terms, the community reads Darl's act in a manner different from his intention. It is important to note as well Faulkner's care in situating the barn burning in the context of a dominant ideology rooted in capitalism that is articulated explicitly in the text. Along these lines, Darl recalls the events leading up to the barn burning in reified terms. He continually refers to Addie as a horse, for example, relegating her to the level of beast of burden or labor commodity. The same is true in his perception of Jewel, who enters the fiery barn and "seems to materialise out of the darkness, lean as a race horse in his underclothes in the beginning of the glare" (*AILD* 218). As the fire rages, Jewel, Mack, and Gillespie attempt to save as much of the property as possible, rescuing mules, cows, and horses from the burning barn. Only after the stock has been saved does Jewel try to retrieve Addie's body from the flames, mounting the coffin as he would his prized stallion and "riding upon it, clinging to it, until it crashes him forward and clear" (222). Sustaining burns during the rescue, Jewel gives off "a thin smell of scorching meat," further indicating the reification that comes from his part in the frantic attempt to preserve Gillespie's property (222).

As a harbinger of social unrest, the barn-burning episode goes directly to the question of Darl's sanity, a central aesthetic and ideological conflict in the novel. Viewing the barn burning strictly in familial terms suggests that Darl is the sanest Bundren—a dubious distinction, at best. After all, Darl is the only one who appears to recognize the madness of the burial journey, which has more to do with satisfying individual needs than fulfilling Addie's last wishes. However, examined within the dominant ideology rooted in capitalism, Darl's act is branded as the ultimate insanity, for it threatens the very foundation of the socioeconomic order: the ownership of private property. Even within the family, Darl is perceived as a threat to this sacred principle. As Anse ponders the threat posed by Darl after the barn burning, Jewel advises, "Catch him and tie him up," and then adds with trepidation, "Goddamn it, do you want to wait until he sets fire to the goddamn team and wagon?" (233). For Jewel, the team and wagon have been invested with added value, given that Anse secured them in a backhanded deal with a Snopes in which he agreed to trade Jewel's stallion without his son's permission. Jewel must protect the team if he has any hope of reversing Anse's deal and protecting his prized property.

While Jewel's urgency to guard his investment largely determines his response to the barn burning, Cash is able to examine Darl's act from a more rational perspective. Still, given his name, it is not surprising that a capitalist mentality informs Cash's interpretation. Initially, Cash tries to reconcile what Darl has done through the logic of exchange value: "Of course it was Jewel's horse was traded to get her that nigh to town, and in a sense it was the value of the horse Darl tried to burn up" (*AILD* 233). When Cash factors in the human dimension, he comes close to making sense of Darl's action; he even admits that "I can almost believe he done right in a way" (233). Despite this bit of sympathy, however, Cash's inclination is to uphold the principle of private ownership: he finally insists that "nothing excuses setting fire to a man's barn and endangering his stock and destroying his property" (233). Later, considering Darl's commitment to the state asylum, Cash experiences the same sort of ambivalence. On the one hand, he insists that "there just aint nothing justifies the deliberate destruction of what a man has built with his own sweat and stored the fruit of his own sweat into" (238). By this logic, destroying capital is always irrational—crazy, by definition. On the other hand, dire straits force him to admit that "I aint so sho that ere a man has the right to say what is crazy and what aint" (238). Although desperate circumstances force Cash to understand, to some extent, the logic of burning the coffin and thus to recognize at least some justification for property destruction, he ultimately cannot oppose the fundamental concept of private ownership that supports the established socioeconomic order. From this perspective, Cash can be viewed as a conflicted subject of capitalism.

The contradiction exposed in Cash's dilemma is analogous to an ideological conflict prevalent in the historical context of the novel. The economic chaos wrought by the market crash forced desperate citizens to weigh the options of social protest, and perhaps revolution, against preservation of the established order based in capitalism. Foremost among America's potential revolutionaries were small farmers, who had endured years of hardship long before the crash. Referring to the initial years of the Depression, Robert S. McElvaine observes, "The clouds of agrarian unrest had been gathering since 1920. Those clouds were mature enough to produce small but powerful storms of violence in the Hoover years" (91). The question on the minds of many small farmers, McElvaine adds, was how to define the nature of violence directed against the established order—as revolution or patriotism. The comments of one small farmer offer lucid illustration of these alternative interpretations: "They say blockading the highways is illegal. I says, 'Seems to me there was a Tea-party in Boston that was illegal too. What about destroying property in Boston harbor when our country was started?'" (qtd. in McElvaine 92). Through the interwoven representation of family and community,

Faulkner is able to raise the same quandary about Darl's act of resistance: Is it an illegal act or an instance of necessary revolution?

If the central ideological question that Faulkner poses with respect to Darl is a timely one, so is the apparent response, which is suggested by Darl's fate. Within a familial context, the novel does evoke noticeable sympathy for Darl as a character whose resistance is motivated by harrowing circumstances. However, the novel shows that this sympathy does not extend as easily to Darl as a representative of social upheaval, as the swift intervention of the state makes clear. Patrick O'Donnell contends that the novel points to state authority as one of the constitutive elements of Bundren civic identity, such as it is. Because the Bundrens feel this identity threatened by Darl, they submit to what O'Donnell, following Louis Althusser, calls the state apparatus—in this case represented by the asylum agents who subdue Darl and take him to Jackson for confinement. As a result, O'Donnell argues, "Darl is the sacrifice paid to the State so that the Bundrens can complete their epic journey and continue with business as usual" (90). While committing Darl to the asylum protects the Bundrens' place in society, it also preserves stability by removing what the community perceives to be an immediate threat to private property and a sign of potential social upheaval. Along these lines, the vexed logic that Faulkner exposes so vividly in Cash's response to the barn burning leads to the submission to state authority as a means of bringing about resolution. Consequently, Darl's committal can be read, on one level, as an ideological response founded on the social concept of private property. The severity of the penalty—Darl essentially loses his rights as a private citizen—reveals the strength of the notion that ownership of private property is a natural and even sacred right not to be challenged in the least. In depicting this deference to state authority, Faulkner illustrates the workings of a dominant ideology that relies on concepts of property and ownership to define the terms of social order.

The effects of this political struggle between revolution and restraint manifest at the level of form as well, exposing the ideological dimensions of Faulkner's aesthetic decisions. Even a cursory reading of the text will confirm that Faulkner carries forward in this novel his interest in certain formal practices associated with high modernism. In a revised version of his 1933 introduction to a proposed edition of *The Sound and the Fury*, Faulkner reflects on the composition of *As I Lay Dying*, calling it a "deliberate book" and adding that "I set out deliberately to write a *tour-de-force*. Before I began I said, I am going to write a book by which, at a pinch, I can stand or fall if I never touch ink again" (*Essays* 297). Faulkner's penchant for formal experimentation in pursuing this goal is suggested by the division of the novel into interior monologues that record events from various perspectives. This multivocal form, as Eric J. Sundquist explains, leaves the text "existing in an analogously fragile state and maintaining its narrative form despite the apparent absence of that substance one might compare to, or identify with, a central point of view embodied in an omniscient narrator" (30–31). The reader is thus left to construct from these various perspectives a meaningful plot that can be sufficiently comprehended; the use of the journey as a unifying device is certainly helpful in this regard. A further nod to modernism is found in the descriptive language of the novel, which employs various degrees of abstraction to evoke vivid and often curious images.[3] For Darl, the sun rising above the horizon is "poised like a bloody egg upon the crest of thunderheads" (*AILD* 40). Probably the most memorable instance of abstraction in the novel is Vardaman's laconic and imagist attempt at signification: "My mother is a fish" (84). Such descriptive tendencies have led to the assertion that certain effects of Faulkner's narrative technique share much in the way of aesthetics with abstract movements in painting such as Cubism.[4]

Certainly one of these common traits is a self-conscious treatment of form displayed primarily in Darl's monologues. Ironically, though, this emphasis often serves the cause of realism as effectively as it does abstraction. Consider the novel's opening paragraph, which illustrates Darl's reliance on spatial points of reference: "The path runs straight as a plumb-line, worn smooth by feet and baked brick-hard by July, between the green rows of laidby cotton, to the cottonhouse in the center of the field, where it turns and circles the cottonhouse at four soft right angles and goes on across the field again, worn so by feet in fading precision" (*AILD* 3). With such visual imagery, Faulkner evokes a stark pastoral aesthetic that anticipates the fusion of post-Impressionist interest in shapes and lines with the visual clarity of social realism found in, say, the Depression paintings of Thomas Hart Benton or the photographs that would comprise the Farm Security Administration collection. In the thirties Benton abandoned the abstract style that he had adopted from post-Impressionism and turned to what many called, in a pejorative sense, "regionalism." Even then, Benton retained post-Impressionist elements—depictions of elongated human bodies and the movement of mundane objects to the foreground, for example—in his treatment of rural subjects and themes from a socially conscious point of view. Many of the FSA photographs display modernist influences in addition to the stark realism valued in the thirties—for instance, the emphasis on mundane objects in the foreground often yields an abstract quality in the photograph, much like the flattening effect of Cubism. In each case, elements of figural placement, order, and design aid in the vivid depiction of rural life. The point here is simply that Darl effectually serves as ground zero for continuing negotiations between the aesthetic ideologies of formalism and social realism inscribed in the representational scheme of *As I Lay Dying*.

As arguably the most enigmatic figure in the novel, Darl is central to an understanding of how key aesthetic decisions constituting the form of the text yield implications in relation to pending cultural politics. We do not have to progress very far into one of Darl Bundren's monologues to get the sense that he is a character *in* the world of the text but not *of* that world. In many respects, Darl is typical of characters found in works of high modernism; his service in World War I, for instance, aligns him with Hemingway's traumatized and alienated soldiers who came home only in a geographical sense. Like the transparent eyeball Emerson describes, Darl is an omnipresent watcher; he even recalls with detailed accuracy conversations he has not witnessed in person. In addition, Darl seems to possess a mystical intuition, much like the one T.P. attributes to Benjy in *The Sound and the Fury*, enabling him to penetrate the facade of secrecy others have constructed. His knowing that Jewel is not Anse's son and his sensing that Dewey Dell is hiding an unwanted pregnancy are cases in point. Darl's manner of speaking also sets him apart from his family and the surrounding community; his considerable gifts of expression wax poetic and reveal a streak of intellectual prowess combined with lyrical mysticism. Considering these gifts, Darl's detachment from a community that prides itself on work rather than introspection is predictable. Tull states the communal verdict, revealing Darl's alienation as a self-fulfilling prophecy: "I have said and I say again, that's ever living thing the matter with Darl: he just thinks by himself too much" (*AILD* 71). The form of Darl's monologues confirms this isolated perspective and leads Donald M. Kartiganer to identify in him a heightened vision that is "sharp, but with the clarity of the disengaged" (*Fragile* 30). Kartiganer emphasizes this sense of disengagement solely within the parameters of the text; however, the broader ideological nature and political consequences of this aesthetic effect are important to consider as well.

Because of Darl's alienation from members of his family and from the community, it is not surprising that his interior perceptions are far removed from those of other characters with a voice in the novel. Nor is it surprising that his perception of the barn burning produces the aesthetic effect of distance. Darl's description illustrates how his preoccupation with form works to resist the social dimensions of his action by introducing a dominant note of abstraction. Having set the raging fire, Darl records its progress with emphasis on spatial design and abstract expression: "The front, the conical façade with the square orifice of doorway broken only by the square squat shape of the coffin on the sawhorses like a cubistic bug, comes into relief" (*AILD* 219). Viewing the burning barn in these terms yields stasis and prevents Darl from anticipating the broader ramifications of his action in the context of social relations. For Darl, the barn burning occurs without social context; from his perspective, the action is suspended like the buzzards he sees circling above the wagon "with an outward semblance of form and purpose, but with no inference of motion, progress or retrograde" (227). Darl surveys the scene in the manner of a painter viewing a canvas. Inspired by creative genius, the barn burning is a work of "art" with significant form that enables Darl to express intense pain over the loss of his mother and the subsequent humiliation that the journey toward burial in Jefferson has caused. Roger Fry introduced the aesthetic concept of "significant form" to develop a theory of representation resistant to the reductive documentary style found in, say, the popular landscapes of nineteenth-century Britain. Instead of documenting a figure as it appears in reality, according to Fry, the artist should strive to represent the figure in a form derived from comprehensive perception, depicting the actual object or scene as well as the emotional response of the artist. For Darl, then, the figure of the "cubistic bug" is a significant form of Addie's coffin. In this regard, Darl is analogous to the solitary artist whose subjective vision subsumes social reality.

With Darl in a kind of solitary confinement reinforced by the form of the text, Cash is left primarily to weigh the consequences of the barn burning in its social context. And, as we have seen, Cash applies the logic of capitalism in attempting to do so, thus rendering Darl himself an abstraction. For those invested in private property, both materially and ideologically, the barn burning transforms Darl from an alienated misfit into a disturbing symbol of social upheaval. Though Darl insists on autonomy for his work of "art," he cannot negate the ties that bind it to social reality. Consequently, by performing an act of resistance with such profound social implications, Darl violates the terms of disengagement governing both the formalist aesthetic sensibility he embodies and the social contract that works ideologically to validate private property. For both offenses, Darl faces confinement motivated by interest in preserving order. Although he is no activist for the class of poor farmers he occupies, Darl's role as a harbinger of revolt nevertheless attracts a considerable amount of dominant-class anxiety and mobilizes powerful forces against him. What emerges from Faulkner's depiction of Darl, and indeed from *As I Lay Dying* as a whole, is a penetrating social vision, revealing much about the ideological means of defining and maintaining the terms of social order favorable to the dominant class.

This feature of Darl's character is further illustrated by a comparison to

Steinbeck's Tom Joad, a literary figure more explicitly representative of the grassroots dissidence that fueled agrarian social unrest and protest in the Depression. Darl Bundren and Tom Joad share in common a mystical quality, although Darl's stems mainly from solipsistic introspection and Tom's from a burgeoning class consciousness fueled by experiencing social injustice firsthand. Both Darl and Tom function as Christ figures: Darl is the "lamb" sacrificed for the salvation of ownership and established order, while Tom is like the mythic Christ, accepting his cup, disappearing in body, and then living on in spirit to inspire apostles of resistance to follow. As Darl moves closer to his sacrificial moment, he spirals further into social disengagement and abstraction. By contrast, Tom's vision in *The Grapes of Wrath* becomes more coherent as he develops deeper political convictions and an increasing commitment to social activism.

The departing words of the characters highlight this fundamental difference between them. Darl's description of his incarceration reveals that he has become alienated even from himself: "Darl has gone to Jackson. They put him on the train, laughing, down the long car laughing, the heads turning like the heads of owls when he passed" (*AILD* 253). Still emphasizing form, Darl observes the asylum officials with typical distancing effect: "Their necks were shaved to a hairline, as though the recent and simultaneous barbers had a chalk-line like Cash's" (253). This effect becomes even more pronounced when Darl articulates resistance to his forced removal, employing imagery that calls to mind the post-Impressionist movement of surrealism. For instance, Darl observes that "the state's money has a face to each backside and a backside to each face" (*AILD* 254). Stream of consciousness then leads Darl to describe a nickel with "a woman on one side and a buffalo on the other; two faces and no back," which then leads to a sexually explicit recollection of a "spy-glass" he looked into during his tour of duty in France: "In it it had a woman and a pig with two backs and no face. I know what that is" (254). Echoing Joyce's Molly Bloom upon his exit from the stage of the text, Darl simply mutters, "Yes yes yes yes yes yes yes yes" (254). The opposite of Darl, Tom Joad moves from isolation and confinement—he has just been released from prison as the novel opens—toward communal identity expressed in Rev. Casey's belief that "a fella ain't got a soul of his own, but on'y a piece of a big one" (Steinbeck 535). Tom's acceptance of this spiritual collectivism leads to the rather more simplistic epiphany that "a fella ain't no good alone" (535) and finally to a direct statement of social activism based in class consciousness: "I'll be ever'where—wherever you look. Wherever they's a fight so hungry people can eat, I'll be there. Wherever there's a cop beatin' up a guy, I'll be there. . . . An' when our folks eat the stuff they raise an' live in the house they build—why, I'll be there. See?" (537). In this instance, the form of *The Grapes of Wrath*, with its balance toward the clarity of social realism, paradoxically renders Tom's departure an arrival, for it is apparent that in his end as an individual character is his beginning as a reminder of the collective struggle of his class to overcome social injustice. Darl leaves on far different terms, the force of his isolated act of resistance diminished in large measure by the progressively abstract form of his final statements and by the prevailing logic of socioeconomic order. Simply put, Tom's final words strive for collective purpose, expressing an individual faith that he can embody the power of the people for the cause of reform, while Darl's gibberish signals his utter isolation from community and the devastating effects of challenging the status quo.

The differences between Darl and Tom—and indeed between *As I Lay Dying* and *The Grapes of Wrath*—are directly related to the contrasting perspectives that Faulkner and Steinbeck bring to bear on the issue of hardship and injustice in rural America. Clearly, Faulkner's view of the Bundrens is a far cry from Steinbeck's approach to the Joads. For Faulkner, the catastrophes that befall the Bundrens—most of them worthy of the Book of Job—are often tinged with black comedy, as in the case of the circling buzzards or of Anse's economical notion to heal Cash's broken leg by "setting" it in concrete. Although Steinbeck's rendering of the Joads drew criticism from many who feared at the time that it bolstered the "Okie" stereotype, Steinbeck's sympathy for the plight of migrants is unmistakable and leads him often to reverence that borders on hagiography. Of course, the chronological distance between the novels is also a distinguishing factor. Faulkner's novel was published in the first year of the Depression, contributing to the establishment of many key themes, while Steinbeck's appeared as the thirties drew to a close. *The Grapes of Wrath* thus bears witness to the suffering in medias res, striving for a level of solidarity befitting Steinbeck's commitment to radical politics and to the cause of proletarian literature. Still, the social insight of Faulkner's novel should not be ignored, for the depiction of Darl Bundren demonstrates Faulkner's capacity to glimpse the specter of revolution and to comprehend the difficulty confronting dissident forces intending to challenge the existing power structure. Based on this dimension, and on the others mentioned above, *As I Lay Dying* reads as arguably the first quintessential Depression novel.

Faulkner explores the revolutionary impulse further in perhaps the most class-conscious work in his canon. "Barn Burning" began in 1938 as a chapter of a novel-in-progress, was subsequently revised and published as a short story a year later, and then later recalled for a cameo appearance in the opening section of *The Hamlet*. Whereas class consciousness is one of many forces at work in *As I Lay Dying*, it functions as the central social and narrative conflict in "Barn Burning." The title of the story establishes this overriding theme by referencing a practice of class warfare with historical resonance and renewed symbolic value in the context of mounting populism, civil unrest, and fundamental social and political reform under the auspices of the New Deal. The story is told from the perspective of Colonel Sartoris ("Sarty") Snopes, a young boy whose coming-of-age unfolds against the backdrop of an intense political struggle shaped by the forces of a transformed socioeconomic order. The young protagonist's name—a volatile fusion of the aristocratic "Sartoris" and the sharecropping "Snopes"—reflects the opposing forces that delineate his maturity as a site of political struggle. Like Cash Bundren, Sarty must weigh the consequences of barn burning, producing a dilemma that pits family loyalty against the material concerns that define the plantocracy.

With "Barn Burning," we find Faulkner once again at the vanguard of a popular trend in American culture. In the second half of the thirties, the plight of the sharecropper was a high-profile cause in American society, inspiring a flurry of activity in the culture industry. Journalists set out to expose the brutal workings of slavery's systemic descendant in articles and photographs. With objectivity difficult to maintain in the climate of the Depression, these assignments resulted in the fusion of creative nonfiction and photography into forms anticipating the documentary film. The most enduring examples of this genre are James Agee and Walker Evans's *Let Us Now Praise Famous Men*, which began as an article for *Fortune* magazine in 1936 but wound up a book published in 1941, and Erskine Caldwell and Margaret Bourke-White's *You Have Seen Their Faces* (1937). Employing photographers such as Evans, Bourke-White, and Dorthea Lange, the Farm Security Administration amassed an impressive collection of pictures documenting the harrowing conditions endured by sharecroppers. Films such as King Vidor's *Our Daily Bread* (1934) and John Ford's adaptation of *The Grapes of Wrath* (1940), as well as March of Time newsreels, demonstrated Hollywood's social conscience on the matter and raised the awareness of the viewing public. Writers chimed in as well, giving unique voice to the plight of sharecroppers and promoting working-class solidarity able to transcend racial divisions in the interest of reform. Riding the wave of proletarian literature, Richard Wright's *Uncle Tom's Children* (1938) offered Depression readers visceral depictions of racial oppression and violence as well as utopian images of black and white sharecroppers uniting against the plantocracy, explicitly under the banner of the Communist Party. With somewhat less intensity, Sterling A. Brown's 1939 poem "Sharecroppers" similarly dramatized the cruel effects of the system and raised a coalition of black and white sharecroppers as an implied possibility, if not yet an actual social formation. As this diverse body of cultural production attests, the figure of the sharecropper was integral in the cultural politics of rural dissidence, embodying the convergent forces of agrarian tradition, class conflict, racial strife, and ideas for social and political reform. Putting Faulkner's "Barn Burning" in this cultural context reveals it to be a timely and wide-ranging examination of the historical, social, economic, and political factors contributing to incendiary conditions in rural America.

As the story begins, Faulkner turns immediately to economics, making it abundantly clear that the marketplace has become the foundation of rural society, for the narrator notes early on that the general store is where the justice of the peace presides. At the outset of the story, Sarty sits on a keg of nails in the store. Displaying an intense desire for consumption, Sarty "knew he smelled cheese, and more: from where he sat he could see the ranked shelves close-packed with the solid, squat, dynamic shapes of tin cans whose labels his stomach read" (*CS* 3). Given his Pavlovian response to the goods, Sarty would be the ideal consumer, if his place in the social hierarchy among the poverty-stricken and nomadic class of sharecroppers did not deny him the necessary purchasing power to access the market economy in general and these products in particular. The image calls to mind Walker Evans's photographs that capture the situational irony of sharecroppers surrounded by advertisements for products they could not afford. Sarty must contend with much more, however, than unfulfilled consumer desire. On the one hand, he is connected to the legendary Colonel Sartoris, who has become a powerful symbol of dominant-class hegemony; on the other hand, he bears the Snopes name and so must weigh the different version of "truth" offered by his father, Abner Snopes, who is the prime agent of social upheaval in the story. In this regard, "Barn Burning" is marked by an intensification of the dueling class sympathies that surface in *As I Lay Dying*, with the economical form of the short story bringing the issue of class conflict to the fore.

Through the course of "Barn Burning," Ab Snopes emerges as a representative of the dispossessed, speaking much more forthrightly and credibly than Anse Bundren about the plight of the small farmer in an exploitative socioeconomic system. This discrepancy when it comes to matters of social and economic justice is due in large measure to the fact that Anse owns a small tract of property and thus has at least some stake in the system, whereas Ab must rent land to make a crop and is thus subject to the inequities built materially and contractually into the system of sharecropping. For this reason, Ab feels even more powerless than Anse to exert any control over his future. Accused but not convicted of burning his landlord's barn at the beginning of the story, Ab is ordered by the court to leave the area so he will no longer remain a threat to property and thus to order and stability. Arriving on the estate of Major De Spain, his new landlord, Ab says with invective, "I reckon I'll have a word with the man that aims to begin to-morrow owning me body and soul for the next eight months" (CS 9). Instead of words, however, Ab much prefers symbolic gestures designed to register opposition to the powerful elite. So, on this particular occasion, Ab arrives with a rather pungent calling card: one of his shoes intentionally smeared with "fresh droppings" (10). Moving past the butler, a linen-clad, elderly black man whose presence calls to mind the historical alliance in the South between blacks and the planter class against poor whites, Ab soils De Spain's imported rug with "the machinelike deliberation of the foot which seemed to bear (or transmit) twice the weight the body compassed" (11). The added weight is symbolic, for Ab's gesture signals class resentment and his resistance to the ideology that confers sanctity on De Spain's property. Naturally, the soiling of the rug elicits an angry response—first from the butler and then from Mrs. De Spain. Having resisted the social pact represented by the butler in the service of De Spain, Ab now redirects his dissidence toward Mrs. De Spain as the embodiment of De Spain's estate. Ordered to leave, Ab turns abruptly on the rug, "leaving a final long and fading smear," which elicits from Mrs. De Spain a "hysteric and indistinguishable woman-wail" suggestive of a sexual violation (12). Later, Major De Spain evokes the same association, engendering his property with the ideology of "pure" southern womanhood. After issuing the terms of Ab's penalty for soiling the rug, the Major reasons that "maybe it will teach you to wipe your feet off before you enter her [Mrs. De Spain's] house again" (16).

Obviously, there is more at stake here than an expensive imported rug, which the major could presumably afford to replace. De Spain's urgency in responding to the incident reveals his recognition of the broader social significance of Ab's defiant gesture. The major knows that Ab has, symbolically at least, staged a revolt and that he must be punished in the name of preserving the respect for private property essential to upholding the social structure. First, De Spain insists that Ab restore the rug to its original condition; in this effort, the Snopeses become mechanistic devices in De Spain's apparatus. Commanded by Ab to clean the rug, his daughters scrub furiously with little regard for its condition, for the outcome resembles the work of "a lilliputian mowing machine" (CS 14). When he returns the rug to De Spain, Ab stomps on the portico with "wooden and clocklike deliberation" (15). Unsatisfied with the result, De Spain lashes out at Ab in a rejoinder that turns the rug into a gauge of economic disparity between landlord and tenant: "It cost a hundred dollars. But you never had a hundred dollars. You never will" (16). With no hope of extracting cash from Ab, De Spain instead defers to the primary source of his control over the tenant—the contractual agreement—and imposes a penalty of twenty bushels as compensation for the rug. Ab's gesture succeeds in at least one respect, then: it forces the establishment of a more material relationship between De Spain's property and the fruits of tenant labor that enabled him to purchase it. Surely knowing that his words and gestures alone will not be enough to tarnish his new landlord, the tenant seeks to employ the power of the court in order to resist De Spain and expose the unjust material reality at the base of De Spain's wealth, power, and status.

The case of *Snopes v. De Spain* is the basis of the story's second trial scene. The defendant accused of barn burning in the first trial, Ab is now the plaintiff, boldly taking his landlord to court and testing the philosophical principle that justice is blind, especially in regard to the boundaries of social class, economic means, and political clout separating the two litigants. Rendered complacent by these divisions, De Spain is shocked at Ab's public display of defiance to authority. Arriving at the courthouse on his horse, he wears an expression of "amazed unbelief" resulting from "the incredible circumstance of being sued by one of his own tenants" (CS 18). As the narrator makes clear, Sarty does not understand fully the nature of the trial; based on the limited legal precedence he knows, Sarty cries out, "He ain't done it! He ain't burnt . . ." (18). In a technical sense, the allusion to barn burning is a nice bit of foreshadowing. But it also serves well to cast Ab's legal action in a similar light, as it were. After the first trial, we learn that Ab views fire as the great equalizer; the narrator explains that "the element of fire spoke to some deep mainspring of [Ab's] being, as the element of steel or of powder spoke to other men, as the one weapon for the preservation of integrity" (8). However, in the second trial, Ab turns to the scales of justice rather than the flames of property destruction to serve as a leveling force in responding to De Spain and furthering his cause to disrupt an established order that he brands unjust and oppressive.

Instead of producing in Ab a newfound trust in the system, however, this trial only reinforces his belief that justice is blind in the sense of not seeing the endemic inequities that favor the powerful over the powerless, the landed gentry over the landless sharecroppers. Even though the verdict amounts to a reduction in the penalty, Ab's integrity suffers a blow because he is once again reminded of his inferior socioeconomic status— this time by the judge, who tells him in open court that "twenty bushels of corn seems a little high for a man in your circumstances to have to pay" (*CS* 18). The judge's decision upholds both the symbolic and material value of De Spain's property and further validates the socioeconomic system that enables him to exploit the labor of tenants like Ab as a means of garnering his wealth. As the judge sends Ab away with the admonition that "you can stand a five-dollar loss you haven't earned yet" (18), Ab is at a loss in more ways than one. Convinced that the justice system is an accomplice in the power structure that bolsters the dominant class as it exploits the tenant class, Ab knows that he must take matters into his own hands if he is to make any lasting impression on his enemy and the system that favors him. For Ab, burning De Spain's barn is the next logical step. After all, barn *razing* stands in direct contrast to barn *raising*—that longstanding agrarian tradition symbolizing communal goodwill and the hope of abundance—and thus serves the dissident Ab Snopes well in this escalating class conflict with the formidable Major De Spain.

That Faulkner should turn to barn burning as the central focus of a story in the late thirties is no coincidence, taking into account relevant historical and cultural factors. Dating back to the eighteenth century in America, barn burning was a powerful material and symbolic form of social protest for those oppressed by the systematic inequities of share-cropping and farm tenancy. In the years immediately preceding Faulkner's "Barn Burning," dissidence had reached a crescendo in rural America, particularly in the South, where the activism of groups such as the South-ern Tenant Farmers' Union (STFU) and the Share Cropper's Union (SCU) mounted resistance to authority in the name of greater social and eco-nomic justice. The STFU initially formed in opposition to the Agricultural Adjustment Act of 1933, which the organization perceived as blatantly fa-vorable to large landowners, but eventually the organization took up the cause of tenants and sharecroppers on a much broader scale. As Jerold S. Auerbach explains of the STFU, "Borrowing some of the tactics of trade unions and the fervor of religious revivals, it quickly became the share-croppers' advocate, teacher, preacher, and lobbyist" (59).[5]

Predictably, influential planters countered dissident moves by employ-ing antiunion, strong-arm tactics such as calling in political favors to have union members arrested. In an exemplary incident, the STFU activist and Methodist minister Ward Rodgers was arrested in 1935 for issuing a call to black and white sharecroppers to stage a violent uprising against planters. Rodgers was subsequently tried and convicted, not by a jury of his peers but by one of planters convened in an Arkansas general store. Although Faulkner may not have been thinking of this particular trial when he wrote "Barn Burning," he could have drawn the scenario from any number of similar incidents that took place in the mid- to late thirties, as labor activists involved with the STFU, the SCU, and others clashed with law enforcement agents acting on the prerogative of the dominant planter class. More Americans started to pay attention to the STFU as a result of the Rodgers incident and the national media coverage that it attracted. The media were especially intrigued by the tactics that local authorities employed to defuse social protest, such as ordinances banning

public speeches not receiving prior approval from officials. In part because of the heightened attention, the STFU had grown to a membership
of some twenty-five thousand by the end of 1935.

By any measure, the STFU reached its apex in 1936, a pivotal year in
which the national spotlight shone even more brightly on the union. With
a congressional investigation of alleged planter infractions under way,
the STFU felt confident enough to organize a major strike in response
to the refusal of planters to accept union wage demands. Tensions came
to a head when police broke through a line of STFU protesters blocking
entrance to the Harahan Bridge in Memphis. Strikers were arrested and
subsequently indentured to planters as a means of paying for court costs.
As a further response, the governor of Arkansas mobilized state rangers
and the National Guard to break the strike. Despite failing in its primary
objective, the STFU could take solace in the considerable headway it had
made by the end of 1936. Due in large measure to STFU activism, FDR
made a campaign promise to address problems of farm tenancy, which
he fulfilled with the passage of the Bankhead-Jones Farm Tenancy Act of
1937. At the close of 1936, the STFU had thirty-one thousand members
in seven states, including local chapters in Faulkner's Mississippi. But,
more important, the STFU had fanned the flames of social unrest and
raised the specter of class warfare—a condition that must have gained
Faulkner's attention, if "Barn Burning" is any indication.

Faulkner's "Barn Burning" represents this political struggle through
Sarty's coming-of-age, as the opposing forces represented by Ab and De
Spain try to reduce Sarty's class consciousness to a lowest common denominator in order to claim his allegiance. But Sarty is incapable of accepting such reductive possibilities, given the complicated familial and
social forces defining his path to maturity. As John T. Matthews argues,
the complexity of Sarty's dilemma "suggests that the simple plot of class
consciousness and conflict fails to cover the multiplicity of exploitative
forms in the South" ("Proletarian" 172). This complexity emerges in the
first trial scene, which marks the beginning of Sarty's initiation and the ensuing struggle to define him in terms of class consciousness. The narrator

explains that Sarty has been summoned to testify in the barn-burning case against his father. Because the primary witness is not present, the landlord is reliant on testimony from Sarty to implicate Ab. "Get that boy up here. He knows," the landlord says in response to the justice's assertion that he lacks the proof to secure a conviction (*CS* 4). Taking the stand, Sarty is confronted with the opposing forces aligned in class conflict—first, the dominant class as represented by the justice and citizen-spectators forming the gallery; second, the tenant class embodied in Ab, who resists making eye contact with his son. That Sarty bears the colonel's name lends him a note of authority in the eyes of the court, as the justice makes clear: "I reckon anybody named for Colonel Sartoris in this country can't help but tell the truth, can they?" (4). Yet Sarty knows that his father has something different in mind: "*He aims for me to lie*, he thought . . . *And I will have to do hit*" (4). As it happens, Sarty gets off the hook, thanks to the judge's appeal to the landlord not to force a young boy to implicate his father. In a relief-induced mania, Sarty hears "the voices coming up to him again through the smell of cheese and sealed meat, the fear and despair of the old grief of blood" (5). The image captures essential elements that exert influence on Sarty through the course of the story: the communal voice of the dominant class, the logic of the marketplace, and blood as a determinant of social class.

While anticlimactic, this opening trial scene is effective in describing the alternative points of view that lay claim to Sarty's allegiance. Fundamentally, Sarty must decide whether to stand in opposition *with* his father or in opposition *to* him. Initially, Sarty draws on the class resentment instilled in him by Ab, referring to the landlord as "his father's enemy" and then as "*our enemy . . . ourn! mine and hisn both! He's my father!*" (*CS* 3). Later, in the midst of the trial, Sarty draws on the same sense of animosity for strength enough to lie, referring to the justice as "*Enemy! Enemy!*" (4). Despite these strong professions of solidarity with his father and opposition to those in authority, this encounter with the justice system plants questions in Sarty's mind about his father and the path of resistance that he forges. This emerging conflict does not escape Ab's notice, as the heavy blow he delivers to Sarty after the trial confirms. Designed to knock some sense into his son, this incident instead prompts Sarty to weigh Ab's values against those expressed by the justice of the peace. In this larger context, Sarty begins to see his father as a creature of pragmatic will, a man of "wolflike independence" whose every association is formed on the principle that "his own actions would be of advantage to all whose interest lay with his" (7). Now that Sarty has witnessed, in every sense of the word, the court's appeal to truth and justice as defining principles of common discipline and order, he can contrast these ideals with his father's defiant deeds. Will Sarty accept the dominant ideology that hails him as a subject with appeals to these core principles? Or will he join his father in viewing them as tools of the powerful that must be resisted by the downtrodden in the name of survival? From Ab's perspective, the answer lies in essentialism, as his exhortation to Sarty after the trial demonstrates: "You're getting to be a man. You got to learn. You got to learn to stick to your own blood or you ain't going to have any blood to stick to you. Do you think either of them, any man there this morning would? Don't you know all they wanted was a chance to get at me because they knew I had them beat? Eh?" (8). Ironically, Ab's call for solidarity relies on a key principle that upholds the power of the dominant planter class—that is, the ideological position equating blood and class in the determination of a "natural" order of social hierarchy. For Ab, then, coming-of-age inevitably means developing class consciousness by recognizing one's place in the pecking order as the first step toward upending that order.

Facing contested definitions of "truth," "justice," and "loyalty," Sarty must consider similar questions in relation to Ab that Cash considers in relation to Darl. Is Ab's barn burning a case of vigilantism, or is it a justifiable act of resistance against oppressive forces that threaten his family's very survival? As a revolutionary figure, is Ab a brave hero fighting for the downtrodden, or is he a terrorist who threatens the order and stability of a capitalist system that holds out the best hope for opportunity? These questions raised in the text suggest that in "Barn Burning," Faulkner represents in narrative terms, as he does in *As I Lay Dying*, key elements of the political struggle unfolding in rural America. As a dynamic force, this political struggle has much the same effect on the text as it does on rural social order and the nation as a whole, bringing disruption and resulting in a state of conflict, upheaval, and anxiety.

Shaped by class divisions, the alternative perspectives represented in "Barn Burning" contribute to a form that can be described as polyphonic. Mikhail Bakhtin's concept of polyphony applies to texts that feature multiple voices interacting in relative discursive autonomy, in contrast to the monologic kind, which are dominated by one voice or perspective. In the polyphonic form, Bakhtin argues, a character can declare independence from the author, taking advantage of the considerable freedom inherent in the textual dynamic. With Dostoevsky as his model, Bakhtin explains that the author of the polyphonic text "creates not voiceless slaves but *free* people, capable of standing *alongside* their creator, capable of agreeing with him and even rebelling against him" (6). In "Barn Burning," Ab Snopes aspires to this condition, exerting a level of independence that threatens to undermine the prerogative of the dominant class and, in turn, alters the form of the text by engendering polyphony. Fittingly, Bakhtin elaborates on this concept in language that fuses analysis of aesthetics and ideology to describe a condition of textual politics. Accordingly, for Bakhtin, the polyphonic text is "a unification of highly heterogeneous and incompatible material . . . with the plurality of consciousness-centers not reduced to a single ideological common denominator" (17). Inherent in Bakhtin's paradigm is a fundamental tension between individual wills and "a unity of a higher order" (21), which makes for striking parallels between the textual condition of polyphony and the political system of democracy. In much the same way that established order in democracy seeks to prevent pluralism from becoming Balkanization, Bakhtinian unity seeks to prevent multiplicity from becoming chaos in the realm of the text. These associations provide useful means of exploring how "Barn Burning," to borrow the words of Bakhtin, represents "not the rising or descending course of an individual personality, but the *condition of society*" (27). Furthermore, Bakhtin's theory illuminates how "Barn Burning" participates in the political process of negotiating and ordering alternative perspectives, exposing the influence of social reality as a constitutive element of its form.

Similarities between polyphony in "Barn Burning" and democracy are evident in the struggle for power taking place in the text. This struggle becomes so fierce, in fact, that it compels the narrator's enlistment, as demonstrated by an increasingly explicit alignment with the dominant ideology. This significant development becomes apparent in the first trial scene, immediately after the justice delivers his verdict to Ab: "Leave this country and don't come back to it" (*CS* 5). Tellingly, the narrator defies the presumption of objectivity inscribed in the narrative form by recording Ab's response with a noticeable bias: "[Ab] spoke for the first time, his voice cold and harsh, level, without emphasis: 'I aim to. I don't figure to stay in a country among people who . . .' he said something unprintable and vile, addressed to no one" (5). Why is Ab's statement "unprintable"? By what standards does the narrator justify this censorship? In this instance, the narrator's silencing of Ab—literally denying him a voice—is both an aesthetic maneuver and a political statement, for it shapes the form of the text to validate the logic of the dominant class, as exhibited in the justice's decision to remove Ab as a potential threat to social order.

Though silenced in this instance, Ab is resilient enough to challenge the multiple layers of authority working to suppress his views on social injustice. Already we have witnessed Ab's talent for the defiant gesture, but he is also capable of articulating incisive statements that expose flaws in the dominant ideology. When Ab and Sarty arrive at the De Spain estate, for example, the narrator attempts to coerce Sarty with the ideological prerogative of the dominant class. Faced with the vista of De Spain's mansion, Sarty supposedly feels "*the spell of this peace and dignity*" (*CS* 10). As Ab moves toward the front steps, the narrator insists that Sarty longs for his father to feel the same way: "*Maybe he will feel it too. Maybe it will even change him now from what he couldn't help but be*" (11). The emphatic use of italics reflects the narrator's coercive attempt to condition Sarty's developing class consciousness so that the young boy understands

De Spain's position to be part of a greater good, a "natural" order. True to the story's polyphonic form, however, the narrator stands repeatedly challenged by Ab—for example, when he undermines the "spell" by exposing the material history of De Spain's mansion: "That's Nigger sweat. Nigger sweat. Maybe it ain't white enough to suit him. Maybe he wants some white sweat with it" (12). This statement is the verbal stain prefiguring the aforementioned literal one that Ab smears on the rug with so much symbolic value. These competing perspectives invite associations between text and context. In terms of rural politics, for instance, Ab's statement points to the possibility of interracial sympathy and even solidarity among sharecroppers; the narrator's anxiety and repressive tactics, in turn, mirror the response of the planter class in its determination to prevent such an alliance from taking shape.

The narrator's alignment with De Spain in the struggle to win Sarty's favor and the social and racial divisions that the story leaves intact distinguish "Barn Burning" from other forms of cultural expression dramatizing the issue of sharecropping in the Depression. Richard Wright's "Fire and Cloud" serves as a particularly instructive example. Published in *Uncle Tom's Children*, "Fire and Cloud" was heavily influenced by the political activities of the SCU in rural Alabama. Drawing on the conventions of proletarian literature, Wright tells the story of a fledgling attempt to form a union by mobilizing the rural poor in social protest against oppression and economic exploitation. For much of the story, "Reds" pressure a rural black minister, Dan Taylor, to endorse the organizational effort as a means of ensuring its credibility and bolstering the numbers of union members and sympathizers. Despite early visions of a throng of marchers dissipating the "white fog" of dominant-class hegemony and an admission to himself that "mabbe them Reds *is* right," Taylor remains reluctant to join the cause officially (158). However, after a vigilante band of whites intent on suppressing union activity kidnaps and brutally whips Taylor, leaving him for dead on the side of the road, he realizes that he and his people must fight back.

In Faulkner's story, as we have seen, Ab's defiance of authority produces considerable anxiety, contributing both to the narrator's involvement in the political struggle and the polyphonic form of the text. The third-person narrator in Wright's story is also drawn away from the objective position and into the intensifying conflict. Unlike Faulkner's narrator, however, Wright's clearly joins the cause of the downtrodden who are trying to mount resistance. Once again, this altered point of view manifests in terms of form. For example, section 7 of "Fire and Cloud" ends with an objective rendering of the scene, as the narrator describes Taylor in the third person: "He lay still, barely breathing, looking at the blurred white faces in the semi-darkness of the roaring car" (195). Section 8, though, has an abrupt shift in perspective in rendering Taylor's predicament, as the narrator describes the aftermath of the beating: "He was confused; it might have been five minutes or it might have been an hour. The car slowed again, turning. He smelt the strong scent of a burning cigarette and heard the sound of other cars, gears shifting and motors throbbing. We mus be at some crossroads. But he could not guess which one" (195). In a form that enacts the political philosophy of collectivism, the governing voice of the story represents the individual dilemma, speaking not just *for* the subject but *with* him, as the shift to first-person plural signals. This fusion of narrator and subject becomes an integral component of the story's form, adding support to its overarching social and political themes. Indicatively, the narrator further describes Taylor's woeful condition: "He found himself on his knees; he had not known when he had started falling; he just found himself on his knees. Lawd, Ahm weak!" (202). It appears that the narrator is quoting Taylor at the end, but the absence of quotation marks removes the separation, the line of division, between them, allowing Taylor's individual condition to be mutually felt and expressed. In contrast to the polyphonic form of Faulkner's story, which frames individual voices locked in intense opposition, Wright's story converges toward monologic condition, representing in terms of narrative form the ideals of collectivism informing the rhetoric of the New Deal and, to a much greater extent, the political movements urging it further leftward.

In contrast to Faulkner's representation of fire as a harbinger of entrenched division, Wright's is a variation on the biblical concept of the transforming flame—in this case, enabling a spiritual and political progression from individual suffering to communal action. With Taylor feeling the crack of the whip, the narrator explains that "the fire flamed all over his body," placing the stress on the isolated experience (200). For Taylor, the fire then turns to righteous indignation forged into an image conveyed with an apocalyptic fervor that the dominant-class sympathies of Faulkner's narrator in "Barn Burning" preclude: "Like a pillar of fire he went through the white neighborhood. Some day theys gonna burn! Some day theys gonna burn in Gawd Awmightys fire! How come they make us suffer so? . . . Fire fanned his hate; he stopped and looked at the burning stars" (204). Marking yet another stage in the progression, Taylor rejoins his family and parishioners a changed man, feeling now "the fire of shame"—a seething anguish over his prior lack of political consciousness (206). But this shame quickly turns into a more productive force, for in Wright's story, as in Faulkner's, the individual consciousness of a child provides a space for defining social and political identity in the context of a broader struggle. Trumpeting his newfound conviction, Taylor prefigures Tom Joad in his exhortation to his young son, Jimmy, that "it's the *people*! Theys the ones whut must be real t us! Gawds wid the people! N the peoples gotta be real as Gawd t us!" (210). Taylor realizes, then, that he must leave the "fiery spot of loneliness" to walk among his people, fanning the flames of inspiration in the community (212). As Taylor tells the throng gathered to march in protest, "Ah cant bear this fire erlone! Ah know whut to do! Wes gotta git close to one ernother! Gawds done spoke! Gods done sent His sign. Now its fer us t ack. . . ." (218). With idealistic zeal, Wright depicts a moment of supreme integration, as a crowd of poor whites merges with the already marching blacks to form a "sea of black and white faces" protesting social injustice (220). "Fire and Cloud" thus culminates in a fully realized representation of the racial solidarity that Ab Snopes points to only indirectly and fleetingly, thus exposing a wide gap between Faulkner's approach and that of writers aligned with proletarian literature.[6]

Conventions of the coming-of-age narrative dictate that the young protagonist endure a trial by fire. For Sarty, that condition holds true both literally and figuratively. Because Sarty's maturity is contested space in a raging class war, the outcome of his initiation is sure to be fraught with political implications. As Faulkner's story draws to a close, the salient question thus becomes: To what extent does Faulkner reconcile the issue of Sarty's divided loyalty? The easy answer, perhaps, is that Sarty's decision to warn De Spain of the imminent barn burning signals that the "spell" has worked its "magic" by luring Sarty away from his father's cause. But matters are rarely so simple in Faulkner's Yoknapatawpha. "Barn Burning" ends instead with Sarty's loyalty still in question. Indicatively, he responds to the gunshots ringing in the distance—for him, announcements of his father's death—by internally eulogizing Ab as a "brave" soldier. Predictably, the narrator intervenes to undermine this sentiment, using supposedly omnipotent attribution to assign "definitive" interpretations to Ab's motivations. For instance, the narrator explains that Sarty would one day come to understand that his father's penchant for barn burning (i.e., his disregard for the concept of private property) was an extension of his exploits during the Civil War, when, according to the narrator, Ab stole horses. In other words, Sarty will one day come to view Ab from the same perspective as the narrator and, by way of association, the dominant class. At the end of the story, when Sarty recalls Ab's military service and declares that "he was brave!" the narrator undermines this sentiment by noting that Ab "had gone to that war a private in the fine old European sense, wearing no uniform, admitting the authority of and giving fidelity to no man or army or flag, going to war as Malbrouck himself did: for booty—it meant nothing and less than nothing to him if it were enemy or booty of his own" (*CS* 24–25). The narrator's interjection works to qualify Sarty's show of respect for his father and to render Ab an unscrupulous individualist rather than a representative of an exploited sharecropping class with cause to revolt against an oppressive system. The narrator's enlistment vividly illustrates at the level of form the ideological imperative of the dominant class to restrain revolutionary forces in the context of unresolved class conflict.

Still, in a story that relies so heavily on judicial metaphor, the jury remains out on whether the effort to suppress Ab's dissidence and thus to restore social and textual order is ultimately successful. Ab's presumed death at the hands of De Spain might be read to signal the victory of restraint over revolution and perhaps even suggest Faulkner's alignment with De Spain. But that would involve imposing rather than inferring a resolution to a conflict that remains, in the context of prevailing literary sentiments in the thirties, woefully unresolved. For this reason, "Barn Burning" offers further evidence of the complexity, contradiction, and even ambivalence that attends Faulkner's treatments of class conflict in rural America. Consider, for example, Faulkner's judgment to displace the barn burning and Ab's encounter with De Spain. Rather than depicting this violent moment vividly, as Faulkner most certainly could have done, he filters the scene through Sarty's perception and thus creates the aesthetic effect of distance and ambiguity. This effect extends the polyphonic form of the text to its very conclusion. For, in the end, Sarty apparently still feels what the narrator earlier calls "the old fierce pull of blood" (*CS* 3), as suggested by the need to redeem his father as a brave soldier. Of course, Ab's legacy calls Sarty to the path of *most* resistance, even after he has sacrificed his father to the "justice" of the planter class. Nevertheless, Sarty's response to the impossible choice he faces is to run away, disappearing into the darkness of his own undeclared allegiance. And, we are told, "he did not look back" (25). Eluding expectations that come with the *bildungsroman* tradition, Sarty, like Huck Finn before him, flees from initiation in the form of socialization. In this respect, Sarty joins his father in exemplifying Bakhtin's theory of the character as independent agent. Without definitive resolution, "Barn Burning" records a contradictory response to the pending social and political issues that Faulkner directly engages. In so doing, Faulkner renders the cultural politics of rural dissidence with a kind of realism cast aside in the utopian endeavors of social realism, which progressed all too often toward foregone conclusions. The uncertain outcome of "Barn Burning" offers not only this reading but also at least one plausible explanation as to why Faulkner, unlike Sarty, is compelled to "look back."

By the time Faulkner revised and incorporated "Barn Burning" into *The Hamlet*, the first installment of the Snopes trilogy, the Depression had entered its twilight. At the time Faulkner was working in earnest on the novel, the Nazi-Soviet Pact, coupled with Franco's victory in Spain, had tempered the political idealism of the Left. The tidal wave of activism that had advanced the Popular Front in the mid-1930s was now part of the orderly current of the New Deal. In rural America, populist fervor had subsided; in the South, the STFU and the SCU had disbanded due to internal politics and reforms that diminished public concerns over the injustices of sharecropping. As the thirties gave way to the forties, rural Americans were less inclined to the revolutionary side of the equation, especially since the New Deal had come through sufficiently, if not always efficiently, with relief as well as measurable improvements in people's lives through ambitious initiatives such as the Civilian Conservation Corps (CCC), the Tennessee Valley Authority (TVA), and the Rural Electrification Association (REA). Now, with America on the road to recovery, attention turned from social protest and the specter of revolution to matters of social policy and political reform. In particular, the social contract implicit in the New Deal became a focal point of political debate. During the worst years of the Depression, warnings about the harmful effects of federal relief had largely fallen on deaf ears. But now there was mounting concern, primarily in the higher sectors of the dominant class, that the New Deal would become irrevocably entrenched in the federal government and in the American psyche. The renewed sense of confidence attending economic recovery inspired appeals for Americans to recall the virtue of self-reliance and to resist the cycle of dependency cited as a by-product of federal relief. Faulkner's revision of "Barn Burning" for *The Hamlet* reveals a progression in concern that coincides remarkably with

the general shift in contemporaneous political debate from issues of social protest to questions of social policy influenced as ever by ideological
conceptions of the relationship between the individual and the state.

In revising "Barn Burning" as the closing episode in the first section of
The Hamlet, Faulkner preserves most of the details from the published
short story. For example, Ab's symbolic gesture of soiling the expensive
rug still signals his incendiary act of class warfare coming in the final
stages of the story. More remarkable are the variations that differenti-
ate one incarnation of the story from the next. Such revision had by this
time become a habitual pattern for Faulkner, as he quite frequently incorporated previously published stories, often written hastily for money,
into the narrative frameworks of his novels. Richard C. Moreland identifies two tendencies in Faulkner's method of revision—either a Freudian
compulsive repetition that resists new critical insight or what Moreland
calls "revisionary repetition." In the case of the latter, Moreland explains,
Faulkner "repeats some structured event, in order somehow to alter that
structure and its continuing power, especially by opening a critical space
for what the subject might *learn* about that structure in the different context of a changing present or a more distant or different past" (4). By
these standards, Faulkner's move from representing the complex nature
of class warfare in "Barn Burning" toward a critical space for examining
a potential remedy in *The Hamlet* qualifies as an instance of revisionary
repetition. That remedy, historically speaking, was the use of federal relief
to temper class conflict and resentment. Despite initial wariness of relief
as a sort of social anesthetic, FDR and Congress were committed to this
tactic by the latter half of the thirties. As unemployment continued to soar
in 1938 after yet another substantial drop in the value of the stock market,
FDR asked Congress for $3 billion to bolster relief agencies such as the
WPA and the FSA; Congress responded with $3.75 billion, and economic
indicators rose within a few months (McElvaine 299; Leuchtenburg 249–
51). This condition of public policy shapes the critical space opened up in
the revision of "Barn Burning," suggesting Faulkner's concern over what
many in the Depression era viewed as a relief-for-peace mentality in con-

structing social policy. Consequently, the complex and palpable tale of class warfare that is "Barn Burning" takes a variant form in *The Hamlet*, reading on one level as a cautionary tale about imperiled self-reliance.

When Faulkner incorporates the events of "Barn Burning" into the opening section of *The Hamlet*, he jettisons the *bildungsroman* in favor of an extended homage to Southwestern Humor that spans the novel, as critics have noted. In this version, the traveling salesman V. K. Ratliff assumes, as he so often does, the storytelling duty within the novel's broader narrative frame.[7] Ratliff recounts the saga of Snopes versus De Spain to a gathering of men on the front porch of Will Varner's general store—the center of commerce and social order in Frenchman's Bend—and then later to Will himself. Sarty bears only brief mention, as Ratliff notes his absence from the Abner Snopes clan and then wonders if the boy has been "mislaid in one of them movings" (26). The condescending and ironic tone employed by Ratliff marks him as a descendant of the narrators found in tales of Southwestern Humor. This genre was politically charged in its original historical and cultural context, with its popular frontier sketches staging a conservative brand of cultural politics in the nineteenth century. Southwestern Humor was active in mounting opposition to Andrew Jackson's vigorous championing of the backwoods "common man" for the stated purpose of realizing America's democratic ideals more fully. A fundamental assumption was inscribed in the form of these tales: that the reader would join with the narrator in a laugh at the expense of the "unsophisticated" subjects, thus forming a pact of mutually understood superiority. Given this cultural history, Faulkner's turn to the genre in the context of the Depression—a time of professed, if not always practiced, concern for uplifting the "forgotten man"—begs the question of whether *The Hamlet* has not only formal but also ideological affinity with its literary forebears.

Faulkner's revision of "Barn Burning" for *The Hamlet* offers a productive means of considering this complex issue. In key respects, the revised story does show traces of Southwestern Humor's political conservatism and ideological endorsement of the ruling elite. Under Ratliff's supervision, for example, the airing of Ab's grievances and the sympathy for his plight pronounced in the original story are missing. While the polyphonic form of "Barn Burning" gives Ab's revolutionary sentiments impetus and agency, the monologic imperative of the revised story, resulting from Ratliff's aspiration to narrative dominance, works to defuse them. Reminiscent of his ancestors in Southwestern Humor, Ratliff tries, often with the aid of *The Hamlet*'s supposedly objective narrator, to cast the Snopeses as the base, mysterious, and innately unscrupulous Other. Consider, for example, how Ratliff transforms the story of Ab's alleged arson into a cautionary tale about the dangers of doing business with a Snopes. Concerned over having done just that, Jody Varner repeatedly interjects the apocalyptic phrase, "Hell fire," exhibiting a noticeably high level of Snopes anxiety induced by Ratliff's rhetorical use of the story. In the wake of this tale, Jody emerges as a fusion of Cash and Jewel Bundren, expressing both chronic ambivalence and an urgent desire to protect his property: "Hell fire. I dont dare say Leave here, and I aint got nowhere to say Go there. I dont even dare have him arrested for fear he'll set my barn afire" (*H* 20). Subsequently, Jody seeks to resolve the dilemma through appeasement, granting Flem's request for a clerking job in the general store. This arrangement is forged under the implicit threat of arson and stands as tenuous at best, if we read Jody's extending and Flem's refusing the offer of a cigar to be a variation on the proverbial sharing of the peace pipe. Ratliff calls the agreement "a fire insurance policy"—a derisive interpretation that differs from Jody's more positive spin on it as "benefits" paid to keep the peace and to grant Flem his independence from sharecropping (25, 27).

Faulkner's pointed references to insurance and benefits in describing this "new deal" between Varner and Snopes resonate more forcefully when placed in the context of that other one being struck at the time of the novel's production to administer direct relief payments and crop subsidies by the federal government to rural folks in need. Advocates of the poor and opponents of the sharecropping system—the STFU, the SCU, and more mainstream organizations, for example—had played an important role in securing these benefits by forcing the issue of social injustice in rural America. As a work of fiction, *The Hamlet* is, of course, more than just a response to a relief-for-peace social philosophy. Nevertheless, we can see in *The Hamlet* Faulkner's recurring use of barn burning highlighting a political conviction in formation. For example, Ratliff's opposition to the hand-up given to Flem—a move Ratliff views as a cowardly handout in response to blackmail—registers an ideological response to debates over the continued viability of the New Deal. This episode also serves as a harbinger in the context of Faulkner's evolving political convictions, prefiguring the impassioned defenses of self-reliance and the harsh attacks against the welfare state that the post–Nobel Prize Faulkner would deliver time and time again. Anxiety over a social order transformed by the desire to get something for nothing is signaled even further by the upending of Southwestern Humor's familiar form. In a complete role reversal, Ratliff finds himself the butt of the joke by novel's end—framed by Flem Snopes and fodder for a comic spectacle, he obsessively delves into the soil for nonexistent treasure, digging himself deeper and deeper, as it were.

As the nation moved from the devastation of the Depression toward war-induced economic recovery, indictments of enduring federal relief projects grew more vocal. Without the urgency of the Depression, many reasoned, these projects lacked sufficient justification and served to perpetuate an underclass dependent on the dole and thus deprived of individual liberty. Taking this line of reasoning, Faulkner issues with his short story "The Tall Men" (1941) an explicit warning against an intrusive federal government—referred to repeatedly in the story as "the Government"—intent on manipulating rural folk and folkways through social engineering. As in "Barn Burning," characters can be read, on one level, to embody certain contemporaneous ideological positions; thus the form of the story serves as a symbolic arena for the political struggle between them. At the outset, "The Tall Men" features local and federal authorities in opposition, represented respectively by the Yoknapatawpha sheriff's marshal, who becomes a chronicler through the course of the story, and the federal investigator on hand to arrest the McCallum twins for evading Selective Service registration. The McCallums are drawn directly from the myth of the yeoman farmer. They are cast as a salt-of-the-earth farming family resistant to federal relief or intervention, preferring instead to live by the credo spoken by Buddy McCallum to a federal farm subsidy agent: "We can make out" (*CS* 57).[8]

The fiercely independent McCallums would have been well suited to another work called "The Tall Men"—staunch Southern Agrarian Donald Davidson's epic poem of the 1920s, which reads as a panegyric to the mythic yeoman farmers and pioneers of Tennessee. Faulkner's short story shares more in common with Davidson's poem than a title; in fact, the story's primary themes of rugged individualism and dogged resistance to what is perceived as monolithic federal authority seem to have been lifted from Southern Agrarianism. This similarity is surprising, given that Faulkner had maintained a safe distance from his regional counterparts. After all, Faulkner was less prone than they to romanticize the southern way of life at the expense of exposing its troubling history. Nevertheless, Faulkner's "The Tall Men" represents an affiliation with the brand of defiance that emerged in *I'll Take My Stand* and progressed through the thirties as an alternative to leftist programs of social and economic reform.

While Southern Agrarianism opposed much of the agenda supported by the STFU, these two resistance movements did share a common enemy in industrialism, which both viewed as a threat to the rural way of life. In addition, both movements expressed a solid commitment to land reform and repeatedly opposed New Deal farm policy. What separated them, however, was a fundamental difference in ideological perspective. As Steve Brown and Jess Gilbert explain, the Southern Agrarians "sought to *reestablish* a Jeffersonian society of individual, independent property owners, one comprised substantially of a single class," while the STFU "looked *forward* to transcending the private property system altogether, toward the cooperative commonwealth" (196–97). In Faulkner's "The Tall Men," the federal investigator's consciousness becomes the disputed territory, much like Sarty's in "Barn Burning," as the text represents this ideological conflict between individualism and collectivism and moves toward definitive resolution and, presumably, foregone conclusion.

When the investigator first appears in the story, he reveals a prejudice against the hill farmers that apparently evolved during his previous work as a relief agent for the WPA. In a lengthy lament, the agent rails against *"these people who lie about and conceal the ownership of land and property in order to hold relief jobs"* (CS 46). Not inclined toward the myth of the yeoman farmer as the embodiment of the region he has come to visit, the agent rather prefers the acquisitive charlatan out to manipulate the relief system for individual profit—the same kind of interpretation that the narrator of "Barn Burning" offers of Ab Snopes. The use of italics calls special attention to the prejudicial views of the investigator, who remains nameless in the story—a feature that upholds his bureaucratic anonymity and his belief in following the letter, rather than the spirit, of the law. The dominance of the investigator's point of view in the story, however, is short lived, as he winds up a straw man in relation to the marshal. Like Sarty, the investigator faces an initiation; however, in "The Tall Men," the nature of this process is much less ambiguous.

The primary reason for this clarity is the dominant ideological position that the marshal achieves through the course of the story. In an extended direct quotation, the marshal effectively assumes control of the narrative and thus claims the moral authority to offer the investigator an object lesson in transcending statistical data and bureaucratic procedure as a means of recognizing the inherent value of individualism. This formal decision precludes alternative points of view, working to render the text monologic. The empowered marshal attempts to sway the investigator as he chronicles the history of the McCallum family in an account noticeably influenced by the yeoman myth and fraught with ideological imperatives rooted in self-reliance and local control. For example, the marshal pinpoints Buddy McCallum's decision to quit raising cotton by noting that "it was when the Government first begun to interfere with how a man farmed his own land, raised his cotton. Stabilizing the price, using up the surplus, they called it, giving a man advice and help, whether he wanted it or not" (*CS* 55). According to the marshal, the McCallums refused to participate in the federal stabilization program because "they just couldn't believe that the Government aimed to help a man whether he wanted help or not, aimed to interfere with how much of anything he could make by hard work on his own land, making the crop and ginning it right here in their own gin, like they had always done" (56). Resonant with the rhetoric of self-reliance, this passage means to expose the logical fallacies of stabilization program policy by the light of McCallum common sense, which the marshal defines and projects.

From the marshal's standpoint, the refusal of the McCallums to participate in the federal program, resulting in the production of two cotton crops prevented from sale on the market, is an indicator of the vast distance between the abstraction of federal policy and the reality of farming. One consequence the marshal identifies is a work ethic endangered by "a fine loud grabble and snatch of AAA [Agricultural Adjustment Act] and WPA and a dozen other three-letter reasons for a man not to work" (*CS* 58). But, on a more philosophical note, he expresses concern that federal intervention diminishes the value of the individual. The marshal thus admonishes the investigator: "The trouble is, we done got into the habit of confusing the situations with the folks. . . . You just went and got yourself all fogged up with rules and regulations. That's our trouble. We done invented so many alphabets and rules and recipes that we can't see anything else; if what we see can't be fitted to an alphabet or a rule, we are lost" (59). This passage calls to mind the critique offered in the introduction to *I'll Take My Stand*, as the Agrarians warn of "super-engineers" intent on denying individual liberty in the name of collectivism (xli). The marshal's implicit plea for empiricism here is punctuated with the burial scene at the end of the story. Buddy McCallum's amputated leg is a visceral symbol of the considerable sacrifices he has made as a toiling small farmer trying to provide for his family and as a veteran of World War I now faced with the prospect of losing his sons in the next major conflict taking shape. Burying this symbol of Buddy's sacrifice, the marshal exhorts, "Life has done got cheap, and life ain't cheap. Life's a pretty durn valuable thing. I don't mean just getting along from one WPA relief check to the next one, but honor and pride and discipline that make a man worth preserving, make him of any value. That's what we got to learn again" (*CS* 61). Aside from the explicit ideological position, the tone of this passage is reminiscent of the most overtly political art produced by advocates of social realism and suggests apparent resolution, in a relatively brief span, of the intense conflict represented in "Barn Burning."

Placing the two stories in juxtaposition, an immediate paradox emerges with respect to issues of representation. In "Barn Burning," the small farmer is a threat to established order; in "The Tall Men," the established order, exemplified by the New Deal, is a threat to the small farmer. Why the complete reversal? There is, of course, the argument that different stories call for different scenarios. But contextual forces are more likely contributing factors, especially taking into account that both stories are essentially written from the perspective of the dominant class. For this reason, it is not surprising that "Barn Burning" is so conflicted, reflecting as it does the fear, turbulence, and ambivalence that surfaced in response to rural dissidence. However, once a sense of order had been restored— or once the farmer had uncocked his rifle, to revise V. F. Calverton's phrase—the farmer could seem from the perspective of the dominant class more threatened than threatening. "The Tall Men" illustrates this point vividly in terms of form and tone. Renewed economic security and social stability offered Faulkner the luxury of extolling once again, with all the passion of a Southern Agrarian, the ideal of the yeoman farmer as a model of rugged individualism rather than a peasant with a pitchfork—or, more to the point, a torch. In keeping with its time, "The Tall Men" radiates with recovered self-assurance, upholding self-reliance as an inherent American virtue under threat of dilution by New Deal collectivism. The divided loyalties driving Cash's and Sarty's tormented introspection thus seem all too easily resolved.

Sentiments expressed by the marshal in "The Tall Men" sound much like the Faulkner to come—the resurrected, post-*Portable* Faulkner of the forties and fifties who emerged from the Great Depression as a vocal advocate of classical liberalism's fundamental tenets of self-reliance and local control. This explicit political conviction was a departure, however, from the ambivalent agrarianism of the thirties so reflective of Faulkner's reluctance to take a clear stand in the midst of socioeconomic crisis and culture war. Unlike the Southern Agrarians to his right and Steinbeck, Caldwell, and Wright to his left, Faulkner charted a moderate approach to the plight of rural America in the thirties—a move seemingly out of touch with the times. In retrospect, though, we can understand how this vantage point gave Faulkner a more comprehensive view of the Depression, yielding nuanced, complex, and at times contradictory treatments of social relations. Engaging the cultural politics of rural dissidence, Faulkner offered to Depression readers complex alternatives to the depictions found in revitalized social realism or, more to the point, newly minted proletarian literature of the thirties. By the light of burning barns, Faulkner's brand of realism exposed the obstacles to fundamental change so many of his critics on the left simply refused to acknowledge: that the farmer with his rifle cocked was more a product of political rhetoric than a reflection of social reality, that the downtrodden and dispossessed in rural America were conflicted in their class consciousness—aspiring upward even as they were beaten down—and that, for all these reasons and more, the revolution was not likely to come. After all, as Faulkner vividly demonstrates in *The Hamlet*, Flem Snopes is not about to set a match to Jody Varner's barn as long as he has in mind owning it someday.

Destruction and Reconstruction

Faulkner's Civil War and the Politics of Recovery

AT THE TIME Faulkner was at work on one of the stories that would eventually become a section of *The Unvanquished*, he wrote to his agent, "As far as I am concerned, while I have to write trash, I dont care who buys it, as long as they can pay the best price I can get" (Blotner, *Selected Letters* 84). Once again, apparently, the two-track writing process was at work, for Faulkner wrote this "trash" during intermittent breaks in the composition of a masterpiece, *Absalom, Absalom!* Initial reception of the two novels favored *The Unvanquished*, but literary history has turned the tables. Richard Gray offers a concise assessment of the reputation of *The Unvanquished* in relation to its formidable counterpart. "Despite attempts by several recent commentators to rehabilitate the book as either a trenchant narrative of maturing or, more personally, the work in which

Faulkner finally came to terms with his father figure," Gray observes, "it is difficult to accept any large claims for its achievement, as either a series of tales or a connected narrative" (227). Gray's contention that *The Unvanquished* is a shadow of *Absalom*, treating many of its key themes but in "radically diminished terms," echoes a common charge (227).[1]

Granted, on the basis of literary achievement defined by distinctions between "high" and "low" art, *The Unvanquished* undoubtedly suffers by comparison to *Absalom*. However, if we put the comparison aside in the interest of reading *The Unvanquished* not just as art but as cultural artifact, then its value increases exponentially—much like that of *Mosquitoes*, as argued in chapter 1. *The Unvanquished* thus reads not merely as an inferior novel in Faulkner's oeuvre but, like *Sanctuary* before it, as a testament to his keen understanding of American popular culture and his savvy use of its trends and lexicon to weigh in on the cultural politics of the day. In the case of *The Unvanquished*, Faulkner taps into a popular project of cultural memory aimed at viewing the concerns of the Depression through the historical lens of the Civil War, focused specifically on the forces of destruction and reconstruction common to both events. Consequently, a compendium of Depression themes is inscribed in the form and content of *The Unvanquished*, rendering it both a productive text for reflecting, in conclusion, on issues examined in this study and, in broader terms, a revealing document of American cultural history. In short, then, reading the politics of Depression recovery into Faulkner's Civil War offers a means of transforming *The Unvanquished* from literary "trash" into something of a cultural treasure.

During the Depression, Americans could find cultural representations of the Civil War in abundance. Several novels appeared on the scene— among them, T. S. Stribling's *The Forge* (1931), *Unfinished Cathedral* (1934), and *The Sound Wagon* (1936); Roark Bradford's *Kingdom Coming* (1933); Caroline Gordon's *None Shall Look Back* (1937); Allen Tate's *The Fathers* (1938); Stark Young's *So Red the Rose* (1934); and, of course, Margaret Mitchell's *Gone with the Wind* (1936). Getting in on the game,

Hollywood produced a bevy of films set during the Civil War. A renewed interest in Abraham Lincoln was reflected in D. W. Griffith's *Abraham Lincoln* (1930) and John Ford's *Young Mr. Lincoln* (1939) and *Abe Lincoln in Illinois* (1940). Stressing reconciliation of "a house divided," *Operator 13* (1934) gave audiences Marion Davies as a Union spy who falls in love with a Confederate soldier, played by Gary Cooper. Shirley Temple and Bill ("Bojangles") Robinson sang and danced against a historical backdrop in *The Littlest Rebel* (1935) and *The Little Colonel* (1935). Films with romanticized depictions of the war included *Jezebel* (1938), starring Bette Davis; *So Red the Rose* (1934), a rushed production based on Young's novel; and, towering above them all, the film adaptation of *Gone with the Wind* (1939), which won a record ten Oscars and added allure to the Golden Year of Hollywood cinema. One national crisis, it seems, prompted American cultural memory to reflect on another as a way of coping with the hardship and hoping for recovery. Depictions of the war thus became active sites for staging cultural politics—spaces for expressing frustration, despair, and uncertainty over Depression suffering, for responding to pressing social, political, and economic issues, and for renegotiating terms for the future of American economy and society. As such, these cultural forms reveal to us now as much—or even more, in some cases—about the time in which they were produced as the historical period represented in them.

For leftists in Depression culture, looking back to the nineteenth century yielded models for emulation in the ongoing effort to achieve a radical fusion of art and politics. Laura Browder offers a thorough and insightful study of this phenomenon in *Rousing the Nation: Culture in Depression America*. Referring to the Civil War and the Depression as "America's two great national dramas," Browder suggests that "it is unsurprising that writers and artists of the thirties, especially those of a radical stripe, often identified strongly with their Civil War counterparts" (1). Browder cites Harriet Beecher Stowe as a prime example of this influence: "Like abolitionist writers before them, radical American writers of the thirties were conscious of the import of their historical moment and of the need to persuade a wide readership of the justice of their cause" (2). For Depression writers involved in the literary class war, as discussed in chapter 2, a fundamental challenge was to make literature an agent of social and political change. For proletarian writers, Stowe's case could be both inspirational and instructive, serving as a testament to the potential for fiction not only to be shaped by immediate social and political conditions but also to reshape them. Mindful of this connection, we can trace a line from Civil War to Depression culture war, with representations of the past informing political discourse in the present.

When moving from left to right on the spectrum of cultural politics, we find further evidence of this transition, dating back to the period of Reconstruction when the southern cult of the Lost Cause surfaced to profess the superiority of agrarian values over the crass materialism resulting from alleged northern genuflection at the altar of industrialism. The South might have lost the military phase of the war, according to the ideological claim, but it would continue to mount resistance on the cultural front. The Twelve Southerners set the terms of this extended conflict for the thirties in the introduction to *I'll Take My Stand*: "Nobody now proposes for the South, or for any other community in this country, an independent political destiny. That idea is thought to have been finished in 1865. But how far shall the South surrender its moral, social, and economic autonomy to the victorious principle of Union?" (x). Presuming to speak for the region as a unified whole, the Southern Agrarians declare in no uncertain terms that the South "scarcely hopes to determine the other sections, but it does propose to determine itself, within the utmost kind of life" and to resist fervently attempts to make the South "an undistinguished replica of the usual industrial community" (x). Because the Agrarians' message was inherently regionalist, separatist, and, at times, racist, their extension of the Civil War into the realm of culture war defined by resistance to industrialism and the "cult of Science," as they cited repeatedly, had the effect of limiting the appeal of their conservative gospel.

Precisely where the Southern Agrarians failed, however, Margaret Mitchell succeeded by leaps and bounds. Mitchell's *Gone with the Wind*, in both novel and film adaptation form, was able to transcend the constraints of regionalism by conveying themes associated with the Civil War and the Lost Cause that resonated in Depression culture and, more to the point, aided the cultural memory project of coping and hoping. In the novel, for example, Mitchell describes Scarlett O'Hara walking the barren fields of Tara in the wake of Sherman's march toward Atlanta. "Hunger gnawed at her empty stomach," Mitchell writes before giving Scarlett a few of her signature lines: "As God is my witness, as God is my witness, the Yankees aren't going to lick me. I'm going to live through this, and when it's over, I'm never going to be hungry again. No, nor any of my folks. If I have to steal or kill—as God is my witness, I'm never going to be hungry again" (421). In the film version, the dramatic effects are heightened to Baroque dimensions, rendering the scene an emphatic punctuation to the second act. Destitute, hungry, and clad in a tattered dress, Scarlett digs furiously into the parched ground against a vista of ominous hues. She finds only a rotten yield that leaves her watering the soil with her tears. Suddenly, she gathers herself, looks up, and then stands up in a show of utter resolve. Her soliloquy comes from the novel almost verbatim, demonstrating a capacity to survive by sheer force of will. The relevance of Scarlett's declaration to the Depression is striking. Except for the word "Yankees," it reads or sounds like one of the numerous testimonials recorded in Depression oral histories.

At this moment, Scarlett undergoes a process of symbolic convergence, standing poised between the forces of destruction and reconstruction and, in so doing, embodying both the Civil War South and Depression America. The issue then becomes not whether Scarlett will emerge from the devastation but, rather, what form she—and, by association, her beloved Tara—will take along the road to recovery. Will her suffering transform her into the hardened and unscrupulous materialist she has vowed to become, if need be? Or will she be able to diminish the effects of destruction by reconstructing the Scarlett and the Tara of old? Motivated by "the spirit of her people who would not know defeat," Scarlett's final decision to return to Tara signals an answer, sending the inherently conservative

message that, contrary to the popular maxim, one can go home again—
that it is possible, like Scarlett, to face tomorrow by charting an idyllic
and ideological return to yesterday (Mitchell 1024). Ostensibly shunning
the acquisitive and materialistic drive visibly on display in her running of
the timber mill and her marriage of convenience to Rhett Butler during
Reconstruction, Scarlett will once again go back to the land—a romantic
manifestation of the desire to make life simpler by breaking free from industrial capitalism's totalizing labyrinth. In this regard, the terms of the
Lost Cause translate to the Depression, enabling Mitchell's narrative to
weigh in on debates over the nature of a reconstructed, post-Depression
America. Not surprisingly, Depression readers and moviegoers consumed
the novel and film with relish, gaining hope and satisfaction from com-
forting reassurances.

With invocations of the Civil War prevalent on both the Right and the
Left in Depression cultural politics, Faulkner offered his contributions
in the mid- to late thirties, resulting in *Absalom* and a series of short
stories published in the *Saturday Evening Post* and subsequently revised
and gathered, along with an additional unpublished story, in novel form
as *The Unvanquished* (1938). Because of its lofty status in the Faulkner
canon, *Absalom* has attracted more critical attention aimed at gauging
Faulkner's Civil War. Published in 1936, the same year as *Gone with
the Wind*, *Absalom* is a counterpoint to the romanticized narratives of
the war, grappling intensely with issues of historiography and race ideology in ways that anticipate the textual anxieties of poststructuralism as
well as the vexed historical consciousness of postmodernism. By contrast,
Mitchell's novel glosses over such issues all too easily with Impressionis-
tic strokes of southern Lost Cause ideology and paternalistic depictions of
slave-master relations. Philip Weinstein defines a fundamental difference
between the two novels in terms of historical perspective, arguing that
"*Gone with the Wind* is written as though the past history it is unfolding
took place recently. The novel never acknowledges its own seventy-five-
year vantage point on the events it records—the pastness of the past."
In *Absalom*, however, "the pastness of the past—its unrecoverability—

is foregrounded" (95). In my view, the collapse in time Weinstein cites is a product of the dynamic discussed above: for Depression audiences, Mitchell's novel said as much about the Depression as the Civil War. While *Absalom* certainly bears many marks of its historical and cultural context, as we have seen in chapter 3, Faulkner creates distance using multiple perspectives and adding layers of historical reflection. Faulkner's *Absalom* is, in many respects, about the Depression, too—just not in the thinly veiled way made possible by Mitchell's monologic and monolithic narrative style.[2]

When we turn from *Absalom* to *The Unvanquished*, however, the story changes—literally and figuratively. Strikingly, this novel features frequent Mitchellesque collapses of time—moments when the events of the past seem closer than they technically can be—as well as nods to the Lost Cause that work to bridge the gap between Tara and Yoknapatawpha that literary history has insisted on maintaining. These effects suggest that what can be called Faulkner's popular style was more immediately responsive to prevailing cultural politics. In many respects, then, Faulkner's Civil War in *The Unvanquished*, like Mitchell's in *Gone with the Wind* and many other cultural forms, could be perceived by readers as dressing up key issues and concerns of the Depression in the trappings of the Civil War. Still, the differences are substantial, reflecting a self-awareness—what Cleanth Brooks calls "a large measure of detachment" (77)—in Faulkner that allows him to think critically about the cultural project he has joined.

At the outset of *The Unvanquished*, Faulkner once again sets out to explore the relationship of the individual to the harsh and indifferent forces unleashed by the march of time. The narrator, Bayard Sartoris, recalls an experience during the war when he and his cohort, Ringo, a slave on the Sartoris estate, created "a living map" of Vicksburg. For Bayard, in retrospect, the map is a symbol of history's general indifference to human conflict and suffering. What seems monumental to the individual, Bayard realizes, is miniscule in the overall scheme of time. In the context of this object lesson, the landscape plays the role of overarching historical consciousness, showing a "passive recalcitrance of topography which outweighs artillery, against which the most brilliant of victories and the most tragic of defeats are but loud noises of a moment" (*U* 3). Bayard recalls the living map endeavor as a "wellnigh hopeless ordeal," a failed attempt to "spend ourselves against a common enemy, time, before we could engender between us and hold intact the pattern of recapitulant mimic furious victory like a cloth, a shield between ourselves and reality, between us and fact and doom" (4). Underscoring this failure for Bayard is the fact that the rebellious slave, Loosh, wiped out the map in one fell swoop, adding for dramatic effect, "There's your Vicksburg" (5). The vast discrepancy between the (barely) living map *of* Vicksburg and the actual events taking place *in* Vicksburg speaks to the older Bayard about the folly of trying to shape history toward therapeutic ends. In a brilliant instance of metacommentary, at the same time Faulkner taps the popular trend of rehearsing the Civil War for Depression America, he points to the futility of doing so—insofar as the project is merely an artificial and ideological coping mechanism.[3]

As he does so often, Faulkner responds to Depression cultural politics through elements of form, crafting Bayard's reflection on the past so that it comments on the present. It is worth emphasizing that *The Unvanquished* was published in the same year as the incendiary Roosevelt administration report citing the South as the nation's top economic problem. This report advanced the cause of using Depression hardship as grounds for stepping up efforts to modernize southern infrastructure and agricultural practices under the auspices of the New Deal. In the novel, as an older Bayard looks back on his childhood experiences, the limited perspective that he had then, and still has now, on chaotically unfolding events becomes pronounced. Through point of view, then, Faulkner challenges the validity of achieving a collective or objective vantage point from which to steer through the course of harrowing developments with any modicum of certainty—the kind of perspective envisioned, as we have seen, in the political rhetoric of the New Deal and, more forcefully, that of the radical Left. In a passage that conflates the Civil War and the

Depression in Mitchellesque fashion, Bayard explains that "we knew a war existed; we had to believe that just as we had to believe the name for the sort of life we had led for the last three years was hardship and suffering. Yet we had no proof of it." In fact, Bayard continues, "we had had thrust into our faces the very shabby and unavoidable obverse of proof" (*U* 94).

The subsequent meditation is rendered in a typically Faulknerian series of randomly associated dependent clauses, suggesting that even now Bayard is unable to shape the traumatic events into an ordered narrative. Instead, he seems to experience them all over again as a rush of sensory stimuli and material objects recorded in atomistic terms. Unable to achieve a controlling viewpoint, Bayard is not so much a subject of history as its object, a device for processing in raw form the whims and indifference of time's progression. Staging another skirmish in the broader literary class war, then, Faulkner crafts a highly individualized and resistant form, responsive at once to the totalizing rhetoric of centralized planning, the sacred element of narrative unity avowed by formalism, the monolithic style associated with Mitchell's romantic conservatism, and the utopian collectivism of proletarian literature. As a tenuously bound reworking of previously published short stories, *The Unvanquished* stages in its very textuality the insoluble problematic of forcing individual entities to conform to abstract notions of unified form or collective identity. The sections may coexist in what Faulkner presents to us as a novel, but inconsistencies in style, tone, and genre frequently remind us that they refuse to cooperate with each other or to obey the dictates of authorial prerogative.

On another level, *The Unvanquished* extends the work of *The Sound and the Fury* into the Depression proper by functioning as a narrative of dispossession. As in *Gone with the Wind*, both familial and regional loss create analogues between the past depicted in *The Unvanquished* and the historical context of its production. Consequently, Faulkner's Granny Rosa Millard, like Mitchell's Scarlett O'Hara, embodies a convergence of Civil War South and Depression America.[4] Like Scarlett, Granny is confronted with the harsh reality of materialism, owing to the dire straits brought on by destructive forces that she can barely process—except, like Bayard, as they come to her in a ground-level flurry. For Granny, the struggle against dispossession plays out in the alternating protection, loss, and recovery of the Sartoris family silver. In Civil War lore, the buried or lost family treasure is an elusive and illusory signifier for once-held status and material wealth. In terms of relating *The Unvanquished* to its Depression context, however, the Sartoris family silver represents economic security and the viability of property rights, assuming that Faulkner's novel does not join L. Frank Baum's *The Wizard of Oz* in staging an allegory of the debate over replacing the gold standard with a bimetallic one. For Bayard, as for Benjy Compson in *The Sound and the Fury*, dispossession imprints memory with trauma, initiating an ongoing struggle between the reality of absence and, in turn, the strong desire for recovery and return. Accordingly, with the trunk of silver stored away for safe burial later, Bayard recollects that "the table was set with the kitchen knives and forks in place of the silver ones, and the sideboard (on which the silver service had been sitting when I began to remember and where it had been sitting ever since except on each Tuesday afternoon, when Granny and Louvinia and Philadelphy would polish it, why, nobody except Granny maybe knew, since it was never used) was bare" (*U* 14).

While the use value of the family silver may be inconsequential, its symbolic value is surely not. This condition becomes apparent as Bayard recalls a moment of profound dispossession and devastation. In the recollected scene, Granny stands toe-to-toe with Loosh, who has just divulged the whereabouts of the silver to a regiment of Union soldiers. When Granny invokes the family's property rights, Loosh fires back, "Let God ax John Sartoris who the man name that give me to him," thus challenging the viability of those rights at a time of socioeconomic upheaval. Faulkner dramatizes the anxiety of the old order in tragicomic terms, as Granny momentarily suspends her moral imperative not to allow swearing. Faced with the loss of the silver, the slaves Loosh and Philadelphy, and the Sartoris mansion, which the Union soldiers leave smoldering in flames, Granny lashes out at the powers she cannot control, joining Bayard and Ringo to shout in trio, "The bastuds! The bastuds!" (*U* 75). This scene of destruction does make way quickly for the reconstruction of Granny, however, putting her and the novel on a timely and tragic course of exploration into matters of social, political, and economic import set against a backdrop of ongoing struggle between chaos and the formerly existing social order.

The loss of the cherished silver and the destruction of the Sartoris estate drive Granny, with parasol defiantly raised, in pursuit of the Union soldiers, sparking within her an intense struggle between what Robert S. McElvaine calls "acquisitive individualism" and "cooperative individualism." Tracing economic philosophy from Adam Smith's *Wealth of Nations* through the Progressive Era in America and, finally, to the Depression, McElvaine highlights philosophical opposition between "moral economics" and an increasingly abstract and scientific acceptance of the marketplace as amoral in the context of the modern capitalist state. For McElvaine, this tension manifests in alternating economic tendencies playing out through the course of American history. Times of prosperity fuel acquisitive individualism, with pronounced emphasis on competition and the profit motive; periods of liberalism or economic downturn inspire cooperative individualism, with its promotion of communal values and cooperation. McElvaine stresses the uniqueness of the Depression as "a time *both* of liberalism and economic collapse"—a mixture adding extra potency to the return of cooperative individualism repressed in the Roaring Twenties (196–202). Through the shrewd and profitable horse-trading scheme emerging from Granny's successful quest to recover the family silver, Faulkner represents these dueling economic practices locked in dialectical conflict. In so doing, he responds ideologically to contemporaneous debates over moral economics constituting part of the broader cultural work of envisioning a post-Depression American economy.

While Granny Rosa Millard is cut from the mold of the formidable southern matriarch prevalent in Civil War romances, there is something of the Depression gangster in her as well. With social hierarchy collapsed, signaled by the fact that the Sartorises and the remaining emancipated slaves now share living quarters, Granny quickly learns, like the gangsters of the thirties, that legitimate means of material gain are simply not possible. At this point, Granny has already been forced to "borrow" (read: steal) horses to get home after an initial failed start to Memphis. The roadside marauders who take Granny's mules have by now taught her a valuable lesson in survival-of-the-fittest skills. Still, Granny's insistence that "I'm going to take care of them [the horses] until I can return them" is suggestive of her need to preserve at least some semblance of moral integrity, even in a vacuum of law and order—or at least of Bayard's need to remember it that way (*U* 77). However, under the overwhelming pressures of socioeconomic disarray—a state of flux rendered vividly through recurring images of dispossessed property (mainly shadowy and hushed bands of emancipated slaves) passing by on the renewed journey to Memphis—moral economics is a luxury Granny can scarcely afford to keep. The second start for Memphis—a narrative of migration—is reminiscent of Scarlett's harrowing escape from Atlanta to Tara, just as Sherman's forces arrive. For both women, the experience instills a steely determination to be among those fit enough to survive by hook or by crook. It becomes the latter when Granny confronts the Yankee Colonel Dick with the demand for the return of her slaves and silver and then benefits from a generous miscalculation on his part. Here we find Granny succumbing to the temptation of acquisitive individualism, even as she tries to conceal the dark conversion with halfhearted professions of personal integrity and divine sanction. "I tried to tell them better," Bayard remembers her saying in reference to the encounter with the Union forces. "You and Ringo heard me. It's the hand of God" (112).

Before long, Granny is in cahoots with a Snopes—the surest sign of lapsed integrity in Faulkner's Yoknapatawpha—and commandeering her black-market operation of forging documents to "borrow" horses from one Union regiment so she can sell them to another. Like Scarlett at the helm of the timber mill, Granny has a grand design on power and profit— an aspect of her character that only Ab Snopes can openly appreciate.

Offering Granny a dubious compliment at best, Ab tips his hat to her illegitimate entrepreneurial spirit, pointing out that "you got to build a bigger pen to hold the stock you aint got no market yet to sell" (*U* 122–23). Expressing sentiments similar to those found in the gangster novels and films, as discussed in chapter 3, Ab celebrates the total absence of law and order that has enabled Granny's operation to prosper. He does so for the purpose of giving ironic instruction to Bayard: "Dont waste your time learning to be a lawyer or nothing; you just save your money and buy you a handful of printed letterheads." (123). Ab's pointed comments serve to fill in the blanks left by Granny's repeated attempts to erase profit motive from her character. "We have been successful so far. Too successful perhaps," Granny says at one point, making both a business decision on a risky plan offered by Ab and a moral judgment on the entire endeavor she has masterminded (126).

As Granny's scheme continues, she progressively tries to shift the balance from the acquisitive individualism side of the equation promoted by Ab to the cooperative individualism one tallied by her conscience. Standing before members of the community who have gathered in church, Granny offers a laconic yet full public confession—"I have sinned. I want you all to pray for me" (*U* 137)—before instituting a quasi relief program founded on the principles of moral economics. Bayard explains the conditions for those seeking the dole from Granny: "Each time Granny would make them tell what they intended to do with the money; and now she would make them tell her how they had spent it, and she would look at the book to see whether they had lied or not" (138). Granny's system thus rivals the cooperative-farming arrangement instituted by Uncle Buck and Uncle Buddy McCaslin, who "had persuaded the white men to pool their little patches of a poor hill land along with the niggers and the McCaslin plantation, promising them in return nobody knew exactly what, except that their women and children did have shoes" (49). Tellingly, though, it is Granny's turn to cooperative individualism, enacted as penance for her earlier acquisitive individualism, that brings her to a most tragic end—at least by Bayard's accounting. Having "made independent and secure almost everyone in the county save herself and her own blood," Granny is tempted into a final deal out of a desire to give the returning John Sartoris a monetary foundation for reconstructing his plantation (151). Duped and then shot to death by Grumby—the absolute embodiment of acquisitive individualism—the heretofore outspoken and seemingly indomitable Granny appears through Bayard's memory as though "she had been made out of a lot of light dry sticks notched together and braced with cord," only to be irrevocably undone and left to fall in "a quiet heap on the floor" (154). On a psychological level, this recollection suggests Bayard's need to translate Granny's violent demise into a quietly abstract image, but one that works as well from an exterior perspective to render Granny as the symbolic detritus of contending economic impulses awakened in her by desperate circumstances.

With the death of Granny Rosa Millard at the close of "Riposte in Tertio," *The Unvanquished* is not the same story—literally or figuratively. The trauma and the narrative vacuum engendered by her destruction leave Faulkner searching for a means of reconstruction for a narrative that now lies, along with Granny, in fractured form. As "Riposte in Tertio" gives way to "Vendeé," *The Unvanquished* moves from tragedy to revenge tragedy, the intermittent moments of comic relief falling somewhat flatter than before, in the aftermath of Granny's demise. At least since the age of Shakespeare's *Hamlet*, the revenge tragedy as a form relies on the avenger's pursuit of the culprit and on the restoration of social order upended by the tragic event. True, Granny's death comes at a time of great upheaval, with the society and way of life she longs to restore lying in utter shambles. But her death and the form of the revenge tragedy do give almost divine sanction in the second half of the novel to the cause of reasserting the old order. That (lost) cause gains the upper hand, as it were, with Bayard's lynching and symbolic dismemberment of Grumby. As we have seen in chapter 3, the lynching films of the thirties rely almost exclusively on class, not race, for fueling conflict in the plot. That is the case as well in *The Unvanquished*, with Grumby rising from the ranks of the class of poor whites to wreak havoc in a Yoknapatawpha County sorely in need, we are led to believe, of a guiding paternal hand. Ironically, that role is played first by the young Bayard, who neutralizes Grumby and thus makes way for the return of his father to handle the rest of Grumby's lot—the nameless, faceless throng corralled, literally put back in its place, by John and Drusilla's commandeering of the ballot box. All that remains is for the revenge tragedy to run its natural course toward death—and so it does for John, who dies by the very same code he lived by. Unlike Hamlet before him, though, Bayard is able to dodge the proverbial bullet of the revenge tragedy form and live to replace his father.

The conclusion of Faulkner's *The Unvanquished* plays out on a strikingly similar stage to the one in Mitchell's *Gone with the Wind*. In Mitchell's novel and the film, as one reared in America almost cannot help but know, Scarlett stands at the bottom of the staircase, having just been dismissed by Rhett Butler for her emotional infidelity. "My dear, I don't give a damn," he says in response to her sudden and convenient discovery of love for him (1023). It is then that she vows—or maybe plots—to get him back by returning to Tara to regroup. Thus, it can be argued, Scarlett merely suspends one form of acquisitive individualism for another. Her idyllic move back to the land then reads as a mere ruse: a self-deceptive means of regaining her capacity to produce what she wants to possess, and a socially symbolic act of recovery in the economy of desire. In *The Unvanquished*, Bayard also stands poised near a staircase, with the defiant Aunt Jenny's words still echoing in his mind as he looks with longing into now mad Drusilla's empty room: "Oh, damn you Sartorises! . . . Damn you! Damn you!" (*U* 254). Aunt Jenny's words merely punctuate what Bayard earlier realized about his tenuous claim on an independent identity and on the Sartoris household. Referring to his father's body lying in virtual state, Bayard recalls that "I didn't need to see him again because he was there, he would always be there" (253). The eponymous "odor of verbena" that permeates the final scene of *The Unvanquished* defies its traditional role as a symbol of purification, reminding us in trademark Faulknerian manner that the past is never really past. Of course, it was Mitchell's Scarlett O'Hara, not Faulkner's Bayard Sartoris, who became a cultural icon in the context of the Depression. That outcome is not surprising when we consider that, in characteristically American fashion, Scarlett is more focused on tomorrow than yesterday and more capable of reinventing herself at a whim.

Faulkner's unenthusiastic reception at the time should not be taken now as evidence of his detachment from the cultural milieu of the 1930s. On the contrary, it might be taken as further indication of Faulkner's sometimes unflinching, often contradictory, but always complex response to contemporaneous issues and events in producing his fiction. Foregrounding this dimension of Faulkner shows how his literary production reads as both timely and timeless—immediately responsive to forces unleashed by a period of national crisis, but far ranging enough to endure and prevail in the annals of literary history. Faulkner's declaration of independence notwithstanding, this fictional cosmos is not wholly the author's own, taking shape as it did from a highly productive, yet ultimately impossible, struggle to achieve artistic autonomy. Regardless of what Faulkner's fiction means for all time, it bears the distinguishing marks of its production at a particular time. In the midst of the Depression, with scores in search of comforting signs that stability and security would return, Faulkner's fiction expressed this longing as well. With dialectical force, however, Faulkner's form of individualism—and, indeed, his individualism of form—resisted at virtually every turn the kind of bold, monolithic, and often reductive representations coming from the Right and the Left in the throes of cultural politics. Along these lines, Faulkner's productive encounter with the Great Depression revealed not only the clash between the old order and the "new order of things" but also the very idea of order itself to be subjects of a supreme American fiction. Consequently, Faulkner reads now as a Depression writer who, in keeping with the times, found his own means of radical and revolutionary expression.

Notes

Introduction. Placement and Perspective: Faulkner and the
Great Depression

1. See Pells, Peeler, Kutulas, and Denning as prime examples of this trend in the study of cultural history.

2. See Kazin; Wald; Nelson, *Repression and Recovery* and *Revolutionary Memory*; Rabinowitz; Coiner; Teres; Browder; and Morgan.

3. A common practice in treatments of the Depression is to mark its beginning with the stock market crash of 1929. Historically speaking, that is a sound move. However, this study begins in advance of that date by looking at two novels published before the crash: *Mosquitoes* and *The Sound and the Fury*. This decision stems from my emphasis on issues and developments related to the literary class war. By the mid- to late twenties, debates in literary theory were already moving urgently toward questions of literature's social engagement, mainly in revision of the expatriate and alienated stances of the "lost generation."

4. John T. Matthews has been a central figure in this trend, as demonstrated by *The Play of Faulkner's Language* and *The Sound and the Fury: Faulkner and the Lost Cause*, as well as articles such as "*As I Lay Dying* in the Machine Age," "Faulkner and Cultural Studies," and "Faulkner and the Culture Industry," among numerous others. See Ross for a study that examines the ideological implications of rhetoric and narrative structure. For productive uses of historical and cultural inquiry in the conduct of ideological analysis, see King, Sundquist, Grimwood, Wadlington, and Carolyn Porter's insightful chapter on Faulkner in her book *Seeing and Being*. Other scholars have emphasized race, class, and gender in framing ideological inquiry. See Davis for a thorough treatment of race ideology. Some of the most intriguing and productive ideological analysis has come from scholars exploring issues of gender by drawing on feminist theory. For an exemplary sampling, see Gwin; Clarke; Fowler; Jones, " 'Like a Virgin': Faulkner, Sexual Cultures, and the Romance of Resistance" and "Desire and Dismemberment: Faulkner and the Ideology of Penetration"; and Donaldson, "Subverting History: Women, Narrative, and Patriarchy in *Absalom, Absalom!*" See Weinstein for a study that foregrounds the concerns of gender and race in its treatment of identity. For innovative treatments focused on material history and class consciousness, see Godden and Railey.

5. At a subsequent Faulkner and Yoknapatawpha Conference, Bleikasten revisited the issue with the same vigor and cautionary urging. See "Faulkner in the Singular," the published version of those remarks.

Chapter 1. History and Culture: Faulkner in Political Context

1. The imperiled condition of self-reliance and the resulting interest in collectivism was apparent on various fronts. As Richard Pells makes clear in a useful summary, the ideological crisis threatening self-reliance fueled wide-ranging discussions of planned society. To varying degrees, endorsements of a move toward collectivism could be found in the editorial pages of the *New Republic* by 1935 and in articles and books by intellectuals at the forefront of social thought, including Lewis Mumford, George Soule, John Dewey, and Ruth Benedict. Neo-Freudians in psychology such as Karen Horney and Harry Stack Sullivan reevaluated key elements of psychoanalysis considered to be too individualistic. In the field of education theory, George Counts and Charles Beard, among others, argued for pedagogical practices that would promote communal responsibility in students, rather than encouraging them to compete on an individual basis for personal gain (Pells 111–18).

2. Defenses of Hoover often stress his active engagement as a counterargument to historical accounts of his indifference. Romasco, for example, argues that Hoover did not "struggle to overcome [the crisis] in some splendid isolation" (133). See also Joan Hoff Wilson for an example of the revisionist approach casting Hoover's policies as antecedents to those of the New Deal.

3. Crafted from a liberal humanist perspective, early chronicles of FDR and the New Deal tend to be favorable, if not laudatory. See, for example, Freidel, *Franklin D. Roosevelt: The Ordeal*; Burns; Schlesinger; and Leuchtenburg, *Franklin Delano Roosevelt*. In the mid-1970s, however, a revisionist challenge emerged as part of the "New Left" studies, casting FDR and the New Deal as too timid in their social policies and programs. Exemplary of this trend is Bellush. Critiques have come from the other side of the political spectrum as well, generally driven by the emergence of antigovernment conservatism inspired by Barry Goldwater and fashioned for the mainstream by Ronald Reagan. For historians of this ideological bent, FDR and the New Deal represent a turn for the worse in American social history, establishing a debilitating welfare state that has replaced self-reliance with a condition of chronic dependence. Fleming and Powell exemplify this conservative brand of historical assessment. Significantly, the two-track line of anti–FDR/New Deal historiography has prompted what can now be deemed the old guard to mount vigorous defenses, as exemplified in Freidel, *Franklin D. Roosevelt: A Rendezvous with Destiny*, and Leuchtenburg, *The FDR Years*.

4. Historians generally agree on the importance of this report as a source of bad feeling between FDR and dissidents in the southern wing of the Democratic Party and as a key rhetorical device in the purge effort. Freidel documents FDR's rhetorical use of the report in trying to paint southern conservatives as obstacles to the sort of progress that could be achieved with the emerging liberal challengers in office (*FDR* 99–101). Noting the unpleasantness and the aggressiveness of the purge effort, Biles recounts that FDR invoked the report while inaugurating a new Rural Electrification Association (REA) project in Barnesville, Georgia. In so doing, FDR publicly endorsed the challenger to the incumbent Democratic senator Walter George, who was seated several feet away. Frederickson explains that in the case of southern lawmakers, "most responded angrily and defensively" to the report and viewed it as "a slur on the entire region" (25), this in spite of the fact that its supporting data had been generated by researchers at major southern universities.

5. See Wolfskill for a comprehensive history of this conservative organization.

6. History has tended to record Coughlin and Long as demagogues and even as harbingers of the potential rise of fascism, which was the subject of so much speculation during the Depression. Schlesinger offers an interpretation that is typical in this regard (15–28, 42–68). However, later historians have tempered the charge of fascism. See, for example, Brinkley, *Voices of Protest*. My interpretation of these figures aligns with McElvaine's in stressing the elements of populism that defined these movements as they attracted an American public that was increasingly concerned with issues of social and economic justice as the effects of the Depression reached into the ranks of the middle class (237–40).

7. Pells offers a common refrain when he defines the Popular Front in America as a project of political expediency carried forward with one eye on the international stage and one on the domestic. For radicals in the mid-1930s, he argues, the Popular Front was an endeavor to recast political rhetoric and social activism in terms more amenable to the mainstream American public. Carrying out this mission, leftist radicals now "earnestly preached the virtues of collective security in international affairs, while on domestic matters they slowly adapted the old socialist ideals to the more conciliatory Popular Front" (294). Taking this pragmatism even further by the election of 1936, radical "desire to fashion a new party gave way to rapprochement with the New Deal" (296). Emphasizing this compromising impulse, Pells defines the Popular Front's influence as negligible, given "that it was never really strong enough to put pressure on or wring concessions from the New Deal" (297). In *Radical Hollywood*, Buhle and Wagner make a different case, however, arguing for greater Popular Front influence based on its alliance with the New Deal to employ cultural production as a way to shape "the public and consumer into self, family member, and citizen" (60). For Buhle and Wagner, the Popular Front thus exerted immeasurable influence as an independent agent rather than as part of the New Deal ideological apparatus. The study of the Popular Front has been susceptible, as Szalay notes, to historical revisionism informed by current politics in the academy. Szalay takes Denning to task for applying the terms "cultural front" and "Popular Front" interchangeably to achieve "a politically safe reinvention of American radicalism, one in which the current academic left gets to discard two twinned versions of statism: the troubled legacy of Stalinism on the one hand, and the presumably hegemonic, mainstream liberalism of the New Deal on the other" (19). While Szalay's point is well taken, this tendency in Denning's account does not discount his thorough demonstration of the Popular Front as a visible force in American culture and, as a result of its alliance with the New Deal, in politics and public policy as well.

8. See Schlesinger 211–43 and McElvaine 250–63 for a more complete description of this phase of New Deal progression.

9. For an informative cultural history of the politics of publishing, see Pells 151–93.

Chapter 2. Decadence and Dispossession: Faulkner and the "Literary Class War"

1. See, for example, Joyce W. Warren and Dauffenbauch.

2. For an early treatment of the interwoven themes of sex and art, see McHaney, "Oversexing the Natural World," and Dunlap. Later examinations have brought gender theory to bear on this line of inquiry. See Rado and Wittenberg, for example. For analysis of ideas related to language, see Matthews, *Play* 45–50, and Hepburn.

3. See, for example, Scott, Carvel Collins, Trouard, and Matthews, *Play* 63–114.

4. The chronological order of the versions has been the source of some critical debate. Citing biographical data, Panthea Reid Broughton convincingly argues that the *Southern Review* version anticipates the *Mississippi Quarterly* version; she distinguishes between the first "romantic introduction" and the "more matter-of-fact" revision ("Faulkner's Cubist Novels" 61n). I choose to emphasize the second version because tensions between subjective and objective point of view correspond to those in the novel, as my reading highlights. For further comparison between the two versions of the introduction, see Broughton, "Economy of Desire."

Chapter 3. Power by Design: Faulkner and the Specter of Fascism

1. My treatment of Faulkner and fascism is similar in some respects to Brinkmeyer's, especially the works cited to establish historical and cultural context. But Brinkmeyer's focus is defined primarily in terms of regional conflict—specifically, "the larger cultural critique of the South by the rest of America (and by some Southerners) that took place from the mid-1930s through World War II—a critique that centered on issues involving the meaning and value of democratic ideology" (74). For Brinkmeyer, the fascist charge against Faulkner and Faulkner's response to fascism must be understood in light of the "democratic revival"—an ideological response in the late thirties and early forties to the rise of fascism abroad and potentially at home. Although my discussion of Faulkner and fascism intersects with Brinkmeyer's at key points, my fundamental approach is different,

concerned as it is with the discourse around fascism as a means of renegotiating the distribution of power in response to the crisis of the Depression.

2. For examples of this line of inquiry, see Jameson, *Fables of Aggression*, and Morrison.

3. Guttman situates this dynamic in the context of social anxieties arising from industrialization in the South. For her, the narrative of Temple's rape corresponds to the cultural narrative of southern industrialization observed by W. J. Cash and articulated in the main by the Southern Agrarians, as mentioned in chapter 2 with regard to Caddy Compson. To reiterate, this narrative traumatically envisions a feminized South being threatened with "rape" by the force of northern industry, thus ideologically sanctioning an aggressively defensive posture on the part of southern men to defend the South's "virtue." See Yaeger, "Beyond," for a broader discussion of the gender ideology informing such narratives. See Roberts, *Faulkner and Southern Womanhood* 109–39 for further discussion of how this gender ideology informs Faulkner's work.

4. See, for example, Bleikasten, "Terror and Nausea," and Scheel.

5. See Watson for a comprehensive discussion of panoptical theory in *Sanctuary*. He establishes this critical framework to analyze the modus operandi of Popeye's control over the Frenchman's Bend bootlegging operation and the Memphis underworld as well as his disruption of law and order in Jefferson.

6. For detailed description and analysis of these films, see Bergman 23–29.

7. The contextual framework of my reading corresponds fundamentally to Sundquist's: "*Sanctuary* is less dependent on Faulkner's native Southern traditions than his other major novels, and it engages more directly than any of them the violent realities of contemporary life, in this case the realities of a country poised at a point of passing from the Roaring Twenties to the Depression Thirties. It belongs emphatically to the genre of 'hard boiled' fiction of that period" (45–46).

8. For an intriguing take on the relationship between race ideology and social upheaval in *Light in August*, see Railey 96–105. My reading of *Light in August* shares with Railey's the basic contention that the novel's central concern is a crisis in social order. However, Railey defines this crisis within a southern paradigm, arguing that it reflects paternalistic anxiety over a transformed socioeconomic system that allows greater mobility. Although I arrive at conclusions similar to Railey's, my path is decidedly different, owing to the historical and cultural context of the Depression in which I situate the novel.

9. Here I summarize a general argument made by Lukács in *The Historical Novel*. See in particular chapter 1, in which Lukács defines the genre and uses Walter Scott's fiction as a means of testing his theory.

10. See Matthews, "Faulkner and Proletarian Literature" 178–86, for an instructive comparison of *Absalom* and Endore's *Babouk*.

Chapter 4. Revolution and Restraint: Faulkner's Ambivalent Agrarianism

1. The motivation for the Bundrens' journey has been a source of debate since the earliest treatments of the novel, often in the process of trying to define its form. While initial reviews often charged Faulkner with condescension in his depiction of poor whites, later assessments pointed to noble intentions that keep the Bundrens moving forward and elevate the narrative to epic status. Robert Penn Warren, for example, observes, "The whole of *As I Lay Dying* is based on the heroic effort of the Bundren family to fulfill the promise to the dead mother to take her body to Jefferson" (105). Likewise, Howe insists that the blend of comedy and tragedy has a cohering effect. Noting that Faulkner approaches the Bundrens with "a comely and tactful gravity, a deep underlying respect," Howe concludes, "an American epic, *As I Lay Dying* is human tragedy and country farce. The marvel is, that to be one it had to be the other" (190–91). Vickery sets the stage for subsequent criticism when she challenges this trend, arguing that "the journey from beginning to end is a travesty of the ritual of internment" because of the Bundrens' behavior (52). Sundquist finds a striking parallel between form and content, defining the novel as a "corpse, a narrative whose form is continually on the verge of decomposition and whose integrity is retained only by heroic imaginative effort" (31). My reading extends this line of critical inquiry by setting Faulkner's depiction of the Bundrens against the backdrop of historical and cultural forces so as to examine the implications of the novel's form.

2. For additional treatments of property destruction as social protest, see Woodward 415 and Wyatt-Brown.

3. Faulkner's style in *As I Lay Dying* has provided grounds for vigorous critical debate. Sundquist succinctly identifies the two most common charges lodged against Faulkner's modernist tendencies: "that the author or narrator (the two are easily confused) has fallen victim to his own fantasies of technique; or that a character or speaker (these two are also easily confused) has been allowed a command of language incommensurate with his place in the novel's realistic or representational scheme" (29). I agree with Sundquist's assessment that these disjunctions are not detriments but rather evidence of striking parallels between formal structure and thematic content. Sundquist defines this fusion in textual terms, noting how instabilities in narrative voice reinforce the theme of disembodiment in the novel. My interest is in defining the fusion in contextual terms—that is, relating

issues of multiple voice and disrupted form to the dynamics of pending cultural politics.

4. See Broughton, "Cubist Novel" and "Faulkner's Cubist Novels." Incidentally, the verse that Faulkner wrote in the infancy of his literary career has also been compared to modern painting in terms of aesthetics. See Lind and Reid for readings along these lines.

5. The historical data relevant to the STFU come from Auerbach. See Grubbs for a more comprehensive social history of this organization's formation and record of activism. I should note that scholars continue to debate the effectiveness of the STFU, with some stressing the failure of the organization to meet basic objectives and others pointing to its significance as a political force reflected not only in the lives of its members but also in the anxieties of the planter class. Without wading too deeply into the waters of that historical argument, I generally agree with the latter school of thought and thus interpret the STFU as a significant movement representative of the potential for social upheaval in rural America. While organizations such as the STFU, the SCU, and the Farmers' Alliance may not have achieved the radical reform they advocated, they were successful in disrupting the status quo enough to bring injustices of the sharecropping system under the national spotlight. Without the work of these dissident organizations, reforms to New Deal agricultural policy might not have taken place. Moreover, while these dissident groups may not have achieved the level of racial solidarity among sharecroppers and small landowners that they desired, the fact that they were working toward it proved significant as a source of anxiety for the ruling planter class, which relied on racial division as a means of maintaining its hegemonic position. For a reading of "Barn Burning" and *Absalom, Absalom!* in the context of the STFU and material labor practices in the South, see Godden 123–29.

6. Godden offers a persuasive explanation for the nature of this rendering in the context of competing forces of racial and class consciousness active in Ab: "Even though Faulkner writes after the interracial activities of the Southern Tenant Farmers' Union (1934–37), he senses that a white tenant who destroys a planter's goods cannot do so in the name of his *whole* class, because that acknowledgement would render his class body more black than white" (126).

7. See, for example, Froelich and McHaney, "What Faulkner Learned." A major point of discussion has been the extent to which V. K. Ratliff speaks—or presumes to speak—with a moral authority that works to uphold communal values and to maintain codes of social conduct. My reading of the ideological function of Ratliff's storytelling draws on the kind of skepticism expressed by Froelich when

he complicates Ratliff's response to Ike Snopes's amorous pursuit of Jack Houston's cow. I agree with Froelich that the reader can fall all too easily into the trap of taking Ratliff at face value, not recognizing the ulterior motives informing his narrative style. Matthews shrewdly analyzes Ratliff's mode of storytelling in the context of nostalgia, assigning an ideological function to the form. For Matthews, Ratliff is fully aware of the baseless nature of his assumptions and values. In this sense, Ratliff's pose as the champion of communal values is but a mask worn for the rhetorical effect of deterring the Snopes's advancement (*Play* 168–69).

8. Carolyn Porter astutely links this recurring theme of yeoman self-reliance in Faulkner's fiction to a tendency in the Falkner family influenced by a contradiction in southern historiography—the ideological maneuver to apply the cosmetics of agrarianism to the base of a southern economic order structured on modes of capitalist production. Historical treatments of the small farmer have been employed frequently toward that end. Specifically, Porter cites the case of Southern Agrarians such as Frank Owsley, who painted an embellished picture of the antebellum South as a democracy of hardworking and content small farmers. This ideological maneuver sought to obscure the actual acquisitive desires of the yeomanry to obtain more land and reap larger profits through increased exploitation of labor and resources. As social concepts and historical figures, Porter argues, both the aristocratic planter and the yeoman farmer have been used to mask the material reality of the more common figure: "the parvenu capitalist entrepreneur of the antebellum Southwest" (211), a supposedly "self-made man" who was invested in the American tradition of progress and thus shared much more in common with his northern industrialist counterpart than the cult of the Lost Cause would allow.

Conclusion. Destruction and Reconstruction: Faulkner's Civil War and the Politics of Recovery

1. Gray cites favorable assessments of *The Unvanquished* such as Edward L. Volpe's *A Reader's Guide to William Faulkner* and Judith Bryant-Wittenberg's *William Faulkner: The Transfiguration of Biography* (411n). Both Volpe and Wittenberg seek to elevate the novel based on its literary merits, but the more persuasive reassessments have been those focused on issues of historical and cultural context. Cleanth Brooks defends the novel as well, citing Faulkner's rendering of the characters as "much more than a glib romanticizing that cannot be sustained and finally breaks down into cold quizzicality" (76).

2. Godden provocatively discounts this distance to argue for explicit and con-

stitutive relations between *Absalom* and the New Deal. Building on the historical argument that the New Deal was, in effect, "the South's 'Second Civil War,' " he points to a signal event in the history of southern labor as crucial to *Absalom*'s production. In Godden's view, Faulkner is compelled to tell the story of Sutpen from 1934 to 1936 because that was when the South's "dependency culture and its labor base were dramatically exposed as economically archaic" (119). While I think Godden ultimately reads too much of the New Deal into Faulkner's Civil War, I must acknowledge a debt to his materialist approach for helping to shape my ideas about Faulkner's mode of historical representation.

3. Faulkner's treatment of history and historiography in *The Unvanquished* has attracted significant critical attention. See Hockbruck for discussion of Faulkner's self-reflexive mode of historical representation in depicting the Civil War. Also, see Lowe for an examination of Faulkner's historical representation in the context of Nietzsche's historical theories.

4. Of course, it could be argued as well that Drusilla is the more appropriate analogue to Scarlett O'Hara, considering the similarity in age and both women's willingness to defy social and cultural conventions, particularly the rigid gender norms imposed by the cult of southern womanhood. Both Granny and Drusilla have inspired examinations of Faulkner's treatment of gender roles—arguably the most interesting studies of *The Unvanquished* to come along in recent years. See, for example, Berg; Clarke, "Gender, War, and Cross-Dressing in *The Unvanquished*"; Roberts, "Precarious Pedestal"; and Yaeger, "Faulkner's 'Greek Amphora Priestess.' "

Bibliography

Adorno, Theodor. *Aesthetic Theory*. Trans. C. Lenhardt. Ed. Gretel Adorno and Rolf Tiedemann. New York: Routledge, 1986.

Aiken, Conrad. "William Faulkner: The Novel as Form." *The Atlantic Monthly* Nov. 1939: 650–54. Rpt. in Hoffman and Vickery 134–42.

Althusser, Louis. "Ideology and the Ideological State Apparatuses." *Essays on Ideology*. London: Verso, 1984. 1–60.

Arnold, Edwin T. "Freedom and Stasis in Faulkner's *Mosquitoes*." *Mississippi Quarterly* 28 (1975): 281–97.

Auerbach, Jerold S. "Southern Tenant Farmers: Socialist Critics of the New Deal." *Labor History* 7 (1966): 3–18. Rpt. in Dubofsky and Burwood 55–70.

Baigell, Matthew, and Julia Williams, eds. *Artists against War and Fascism: Papers of the First American Artists' Congress*. New Brunswick: Rutgers University Press, 1986.

Bakhtin, Mikhail. *Problems of Dostoevsky's Poetics.* Trans. Caryl Emerson. Minneapolis: University of Minnesota Press, 1984.

Bellush, Bernard. *The Failure of the NRA.* New York: W. W. Norton, 1975.

Benjamin, Walter. "The Work of Art in the Age of Mechanical Reproduction." *Illuminations.* New York: Harcourt Brace Jovanovich, 1968. Rpt. in *Film Theory and Criticism: Introductory Readings.* 4th ed. Ed. Gerald Mast, Marshal Cohen, and Leo Braudy. New York: Oxford University Press, 1992. 665–81.

Berg, Allison. "The Great War and the War at Home: Gender Battles in *Flags in the Dust* and *The Unvanquished.*" *Women's Studies* 22 (1993): 441–53.

Bergman, Andrew. *We're in the Money: Depression America and Its Films.* New York: Harper and Row, 1971.

Biles, Roger. *The South and the New Deal.* Lexington: University of Kentucky Press, 1994.

Bingham, Emily S., and Thomas A. Underwood. Introduction. *The Southern Agrarians and the New Deal.* Ed. Bingham and Underwood. Charlottesville: University of Virginia Press, 2001. 1–33.

Blanchard, Margaret. "The Rhetoric of Communion: Voice in *The Sound and the Fury.*" *American Literature* 41 (1970): 555–65. Rpt. in *William Faulkner's* The Sound and the Fury: *A Critical Casebook.* Ed. André Bleikasten. New York: Garland, 1982. 123–33.

Bleikasten, André. "Faulkner and the New Ideologues." Kartiganer and Abadie, *Faulkner and Ideology* 3–21.

———. "Faulkner in the Singular." Kartiganer and Abadie, *Faulkner at 100* 204–18.

———. *Faulkner's As I Lay Dying.* Trans. Roger Little. Bloomington: Indiana University Press, 1973.

———. *The Most Splendid Failure: Faulkner's* The Sound and the Fury. Bloomington: Indiana University Press, 1976.

———. "Terror and Nausea: Bodies in *Sanctuary.*" *Faulkner Journal* 1 (1985): 17–29.

Bloom, James. *Left Letters: The Culture Wars of Mike Gold and Joseph Freeman.* New York: Columbia University Press, 1992.

Blotner, Joseph. *Faulkner: A Biography.* 2 vols. New York: Random House, 1974.

———. *Faulkner: A Biography, One-Volume Edition.* New York: Random House, 1984.

———, ed. *Selected Letters of William Faulkner.* New York: Random House, 1977.

Blotner, Joseph, and Frederick L. Gwynn, eds. *Faulkner in the University*. Charlottesville: University of Virginia Press, 1959.

Brinkley, Alan. *The End of Reform: New Deal Liberalism in Recession and War*. New York: Alfred A. Knopf, 1995.

———. *Voices of Protest: Huey Long, Father Coughlin, and the Great Depression*. New York: Knopf, 1982.

Brinkmeyer, Robert H. "Faulkner and the Democratic Crisis." Kartiganer and Abadie, *Faulkner and Ideology* 70–94.

Brooks, Cleanth. *William Faulkner: The Yoknapatawpha Country*. New Haven: Yale University Press, 1963.

Browder, Laura. *Rousing the Nation: Radical Culture in Depression America*. Amherst: University of Massachusetts Press, 1998.

Brown, Steve, and Jess Gilbert. "Alternative Land Reform Proposals in the 1930s: The Nashville Agrarians and the Southern Tenant Farmers' Union." *Agricultural History* 55 (1981): 351–69. Rpt. in Dubofsky and Burwood 191–209.

[Broughton], Panthea Reid. "The Cubist Novel: Toward Defining the Genre." Fowler and Abadie 36–58.

———. "Faulkner's Cubist Novels." Fowler and Abadie 59–94.

———. "The Economy of Desire: Faulkner's Poetics, from Eroticism to Post-Impressionism." *The Faulkner Journal* 4 (1988–89): 159–77.

Buhle, Paul, and Dave Wagner. *Radical Hollywood: The Untold Story behind America's Favorite Movies*. New York: New Press, 2002.

Bürger, Peter. *Theory of the Avant-Garde*. Trans. Michael Shaw. Minneapolis: University of Minnesota Press, 1984.

Burns, James MacGregor. *Roosevelt: The Lion and the Fox*. New York: Harcourt, Brace, and World, 1956.

Caldwell, Erskine. *Tobacco Road*. Athens: University of Georgia Press, 1960.

Calverton, V. F. "The Farmer Cocks His Rifle." *Modern Quarterly* 7 (1934): 727–31.

Cash, Wilbur J. *The Mind of the South*. New York: Vintage, 1941.

City Streets. Dir. Rouben Mamoulian. Paramount, 1931.

Clarke, Deborah. "Gender, War, and Cross-Dressing in *The Unvanquished*." Kartiganer and Abadie, *Faulkner and Gender* 228–51.

———. *Robbing the Mother: Women in Faulkner*. Jackson: University Press of Mississippi, 1994.

Cohen, Philip. "Faulkner Studies and Ideology Critique in the 1990s." *Mississippi Quarterly* 49 (1996): 633–54.

Coiner, Constance. *Better Red: The Writing and Resistance of Tillie Olsen and Meridel Le Sueur*. New York: Oxford University Press, 1995.

Collins, Carvel. "The Interior Monologues of *The Sound and the Fury*." *The Merrill Studies in* The Sound and the Fury. Columbus, Ohio: Charles E. Merrill, 1970. 89–101.

Collins, Seward C. "Editorial Notes." *The American Review* 1 (1933): 122–27.

Cook, Sylvia Jenkins. *From Tobacco Road to Route 66: The Southern Poor White in Fiction*. Chapel Hill: University of North Carolina Press, 1976.

Cowley, Malcolm. *Exile's Return*. New York: Viking, 1951.

———, ed. *The Faulkner-Cowley File: Letters and Memories, 1944–1962*. New York: Viking, 1966.

———, ed. *The Portable Faulkner*. New York: Penguin, 1977.

Dauffenbauch, Claus. "A Portrait of the Artist as a Young Aesthete: Faulkner's *Mosquitoes*." *American Studies* 42 (1997): 547–58.

Davidson, Donald. "The Grotesque." *Tennessean* 3 July 1927: 7. Rpt. in Inge 20.

Davis, Thadious M. *Faulkner's "Negro": Art and the Southern Context*. Baton Rouge: Louisiana State University Press, 1983.

———. "Two Mississippi Novels." *Tennessean* 14 Apr. 1929: 7. Rpt. in Inge 26–28.

———. "William Faulkner." *Tennessean* 11 Apr. 1926: 6. Rpt. in Inge 12–13.

Denning, Michael. *The Cultural Front: The Laboring of American Culture in the Twentieth Century*. New York: Verso, 1997.

Dennis, Lawrence. *The Coming American Fascism*. New York: Harper and Brothers, 1936.

Dinnerstein, Leonard. *Antisemitism in America*. New York: Oxford, 1994.

Donaldson, Susan V. "Subverting History: Women, Narrative, and Patriarchy in *Absalom, Absalom!*" *Southern Quarterly* 26 (1988): 19–32.

Dubofsky, Melvyn, and Stephen Burwood, eds. *Agriculture during the Great Depression*. New York: Garland Publishing, 1990.

Dunlap, Mary M. "Sex and the Artist in *Mosquitoes*." *Mississippi Quarterly* 22 (1969): 190–206.

Duvall, John. *Faulkner's Marginal Couple: Invisible, Outlaw, and Unspeakable Communities*. Austin: University of Texas Press, 1990.

Eagleton, Terry. *Ideology: An Introduction*. New York: Verso, 1991.

———. *The Ideology of the Aesthetic*. Malden, Mass.: Blackwell, 1990.

Ekirch, Arthur A. *Ideologies and Utopias: The Impact of the New Deal on American Thought*. Chicago: Quadrangle, 1969.

Engels, Friedrich. Letter to Margaret Harkness. N.d. Rpt. in "Marx and Engels on Balzac." Ed. Friedrich Schiller. Trans. H. Scott. *International Literature* 3 (1933): 113–24.

Fadiman, Clifton. *Party of One*. New York: World Publishing, 1955.

Farrell, James T. "The Faulkner Mixture." *New York Sun* 7 Oct. 1932: 29. Rpt. in Inge 83–84.

Faulkner, William. *Absalom, Absalom! The Corrected Text*. 1936. New York: Vintage International, 1990.

———. *As I Lay Dying: The Corrected Text*. 1930. New York: Vintage International, 1985.

———. *Collected Stories of William Faulkner*. New York: Vintage, 1977.

———. *Essays, Speeches, and Public Letters*. Ed. James B. Meriwether. New York: Random House, 2004.

———. *The Hamlet: The Corrected Text*. Ed. Noel Polk. 1940. New York: Vintage, 1964.

———. Introduction. *Sanctuary*. 1931. New York: The Modern Library, 1932.

———. "An Introduction to *The Sound and the Fury*." *A Faulkner Miscellany*. Ed. Noel Polk. Jackson: University Press of Mississippi, 1974.

———. *Light in August*. 1932. New York: Vintage, 1959.

———. *Mosquitoes*. 1927. New York: Liveright, 1955.

———. *Sanctuary: The Corrected Text*. Ed. Noel Polk. 1931. New York: Vintage International, 1993.

———. *Sanctuary: The Original Text*. 1931. Ed. Noel Polk. New York: Random House, 1981.

———. *The Sound and the Fury*. 1929. New York: Vintage, 1984.

———. *The Unvanquished: The Corrected Text*. 1938. Ed. Noel Polk. New York: Vintage, 1965.

Filreis, Alan. *Modernism from Right to Left: Wallace Stevens, the Thirties, and Literary Radicalism*. New York: Cambridge University Press, 1994.

Foley, Barbara. *Radical Representations: Politics and Form in U.S. Proletarian Fiction, 1929–1941*. Durham: Duke University Press, 1993.

Foucault, Michel. *Discipline and Punish: The Birth of the Prison*. Trans. Alan Sheridan. New York: Vintage Books, 1979.

Fowler, Doreen. *Faulkner: The Return of the Repressed*. Charlottesville: University of Virginia Press, 1997.

Fowler, Doreen, and Ann J. Abadie, eds. *"A Cosmos of My Own": Faulkner and Yoknapatawpha, 1980*. Jackson: University Press of Mississippi, 1981.

————. *Faulkner and Popular Culture: Faulkner and Yoknapatawpha, 1988.* Jackson: University Press of Mississippi, 1990.

Frederickson, Kari. *The Dixiecrat Revolt and the End of the Solid South, 1932–1968.* Chapel Hill: University of North Carolina Press, 2001.

Freeman, Joseph. Introduction. *Proletarian Literature in the United States: An Anthology.* Ed. Granville Hicks et al. New York: International Publishers, 1935. 9–28.

Freidel, Frank. *FDR and the South.* Baton Rouge: Louisiana State University Press, 1965.

————. *Franklin D. Roosevelt: A Rendezvous with Destiny.* New York: Back Bay, 1991.

————. *Franklin D. Roosevelt: The Ordeal.* Boston: Little, Brown, 1954.

Froelich, Peter Alan. "Faulkner and the Frontier Grotesque: *The Hamlet* as Southwestern Humor." Kartiganer and Abadie, *Faulkner in Cultural Context* 218–40.

Fury. Dir. Fritz Lang. MGM, 1936.

Gabriel over the White House. Dir. Gregory LaCava. MGM, 1933.

Geismar, Maxwell. *Writers in Crisis: The American Novel between Two Wars.* Boston: Houghton Mifflin, 1942.

Godden, Richard. *Fictions of Labor: William Faulkner and the South's Long Revolution.* Cambridge: Cambridge University Press, 1997.

Gold, Michael. "Hemingway—White Collar Poet." *New Masses* Mar. 1928: n.p. Rpt. in Gold, *Mike Gold* 160–63.

————. *Mike Gold: A Literary Anthology.* Ed. Michael Folsom. New York: International, 1972.

————. "Proletarian Realism." *New Masses* Sep. 1930: 5. Rpt. in Gold, *Mike Gold* 206–9.

————. "Wilder: Prophet of the Genteel Christ." *New Republic* 22 Oct. 1930: 266–67. Rpt. in Gold, *Mike Gold* 200–203.

Gray, Richard. *The Life of William Faulkner.* Cambridge, Mass.: Blackwell Publishers, 1994.

Grubbs, Donald H. *Cry from the Cotton: The Southern Tenant Farmers' Union and the New Deal.* Chapel Hill: University of North Carolina Press, 1971.

Guttman, Sondra. "Who's Afraid of the Corncob Man? Masculinity, Race, and Labor in the Preface to *Sanctuary.*" *Faulkner Journal* 15 (1999–2000): 15–34.

Gwin, Minrose. *The Feminine and Faulkner: Reading (beyond) Sexual Difference.* Knoxville: University of Tennessee Press, 1990.

Hanley, Lawrence F. "Popular Culture in Crisis: King Kong Meets Edmund Wilson." *Radical Revisions: Rereading Thirties Culture.* Ed. Bill Mullen and Sherry Linkon. Chicago: University of Illinois Press, 1996.

Hanson, Philip J. "The Logic of Anti-Capitalism in *The Sound and the Fury.*" *Faulkner Journal* 7 (1991–92): 3–27.

Hepburn, Kenneth William. "Faulkner's *Mosquitoes*: A Poetic Turning Point." *Twentieth-Century Literature* 17 (1971): 19–28.

Hicks, Granville. *The Great Tradition: An Interpretation of American Literature since the Civil War.* 1933. Chicago: Quadrangle, 1969.

Hockbruck, Wolfgang. "Writing the Civil War in William Faulkner's *The Unvanquished.*" *Revisioning the Past: Historical Self-Reflexivity in American Short Fiction.* Ed. Bernd Engler and Oliver Scheiding. Trier, Germany: Wissenschaftlicher, 1998. 211–30.

Hoffman, Frederick J., and Olga Vickery, eds. *William Faulkner: Three Decades of Criticism.* East Lansing: Michigan State University Press, 1960.

Hoover, Herbert. *The Challenge to Liberty.* New York: Scribner's, 1934.

Houck, Davis W. *Rhetoric as Currency: Hoover, Roosevelt, and the Great Depression.* College Station: Texas A and M University Press, 2001.

Howard, June. *Form and History in American Literary Naturalism.* Chapel Hill: University of North Carolina Press, 1985.

Howe, Irving. *William Faulkner: A Critical Study.* Chicago: University of Chicago Press, 1975.

I'll Take My Stand: The South and the Agrarian Tradition. 1930. Baton Rouge: Louisiana State University Press, 1977.

Inge, Thomas M. *William Faulkner: The Contemporary Reviews.* New York: Cambridge University Press, 1995.

Jameson, Frederick. *Fables of Aggression: Wyndham Lewis, the Modernist as Fascist.* Berkeley: University of California Press, 1979.

———. *The Political Unconscious: Narrative as Socially Symbolic Act.* Ithaca: Cornell University Press, 1981.

Jehlen, Myra. *Class and Character in Faulkner's South.* New York: Columbia University Press, 1976.

Jellison, Charles A., ed. *Tomatoes Were Cheaper: Tales from the Thirties.* Syracuse: Syracuse University Press, 1977.

Jones, Anne Goodwyn. "Desire and Dismemberment: Faulkner and the Ideology of Penetration." Kartiganer and Abadie, *Faulkner and Ideology* 129–71.

———. " 'Like a Virgin': Faulkner, Sexual Cultures, and the Romance of Resistance." Kartiganer and Abadie, *Faulkner in Cultural Context* 39–74.

Karl, Frederick R. Introduction. *Mosquitoes*. By Faulkner. New York: Liveright, 1997. 1–7.

Kartiganer, Donald M. *The Fragile Thread: The Meaning of Form in Faulkner's Novels*. Amherst: University of Massachusetts Press, 1979.

———. Introduction. Kartiganer and Abadie, *Faulkner and Ideology* vii–xxviii.

Kartiganer, Donald M., and Ann J. Abadie, eds. *Faulkner and the Artist: Faulkner and Yoknapatawpha, 1993*. Jackson: University Press of Mississippi, 1996.

———. *Faulkner at 100: Faulkner and Yoknapatawpha, 1997*. Jackson: University Press of Mississippi, 2000.

———. *Faulkner in Cultural Context: Faulkner and Yoknapatawpha, 1995*. Jackson: University Press of Mississippi, 1997.

———. *Faulkner and Gender: Faulkner and Yoknapatawpha, 1994*. Jackson: University Press of Mississippi, 1996.

———. *Faulkner and Ideology: Faulkner and Yoknapatawpha, 1992*. Jackson: University Press of Mississippi, 1995.

———. *Faulkner and the Natural World: Faulkner and Yoknapatawpha, 1996*. Jackson: University Press of Mississippi, 1999.

Kawin, Bruce F. *Faulkner and Film*. New York: Frederick Ungar Publishing, 1977.

Kazin, Alfred. *On Native Grounds: An Interpretation of Modern American Prose Literature*. New York: Harcourt, Brace, Jovanovich, 1995.

Kennedy, David M. *Freedom from Fear: The American People in Depression and War, 1929–1945*. New York: Oxford University Press, 1999.

Kern, Stephen. *The Culture of Time and Space, 1880–1918*. Cambridge: Harvard University Press, 1983.

Kutulas, Judy. *The Long War: The Intellectual People's Front and Anti-Stalinism, 1930–1940*. Durham: Duke University Press, 1995.

Lacan, Jacques. *The Four Fundamental Concepts of Psychoanalysis*. Ed. Jacques-Alain Miller. Trans. Alan Sheridan. New York: W. W. Norton, 1977.

Langford, Gerald. *Faulkner's Revision of* Sanctuary: *A Collation of the Unrevised Galleys and the Published Book*. Austin: University of Texas Press, 1972.

Leach, William. *Land of Desire: Merchants, Power, and the Rise of a New American Culture*. New York: Pantheon, 1993.

Leuchtenburg, William E. *The FDR Years: On Roosevelt and His Legacy*. New York: Columbia University Press, 1997.

———. *Franklin Delano Roosevelt and the New Deal, 1932–1940*. New York: Harper and Row, 1963.

Lind, Ilse Dusoir. "The Effect of Painting on Faulkner's Poetic Form." *Faulkner, Modernism, and Film: Faulkner and Yoknapatawpha, 1978*. Ed. Evans Harrington and Ann J. Abadie. Jackson: University Press of Mississippi, 1979. 127–48.

Little Caesar. Dir. Mervyn LeRoy. Warner Brothers, 1930.

Lovett, Robert Morse. "Liberalism and the Class War." *Modern Quarterly* 4 (1927–28): 191–94.

Lowe, John. "*The Unvanquished*: Faulkner's Nietzschean Skirmish with the Civil War." *Mississippi Quarterly* 46 (1993): 407–36.

Lukács, Georg. *The Historical Novel*. Trans. Hannah Mitchell and Stanley Mitchell. Boston: Beacon, 1962.

———. "Realism in the Balance." Trans. Rodney Livingstone. *Aesthetics and Politics: The Key Texts of the Classic Debate within German Marxism*. New York: Verso, 1971. 28–59.

Marx, Karl. *Economic and Philosophic Manuscripts of 1844*. Trans. Martin Milligan. New York: International Publishers, 1964.

———. *The Eighteenth Brumaire of Louis Bonaparte*. Ed. C. P. Dutt. New York: International Publishers, n.d.

Matthews, John T. "*As I Lay Dying* in the Machine Age." *National Identities and Post-American Narratives*. Ed. Donald E. Pease. Durham: Duke University Press, 1994. 69–94.

———. "Faulkner and Cultural Studies." *Faulkner Journal* 7 (1991–92): 1–2.

———. "Faulkner and Proletarian Literature." Kartiganer and Abadie, *Faulkner in Cultural Context* 166–90.

———. "Faulkner and the Culture Industry." *The Cambridge Companion to William Faulkner*. Ed. Philip M. Weinstein. New York: Cambridge University Press, 1995. 51–74.

———. *The Play of Faulkner's Language*. Ithaca: Cornell University Press, 1982.

———. *The Sound and the Fury: Faulkner and the Lost Cause*. Boston: Twayne, 1990.

———. "Whose America? Faulkner, Modernism, and National Identity." Urgo and Abadie 70–92.

McCann, Sean. *Gumshoe America: Hard-Boiled Crime Fiction and the Rise and Fall of New Deal Liberalism*. Durham: Duke University Press, 2000.

McElvaine, Robert S. *The Great Depression: America, 1929–1941*. New York: Times Books, 1993.

McHaney, Thomas L. "Oversexing the Natural World: *Mosquitoes* and *If I Forget Thee, Jerusalem* [*Wild Palms*]." Kartiganer and Abadie, *Faulkner and the Natural World* 19–44.

———. "What Faulkner Learned from the Tall Tale." *Faulkner and Humor:*

Faulkner and Yoknapatawpha, 1984. Ed. Doreen Fowler and Ann J. Abadie. Jackson: University Press of Mississippi, 1986. 110–35.

McMillen, Neil R., and Noel Polk. "Faulkner on Lynching." *The Faulkner Journal* 8 (1992): 3–14.

Meriwether, James B., and Michael Millgate, eds. *Lion in the Garden: Interviews with William Faulkner, 1926–62*. New York: Random House, 1968.

Millgate, Michael. *The Achievement of William Faulkner*. 1966. Lincoln: University of Nebraska Press, 1978.

Minter, David. *A Cultural History of the American Novel: Henry James to William Faulkner*. Cambridge: Cambridge University Press, 1994.

Mitchell, Margaret. *Gone with the Wind*. 1936. New York: Warner Books, 1993.

Moreland, Richard C. *Faulkner and Modernism: Rereading and Rewriting*. Madison: University of Wisconsin Press, 1990.

Morgan, Stacy I. *Rethinking Social Realism: African American Art and Literature, 1930–1953*. Athens: University of Georgia Press, 2004.

Morrison, Paul. *The Poetics of Fascism: Ezra Pound, T. S. Eliot, and Paul de Man*. New York: Oxford University Press, 1996.

Mumford, Lewis. Foreword. *Planned Society: Yesterday, Today, and Tomorrow*. Ed. Findlay MacKenzie. New York: Prentice-Hall, 1937.

———. "Opening Address." First American Artists Congress. Town Hall, New York City. 14 Feb. 1936. Rpt. in Baigell and Williams 62–64.

Murphy, James. *The Proletarian Moment: The Controversy over Leftism in Literature*. Urbana: University of Illinois Press, 1991.

Nelson, Cary. *Repression and Recovery: Modern American Poetry and the Politics of Cultural Memory, 1910–1945*. Madison: University of Wisconsin Press, 1989.

———. *Revolutionary Memory: Recovering the Poetry of the American Left*. New York: Routledge, 2001.

O'Donnell, Patrick. "Between the Family and the State: Nomadism and Authority in *As I Lay Dying*." *Faulkner Journal* 7 (1991–92): 83–94.

Peeler, David. *Hope among Us Yet: Social Criticism and Social Solace in Depression America*. Athens: University of Georgia Press, 1987.

Pells, Richard H. *Radical Visions and American Dreams: Culture and Social Thought in the Great Depression*. New York: Harper and Row, 1973.

Polk, Noel. *Children of the Dark House: Text and Context in Faulkner*. Jackson: University Press of Mississippi, 1996.

Porter, Carolyn. "Faulkner's America." *Seeing and Being: The Plight of the Par-*

ticipant Observer in Emerson, James, Adams, and Faulkner. Middletown: Wesleyan University Press, 1981.

Porter, Dennis. *The Pursuit of Crime: Art and Ideology in Detective Fiction*. New Haven: Yale University Press, 1981.

Powell, Jim. *FDR's Folly: How Roosevelt and His New Deal Prolonged the Depression*. New York: Crown Forum, 2003.

The Public Enemy. Dir. William Wellman. Warner Brothers, 1931.

Rabinowitz, Paula. *Labor and Desire: Women's Revolutionary Fiction in Depression America*. Chapel Hill: University of North Carolina Press, 1991.

Rado, Lisa. " 'A Perversion That Builds Chartres and Invents Lear Is a Pretty Good Thing': *Mosquitoes* and Faulkner's Androgynous Imagination." *Faulkner Journal* 9 (1993–94): 13–30.

Rahv, Philip. "Excerpts from 'The Literary Class War.' " *New Masses* Aug. 1932: 281–83.

Railey, Kevin. *Natural Aristocracy: History, Ideology, and the Production of William Faulkner*. Tuscaloosa: University of Alabama Press, 1999.

Reid, Panthea. "The Scene of Writing and the Shape of Language for Faulkner When 'Matisse and Picasso Yet Painted.' " Kartiganer and Abadie, *Faulkner and the Artist* 82–109.

Roberts, Diane. *Faulkner and Southern Womanhood*. Athens: University of Georgia Press, 1994.

———. "A Precarious Pedestal: The Confederate Woman in Faulkner's *The Unvanquished*." *Journal of American Studies* 26 (1992): 233–46.

Rodgers, Daniel T. *Atlantic Crossings: Social Politics in a Progressive Era*. Cambridge: Harvard University Press, 1998.

Romasco, Albert. *The Poverty of Abundance: Hoover, the Nation, the Depression*. New York: Oxford University Press, 1965.

Roosevelt, Eleanor. "Helping Them to Help Themselves." *The Rotarian* 56 (1940): 8–11. Rpt. in *New Deal Network*. Franklin and Eleanor Roosevelt Institute, New York. 25 Mar. 2000 <http://newdeal.feri.org/texts/534.htm>.

Roosevelt, Franklin D. "The Forgotten Man." Albany, New York. 7 Apr. 1932. *New Deal Network*. 25 Mar. 2000 <http://newdeal.feri.org/texts/456.htm>.

———. "Greater Freedom and Greater Security." Washington, D.C. 30 Sep. 1934. *New Deal Network*. 25 Mar. 2000 <http://newdeal.feri.org/texts/384.htm>.

———. "Inaugural Address." Washington, D.C. 4 Mar. 1933. *New Deal Network*. 25 Mar. 2000 <http://newdeal.feri.org/texts/62.htm>.

———. "Nomination Address." Chicago. 2 July 1932. *New Deal Network.* 25 Mar. 2000 <http://newdeal.feri.org/texts/61.htm>.

———. "Outlining the New Deal Program." Washington, D.C. 7 May 1933. *New Deal Network.* 25 Mar. 2000 <http://newdeal.feri.org/texts/380.htm>.

———. "The Purpose and Foundations of Recovery." Washington, D.C. 24 July 1933. *New Deal Network.* 25 Mar. 2000 <http://newdeal.feri.org/texts/381.htm>.

———. "The Works Relief Program." Washington, D.C. 28 Apr. 1935. *New Deal Network.* 25 Mar. 2000 <http://newdeal.feri.org/texts/385.htm>.

Ross, Stephen M. *Fiction's Inexhaustible Voice: Speech and Writing in Faulkner.* Athens: University of Georgia Press, 1989.

Rubin, Louis, Jr. "William Faulkner: Why the Very Idea!" Kartiganer and Abadie, *Faulkner and Ideology* 329–52.

Rukeyser, Muriel. "The Virtuosity of William Faulkner." *New Masses* 22 May 1934: 27. Rpt. in Inge 114–15.

Scheel, Kathleen M. "Incest, Repression, and Repetition-Compulsion: The Case of Faulkner's Temple Drake." *Mosaic* 30 (1997): 39–55.

Schlesinger, Arthur M., Jr. *The Age of Roosevelt: The Politics of Upheaval.* New York: Houghton Mifflin, 1960.

Schwartz, Lawrence H. *Creating Faulkner's Reputation: The Politics of Modern Literary Criticism.* Knoxville: University of Tennessee Press, 1988.

Scott, Evelyn. "On William Faulkner's *The Sound and the Fury.*" *Critical Essays on William Faulkner: The Compson Family.* Ed. Arthur Kinney. Boston: G. K. Hall, 1982. 115–18.

The Secret Six. Dir. George Hill. MGM, 1932.

Shouse, Jouett. "American Liberty League." 1934. *The American Liberty League.* The Jouett Shouse Collection. Modern Political Archives Division of Special Collections and Archives, University of Kentucky Libraries, Lexington. 26 Feb. 2001 <http://www.uky.edu/Libraries/Special/mpa/shouse-all-all.html>.

Smith, Albert C. " 'Southern Violence': Arson as Protest in Black-Belt Georgia, 1865–1910." *Journal of Southern History* 51 (1985): 527–64.

Steinbeck, John. *The Grapes of Wrath.* New York: Penguin, 1967.

Sullivan, Patricia. *Days of Hope: Race and Democracy in the New Deal Era.* Chapel Hill: University of North Carolina Press, 1996.

Sundquist, Eric J. *Faulkner: The House Divided.* Baltimore: Johns Hopkins University Press, 1983.

Swados, Harvey. *The American Writer and the Great Depression.* Indianapolis: Bobbs-Merrill, 1966.

Swing, Raymond Gramm. *The Forerunners of American Fascism*. New York: J. Messner, 1935.

Szalay, Michael. *New Deal Modernism: American Literature and the Invention of the Welfare State*. Durham: Duke University Press, 2000.

Tate, Allen. "Three Types of Poetry." *New Republic* 14 Mar. 1934: 126–28.

———. "Three Types of Poetry: II." *New Republic* 28 Mar. 1934: 180–82.

———. "Three Types of Poetry: III." *New Republic* 11 Apr. 1934: 237–40.

Teres, Harvey M. *Renewing the Left: Politics, Imagination, and the New Left*. New York: Oxford University Press, 1996.

Terkel, Studs. *Hard Times: An Oral History of the Great Depression*. New York: Pantheon, 1986.

They Won't Forget. Dir. Mervin LeRoy. Warner, 1937.

Thomas, Gordon, and Max Morgan-Witts. *The Day the Bubble Burst: A Social History of the Wall Street Crash of 1929*. New York: Doubleday, 1979.

Thompson, Alan R. "The Cult of Cruelty." *Bookman* 74 (1932): 477–87.

Tolnay, Stewart E., and E. M. Beck. *A Festival of Violence: An Analysis of Southern Lynchings, 1882–1930*. Urbana: University of Illinois Press, 1992.

Trilling, Lionel. "Mr. Faulkner's World." *Nation* 4 Nov. 1931: 491–92. Rpt. in Inge 69–70.

Trouard, Dawn. "Faulkner's Text Which Is Not One." *New Essays on* The Sound and the Fury. Ed. Noel Polk. New York: Cambridge University Press, 1993. 23–69.

Urgo, Joseph. *Faulkner's Apocrypha: A Fable, Snopes, and the Spirit of Human Rebellion*. Jackson: University Press of Mississippi, 1989.

Urgo, Joseph, and Ann J. Abadie. *Faulkner in America: Faulkner and Yoknapatawpha, 1998*. Jackson: University Press of Mississippi, 2001. 70–92.

Vickery, Olga. *The Novels of William Faulkner: A Critical Interpretation*. Baton Rouge: Louisiana State University Press, 1964.

Wald, Alan M. *Writing from the Left: New Essays on Radical Culture and Politics*. New York: Verso, 1994.

Walton, Edna Lou. "The Snopeses Move Up." *New Masses* 16 Apr. 1940: 27. Rpt. in Inge 216–17.

Warren, Joyce W. "Faulkner's 'Portrait of the Artist.'" *Mississippi Quarterly* 19 (1966): 121–31.

Warren, Robert Penn. Introduction. *Faulkner: A Collection of Critical Essays*. Ed. Warren. Englewood Cliffs, N.J.: Prentice-Hall, 1966.

Watkins, T. H. *The Hungry Years: A Narrative History of the Great Depression*. New York: Holt, 1999.

Watson, Jay. *Forensic Fictions: The Lawyer Figure in Faulkner*. Athens: University of Georgia Press, 1993.

Weinstein, Philip M. *Faulkner's Subject: A Cosmos No One Owns*. New York: Cambridge University Press, 1992.

Wiegman, Robyn. *American Anatomies: Theorizing Race and Gender*. Durham: Duke University Press, 1995.

Wild Boys of the Road. Dir. William Wellman. Warner, 1933.

Williams, Leonard. *American Liberalism and Ideological Change*. DeKalb: Northern Illinois University Press, 1991.

Williams, Raymond. *Marxism and Literature*. Oxford: Oxford University Press, 1977.

Wilson, Edmund. *Axel's Castle*. New York: Scribners, 1931.

———. "The Literary Class War: I." *New Republic* 27 Apr. 1932: 319–23.

Wilson, Joan Hoff. *Herbert Hoover, Forgotten Progressive*. Long Grove, Ill.: Waveland Press, 1992.

Wittenberg, Judith Bryant. "Configurations of the Female and Textual Politic in *Mosquitoes*." *Faulkner Studies* 1 (1991): 1–19.

Wolfskill, George. *The Revolt of the Conservatives: A History of the American Liberty League, 1934–1940*. New York: Houghton Mifflin, 1962.

Woodward, C. Vann. *Origins of the New South, 1877–1913*. Baton Rouge: Louisiana State University Press, 1951.

Wyatt-Brown, Bertram. "Community, Class, and Snopesian Crime: Local Justice in the Old South." *Class, Conflict, and Consensus: Antebellum Southern Community Studies*. Ed. Orville Vernon Burton and Robert C. McMath. Westport, Conn.: Greenwood Press, 1982. 173–206.

Yaeger, Patricia. "Beyond the Hummingbird: Southern Women Writers and the Southern Gargantua." *Haunted Bodies: Gender and Southern Texts*. Ed. Anne Goodwyn Jones and Susan V. Donaldson. Charlottesville: University Press of Virginia, 1997. 287–318.

———. "Faulkner's 'Greek Amphora Priestess': Verbena and Violence in *The Unvanquished*." Kartiganer and Abadie, *Faulkner and Gender* 197–227.

Zender, Karl. *Faulkner and the Politics of Reading*. Baton Rouge: Louisiana State University Press, 2002.

Index

Abe Lincoln in Illinois (film), 223
Abraham Lincoln (film), 223
Absalom, Absalom! (Faulkner): as
  allegory of antifascism, 162–72;
  Civil War depiction in, 168–69,
  226; comparison of, with *Gone
  with the Wind*, 226–27; comparison
  of, with *The Unvanquished*,
  221–22, 227; cultural context
  of, 162–65, 167–68, 226–27;
  Haitian slaves in, 166–69;
  history in, 163, 170; and map of
  Yoknapatawpha County, 47–48;

narrative structure of, 53; and
  race ideology, 169–70; and Rosa
  Coldfield's narrative, 10, 164, 168;
  Sutpen's Hundred in, 162, 164–66,
  168–69
Agee, James, 195
American Artists' Congress, 160
American Individualism (Hoover), 22
American Liberty League, 31–33, 53
American Review, 41
American Writers' Congress, 161
Anderson, Sherwood, 17, 68. *See also*
  Fairchild, Dawson